# THE BIRDER'S GUIDE
# TO VANCOUVER
## AND THE LOWER MAINLAND

# THE BIRDER'S GUIDE TO VANCOUVER

## AND THE LOWER MAINLAND

### REVISED AND EXPANDED EDITION

**NATURE VANCOUVER**

EDITED BY **COLIN CLASEN**

**HARBOUR PUBLISHING**

# CONTENTS

Previous pages: Greater
Yellowlegs. Jim Martin

This spread: Ospreys have
been nesting annually at
Maplewood since 1991.
John Lowman

# FOREWORD

WRITING THESE WORDS ON INTERNATIONAL MIGRATORY BIRD DAY, 2015, it's hard to imagine a finer setting than Vancouver and the Lower Mainland to celebrate the annual wave of migrants that sweep north through the continent in spring. It's not just spring that's good for birding here; we're fortunate to have great birding year-round. For Lower Mainlanders and for visitors, there is no shortage of good, productive places to go birding. Having choices is fine when you live in an area. You can always try somewhere else the next day, or the next week. But for visitors, so much choice is a real challenge if they have only a day or two to explore.

Although the landscape is huge—Boundary Bay to the south, the Fraser Valley to the east, the Strait of Georgia to the west, and the North Shore Mountains to the north—it is nonetheless possible, in a single day, to travel and bird from mountains to mud flats, from forests to farmlands, and from shorelines to city parks. And you can enjoy whole suites of birds in each location.

Birdlife spectacles are many here. Hundreds of Bald Eagles and other raptors winter on Boundary Bay as huge rafts of waterfowl crowd our shorelines. Wheeling flocks of shorebirds fill the skies, and tens of thousands of Snow Geese come and go to and from Arctic Russia in spring and fall. Spring birding provides wave after wave of migrants, and summer offers a diversity of breeding species from mountains to lowlands.

So what can a guide like this one offer to both residents and visitors? It can answer some key questions: What are my choices? What can I expect to see at this location? Are some locations seasonal and some good year-round? Do I want to see mountain birds or marsh inhabitants? Where and when might I find Sharp-tailed Sandpipers? Where am I likely to find Western Tanagers? How about Golden-crowned Sparrows? Red-breasted Sapsuckers? Where should I go next?

This guide will answer all these questions as well as offer many enticements to explore birding locations throughout the region, whether you are a resident of the Lower Mainland or a visitor.

*George Clulow, President, BC Field Ornithologists, May 2015.*

Opposite: An adorable Northern Saw–whet Owl at the George C. Reifel Migratory Bird Sanctuary. Jim Martin

Following pages: The Steller's Jay is a member of the highly intelligent corvid family of birds. John Lowman

# ACKNOWLEDGEMENTS

THE EFFORTS OF MANY PEOPLE HAVE GONE INTO THE PREPARATION OF this book, which has been thoroughly revised, updated and rewritten since it was last published by Nature Vancouver (Vancouver Natural History Society) in 2001. The revised edition includes four new general information sections and two new birding locations.

Thank you to the BC Waterfowl Society (managers of the George C. Reifel Migratory Bird Sanctuary), whose generous financial donation helped make this new edition possible.

Thank you to the following individuals who generously contributed their time and expertise to this project:

- The original authors and updaters of birding location sections in the 2001 edition, many of whom were not able to participate this time due to constraints of time, distance or availability. Their prior work is greatly appreciated, since it formed the foundation for most of the sections that have now been updated by others. They are: Gerry Ansell, Dick Cannings, John and Shirley Dorsey, Kyle Elliott, Christine Hanrahan, John Ireland, Dale Jensen, Hue Mackenzie, Jo Ann Mackenzie, Martin McNicholl, Robin Owen, Mary Peet-Leslie, Allen Poynter, Michael Price, Val Schaefer, Brian Scott, Rick Toochin, Wayne Weber and the late Jack Williams.

- The updaters and revisers of birding location and other sections in the 2016 edition. They are: Catherine J. Aitchison, Patricia M. Banning-Lover, Tom Bearss, Kevin Bell, Christine Bishop, Quentin Brown, Margaret Butschler, Peter Candido, John Chandler, George Clulow, Larry Cowan, Adrian Grant Duff, Kathleen Fry, Carlo Giovanella, Tineke Goebertus, Elaine Golds, Al Grass, Jude Grass, Eric Greenwood, Annabel Griffiths, Jeremiah Kennedy, Derek Killby, Ken Klimko, Rob Lyske, Hilary Maguire, Bill Merilees, David Mounteney, Anne Murray, Monica Nugent, Thomas Plath, Ilya Povalyaev, Varri Raffan, Bev Ramey, John Reynolds, June Ryder, David Schutz, Brian Self, Terry Slack, Daphne Solecki, Richard Swanston, Mike Tabak, Ian Thomas, Mike Toochin, Sharon Toochin, Danny Tyson, Wim Vesseur, Maureen Vo, Liz Walker, Randy Walker, Steffany Walker and Mark Wynja.

- The authors of the new birding location sections in the 2016 edition, namely, Carlo Giovanella for "Kwomais Point Park," Derek Killby for "Lonsdale Quay

Surf Scoters have a clown-faced look and often form large rafts on the ocean. John Gordon

and Kings Mill Walk Park," Brian Self for "North 40 Park Reserve" and Randy Walker for "Brydon Lagoon."

- George Clulow, current President of the BC Field Ornithologists, for authoring the new *Foreword* and updating the *Introduction*.
- Larry Cowan for updating the *Seasonal Status of Vancouver Birds*. This bar-graph species checklist was originally produced for Nature Vancouver by Rick Toochin, with original computer design and data entry by Tom Brown and Kyle Elliott.
- Tom Plath, Mike Tabak, Mike and Sharon Toochin, Danny Tyson and Mark Wynja for updating the *Selected List of Vancouver Bird Species*, originally written by Wayne Weber.
- Members of the birding community and Nature Vancouver who donated:
  - Bird photos: Glenn Bartley, Peter Candido, Colin Clasen, Liron Gertsman, Greg Gillson, John Gordon, Mark Habdas, Virginia Hayes, Michelle Lamberson, Joan Lopez, John Lowman, Jim Martin, Ilya Povalyaev, David Schutz, Tak Shibata, Mike Tabak
  - Location photos: Colin Clasen, David Cook, Al and Jude Grass, Mark Habdas, Bill Kinkaid, Ken Klimko, Ron Long, Joan Lopez, John Lowman, Jim Martin, Nancy Prober
- Cartographer Gavin Castle for the new set of colour maps, which are a great enhancement to the new edition.
- Marion Coope for her help with the initial stages of editing the new edition.
- Marguerite Mousseau for her assistance with the initial coordination and organization of the updating of the book, including selection of photos, initial contact with the publisher and the search for a cartographer.
- Jeremy McCall for handling the contracts (and attending key meetings) with the publisher and cartographer, as well as finding an experienced cartographer and sourcing additional funding.
- Colin Clasen for contacting original authors, sourcing new updaters, compiling and editing the text, contacting photographers, reviewing and selecting photos and ongoing coordination with the publisher and cartographer.
- Daphne Nagorsen and Maureen Shaw for copy editing and reviewing the text.
- The Board of Directors and the Birding Section Committee of Nature Vancouver for their support.
- Harbour Publishing staff for their professionalism, friendliness and helpful guidance. They have our sincere gratitude for their patience, cooperation, flexibility and attention to detail.

# INTRODUCTION

THE VANCOUVER AREA IS ONE OF THE MOST SPECTACULAR PLACES IN North America to observe birds. It contains a vast array of habitats: mountain and lowland forests, bogs, freshwater lakes and streams, marine inlets and bays, brackish marshes, mud flats and rocky shorelines. Over 260 species of birds may be seen here annually, and over 400 species have been recorded more than once.

In addition to providing marvellous birding opportunities in a diversity of habitats, the Fraser River estuary, south of the city, is also a major staging area on the Pacific Flyway. Millions of shorebirds and waterfowl pass through here in the spring and fall on their migratory routes between Siberia, Alaska and northern Canada, and California, Central America and South America. Tens of thousands also spend the winter, joined by an impressive array of species and numbers of raptors.

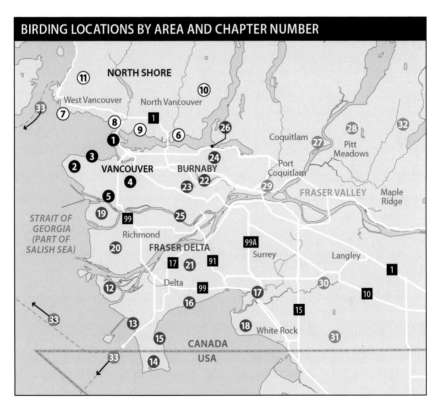

**BIRDING LOCATIONS BY AREA AND CHAPTER NUMBER**

Circled numbers refer to birding locations listed in the Contents.

Boxed numbers refer to the official highway numbers.

# THE ECOLOGY OF GREATER VANCOUVER

GREATER VANCOUVER'S NATURAL ENVIRONMENT ENCOMPASSES FOUR large systems:

**Along the mountainous North Shore,** large forests of western hemlock, western red cedar and Douglas-fir extend for 50 km between the Strait of Georgia (part of the Salish Sea*) and Pitt Lake. This area is full of ravines and canyons, and there are three large freshwater lakes (Capilano, Seymour and Coquitlam) that provide drinking water to Vancouver-area residents.

**Along the shorelines,** the coastal/intertidal area is rich in marine life. Brackish marshes are found at Roberts Bank and Sturgeon Bank to the west of the cities of Delta and Richmond. Huge intertidal mud flats dominate Boundary Bay and Semiahmoo Bay to the south, with smaller ones at Maplewood Flats and Port Moody along Burrard Inlet. Rocky shorelines border most of West Vancouver and Indian Arm.

**The major freshwater environment** is created by the Fraser River system. As the river passes through Greater Vancouver, it divides into three arms. The South Arm, the largest of the three, carries 80 percent of the water flow. Other important freshwater systems associated with the Fraser River are the Brunette River watershed, which includes Burnaby Lake and Deer Lake. To the east of the city, Pitt Lake, the Pitt River and the Coquitlam River all enter the Fraser from the north. The Salmon River, which runs through Langley, enters the Fraser from the south at Fort Langley.

**Where the fresh water meets the sea,** the Fraser River estuary is formed from the confluence of the main river and numerous creeks and rivers, including the Little Campbell, Serpentine and Nicomekl Rivers and their flood plains. The Fraser River delta, which covers 590 square km, is the largest delta on Canada's West Coast. Burns Bog in Delta, and Sea and Iona islands in Richmond, also form part of this system.

Birdlife in the Vancouver area is changing because of rapid human population growth. Almost 60 percent of the population of British Columbia, about 2.6 million people (2011 figures), is concentrated in the lower Fraser River basin, where urban sprawl has resulted in considerable loss of habitat. The dyking of wetlands is a major concern. Over the last 120 years, 70 percent of the original freshwater marshes and 90 percent of the saltwater and brackish marshes have been lost.

Although human-caused habitat alteration and loss have had major negative effects on birdlife, the Vancouver area, like other areas of North America, has also felt the impact of non-native bird and mammalian species. European Starlings

**Sanderling inspecting a crab claw.** David Schutz

and eastern gray squirrels, for example, have been implicated in bird declines. However, on the plus side, dedicated conservation work has seen the re-establishment of Purple Martin colonies throughout the region from where they had been extirpated. No longer suffering from various forms of persecution, Bald Eagles have returned in spectacular numbers.

Many parks and sanctuaries have been created in an effort to preserve and encourage birdlife. The Metro Vancouver Parks system now preserves 14,500 hectares (ha) of land comprising 22 regional parks, 4 regional park reserves, 2 ecological conservancy areas and 5 regional greenways. All contain large areas of valuable bird habitat. There are many municipal parks as well, including the famous Stanley Park in Vancouver's West End. Wildlife refuges include George C. Reifel Migratory Bird Sanctuary in Ladner and Pitt-Addington Marsh Wildlife Management Area in Pitt Meadows/Coquitlam. A number of very large provincial parks occupy areas of the North Shore Mountains, including Cypress, Mount Seymour, Pinecone-Burke and Golden Ears provincial parks.

From fields and forests alive with passerines, to wetlands with vast, wheeling flocks of shorebirds, to huge rafts of sea and bay ducks crowding the waters, and skies with hunting raptors, the diverse habitats of the Vancouver area provide exciting opportunities to watch birds in all seasons.

# HOW TO USE THIS BOOK

All contact information provided is current at the time of writing. The sites described here are grouped by general location in the Vancouver area.

A wide range of habitats is represented. Descriptions for each location contain an overview of the species a birder can expect to find there.

These are some of the favourite spots of members of Nature Vancouver. A site map is provided for ease in locating key roads, paths and other features at each location. Each section contains directions for getting to the site by car from downtown Vancouver.

Since bus and ferry schedules and routes occasionally change, we highly recommend accessing the most up-to-date and reliable information by going to the TransLink and BC Ferries websites listed in the *Public Transit and Weather Information* section of this guide.

Metric measurements are used in all sections, except for the *Tides* section, where both metric and imperial measurements are provided. The abbreviations used are as follows:

m=metre (1 metre=39 inches=3 inches more than 1 yard)
km=kilometre (1 kilometre=0.6 mile)
ha=hectare (1 hectare=2.5 acres)
ft=foot
Mountain elevation example: 1,000 metres=3,280 feet

Nature Vancouver conducts about 150 field trips of various types annually, and visitors are welcome to attend as an introduction to nature in the Vancouver area. Information about upcoming trips, membership and special events is available on the Nature Vancouver website (naturevancouver.ca).

Also see the *Nature-Related Organizations* section for more information on Nature Vancouver and other local and provincial organizations.

Since the last edition of this guide, the advent of digital photography has substantially increased the number of wildlife photographers in the field. However, there are concerns that the pursuit of the perfect shot may at times conflict with the welfare of the birds and their habitats. To address these concerns, we have added sections entitled *Birding and Bird Photography Etiquette* and *Reporting Obvious Harassment of Wildlife*.

Another new section, *Online Resources to Increase Your Birding Success*, helps birders find information on the latest bird sightings in our region and promotes the use of eBird (eBird.org) to record sightings permanently, while at the same time making a contribution to bird science.

And finally, due to an increasing number of questions about birds of prey seen with either wing-tags or colour-coded leg bands, we've included information about where to report these sightings.

*The name Salish Sea, officially adopted in 2009 by the governments of British Columbia and Washington State, pays tribute to the indigenous Coast Salish peoples of the area. It encompasses the various water and land bodies of this trans-national region, including the Strait of Georgia, the Strait of Juan de Fuca, Puget Sound, the Gulf Islands, the San Juan Islands and north to Johnstone Strait.*

*Written by Val Schaefer. Revised by Catherine J. Aitchison, 2001.*
*Significant revisions by George Clulow, 2015.*

## Legend to maps

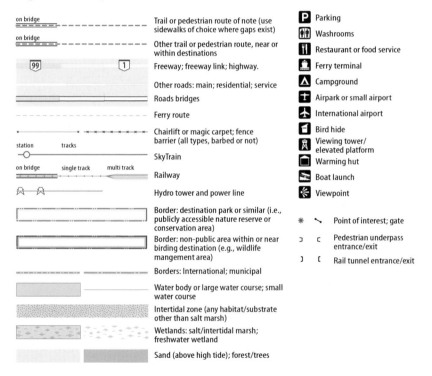

| | |
|---|---|
| on bridge / Trail or pedestrian route of note (use sidewalks of choice where gaps exist) | **P** Parking |
| on bridge / Other trail or pedestrian route, near or within destinations | 🚻 Washrooms |
| 99 1 / Freeway; freeway link; highway. | 🍴 Restaurant or food service |
| Other roads: main; residential; service | ⚓ Ferry terminal |
| Roads bridges | △ Campground |
| Ferry route | ✈ Airpark or small airport |
| station tracks / Chairlift or magic carpet; fence barrier (all types, barbed or not) | ✈ International airport |
| SkyTrain | Bird hide |
| on bridge single track multi track / Railway | Viewing tower/ elevated platform |
| Hydro tower and power line | Warming hut |
| Border: destination park or similar (i.e., publicly accessible nature reserve or conservation area) | Boat launch |
| Border: non-public area within or near birding destination (e.g., wildlife mangement area) | Viewpoint |
| Borders: International; municipal | ✳ ↘ Point of interest; gate |
| Water body or large water course; small water course | ⊐ ⊏ Pedestrian underpass entrance/exit |
| Intertidal zone (any habitat/substrate other than salt marsh) | ] [ Rail tunnel entrance/exit |
| Wetlands: salt/intertidal marsh; freshwater wetland | |
| Sand (above high tide); forest/trees | |

Note: It was announced in late 2015 that the George Massey ("Deas Island") Tunnel, crossing the Fraser River between Richmond and Delta, will be replaced by a bridge, with completion expected by 2022.

# 1. STANLEY PARK

## INTRODUCTION

STANLEY PARK, ARGUABLY THE MOST FAMOUS URBAN PARK IN CANADA, is a 405 ha peninsula of beautiful forests, gardens, freshwater lakes and saltwater shorelines, located next to Vancouver's densely populated West End. It was established in 1888, only two years after the City of Vancouver was incorporated. Although the park has a history of disturbance—partial logging in the 1860s, Typhoon Frieda in 1962, a major destructive windstorm in December 2006, recreational development and tree removal—it still has some good examples of relatively undisturbed old-growth forest. These stands consist of western red cedar, western hemlock and Douglas-fir. About two-thirds of the roughly 250 ha of forest is classified as mature coniferous (over 100 years old). The remainder of the park is given over to gardens and recreational areas, including a pitch-and-putt golf course, the Vancouver Aquarium, beaches, picnic areas and playing fields. An extensive trail system winds throughout the park.

The Stanley Park Seawall walk is continually expanding and it is now possible to walk from the downtown harbour side, all the way around Stanley Park past

Stanley Park Seawall and rocky shoreline. David Cook

English Bay to False Creek. The seawall can become very crowded, especially on summer weekends. Walking or bicycling along the seawall may be particularly rewarding in late fall, winter or early spring, as the waters off the seawall are prime habitat for ducks, loons, grebes and cormorants. With more than 230 species of birds reliably reported from the park, and new ones added every year, it has been a favourite birding area of Vancouverites for generations.

## DIRECTIONS

Only about 1.5 km from downtown Vancouver, Stanley Park is easily reached on foot by walking west along any street through the residential area of the West End. Robson Street, Davie Street and Beach Avenue are three of the main east–west streets.

From downtown by car, drive west on Georgia Street and take the Stanley Park exit to the right, opposite Lost Lagoon. From the Burrard Street Bridge/False Creek area, head northwest along English Bay on Beach Avenue. The drive that encircles

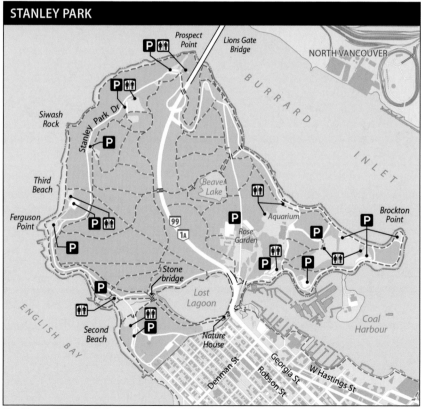

**STANLEY PARK**

Note: The park offers many food services, and there is additional parking available in various sections along the park's roadsides.

the park is one-way counter-clockwise. From North or West Vancouver, drive south across the Lions Gate Bridge (Highway 99) and turn right immediately after entering the park. This exit joins the park drive near Prospect Point, but it is closed during morning rush hours to discourage commuter traffic. There are numerous parking areas along the drive. Pay parking is in effect throughout the park, even on the roadways, so make sure you display your receipt on your dashboard.

There is regular bus service to Stanley Park from downtown Vancouver; for the latest information, please use the TransLink website (translink.ca).

Stanley Park can also be toured by bicycle, especially along the seawall, but be careful, as bicycles must go counter-clockwise around the seawall.

The Stanley Park Nature House, run by the Stanley Park Ecology Society, is located on the southeast shore of Lost Lagoon, near the corner of Chilco and Alberni streets. This is not obvious from street level. Park maps, bird checklists, nature books and general park information are available there. Just type "Stanley Park Nature House" into your web browser or call 604-257-8544 for complete details about their location, hours and programs. They organize a waterfowl count on Lost Lagoon every Saturday at 9 a.m. (free of charge), a monthly bird count on the second Sunday of each month at 10 a.m. and a 2-hour *Discovery Walk* on Sundays at 1 p.m. (for a small fee). On the last Sunday of each month (excluding December), an expert birder leads a 2-hour *Birds of a Feather* walk starting at 9 a.m.

## BIRD SPECIES

### Winter

Lost Lagoon is perhaps the most familiar birding spot in Stanley Park. From late September to early May, the lagoon teems with water birds. These are mainly diving ducks, but there are also many **Canada Geese**, **Mallards**, **American Coots** and smaller numbers of other species. The most common diving ducks are the **Lesser Scaup**, **Common Goldeneye** and **Barrow's Goldeneye**. Most of the goldeneyes use the lagoon as a nighttime roost, departing at dawn and returning in late afternoon. The **Lesser Scaup** seems to do the opposite, apparently feeding elsewhere at night and sleeping in the lagoon during the day. The park's wing-clipped **Mute Swans** (a European species) have not been successful nesters in the past few years, and only two survive, now fed by park staff. They remain a captive species and are not "countable."

A few **Canvasbacks** are sometimes present in Lost Lagoon, and this is one of the more reliable places in Vancouver to find a **Ring-necked Duck** or **Redhead**. Occasionally, a very rare duck shows up. The first **Tufted Duck** ever seen in Canada was sighted here in 1961, and one of these rare old-world ducks has been present for part of the occasional winter in recent years. In 1991 a small marsh was con-

A perfect freeze–frame of the full wingspread of an adult Bald Eagle. John Lowman

structed in one corner of Lost Lagoon opposite the Nature House. It now acts as a winter home to the *Virginia Rail*, which nests in Beaver Lake. In the spring, migrating warblers are attracted to this habitat and the *Red-winged Blackbird* nests in the bamboo and cattails. In the past few years, *Anna's Hummingbird* has become much more common, and there have been one or more successful nests near the marsh for several years.

Do not miss the stone bridge that crosses the creek at the west end of Lost Lagoon, as it is a great spot for winter birding. The tangle of shrubbery next to the bridge contains several feeders that are usually hopping with *Dark-eyed Juncos*, *Song* and *Fox Sparrows*, *Spotted Towhees*, *Black-capped Chickadees*, *Red-winged Blackbirds* and an occasional *Golden-crowned* or *White-crowned Sparrow*. The feeders often allow close looks at normally shy forest birds like the *Chestnut-backed Chickadee* and *Red-breasted Nuthatch*. Sometimes they will even eat from your hand, especially if you have black-oil sunflower seeds. Closer inspection of the shrubbery will usually reveal more birds. A *Virginia Rail* has wintered here for several seasons and a *Harris's Sparrow* has turned up also. The *Wood Duck* and *American Wigeon* can usually be seen in the water near here.

The coniferous forests that cover much of Stanley Park are often very quiet in winter. You may walk for more than a kilometre without seeing a bird, and then suddenly find yourself surrounded by a mixed-species feeding flock. These flocks usually include *Golden-crowned* and *Ruby-crowned Kinglets*, *Black-capped* and *Chestnut-backed Chickadees*, a *Brown Creeper* or two and often a *Red-breasted Nuthatch* or a *Downy* or *Hairy Woodpecker*. The frantic activity lasts a few moments and then all is silent again. Along the dank and often dripping trails, you may be lucky enough to spot a *Red-breasted Sapsucker* or a *Pileated Woodpecker*, but there are generally more land birds around the alder stands and ornamental plantings than in the coniferous forest.

In winter, a walk along the Stanley Park Seawall allows you to see impressive numbers of diving ducks, especially the *Surf Scoter* and *Barrow's Goldeneye*. Other common winter water birds include the *Horned* and *Red-necked Grebe*, *Double-crested* and *Pelagic Cormorant*, *American Wigeon*, *Greater Scaup*, *Black Scoter*, *Common Goldeneye*, *Bufflehead*, *Red-breasted Merganser*, *Glaucous-winged*, *Mew* and *Thayer's Gull* and *Pigeon Guillemot*. Other species are more localized. A few *Western Grebes*, *Long-tailed Ducks* and *Red-throated* and *Common Loons* usually winter out in English Bay. The *Harlequin Duck* may be sighted on rocky areas of the shoreline from Ferguson Point to Prospect Point, and a *Brandt's Cormorant* might be seen on the shoal markers on the harbour side of the park near Brockton Point. At low tide, *Black Turnstones* and *Sanderlings* are possible on the rocks near Ferguson Point, sometimes accompanied by a *Rock Sandpiper* or (rarely) a *Surfbird*. Any group of *American Wigeon* is worth checking out for the occasional *Eurasian Wigeon*. During at least four winters, a *King Eider* has accompanied the flocks of *Surf Scoters* in English Bay, and a *Common Eider* has also spent a winter in their company.

## Spring

Spring migration extends from late February, when most of the *American Robin* population arrives, to the first week of June, when a few straggling *Western Wood-Pewees*, *Western Tanagers* and *Wilson's Warblers* may still be passing through. However, the peak occurs in late April and early May, when the park may be almost choked with birds some days. The commonest species are the *White-crowned* and *Golden-crowned Sparrow* and the *Yellow-rumped* and *Wilson's Warbler*, which may exceed 100 in a day. Look for migrating songbirds along forest edges and ornamental plantings (for example, the gardens around the Lost Lagoon pitch-and-putt course) and in the willows at the edge of Lost Lagoon. You can also see them in forested areas, especially among stands of flowering bigleaf maple trees near Brockton Point and Third Beach. Bigleaf maple flowers, which reach their peak in late April, offer a ready supply of insects for the hungry warblers.

Other species of land birds that migrate through Stanley Park include the *Vaux's Swift*; *Rufous Hummingbird*; *Western Wood-Pewee*; *Tree Swallow*; *Ruby-crowned Kinglet*; *Townsend's Solitaire*; *Hermit* and *Varied Thrush*; *American Pipit*; *Cassin's* and *Warbling Vireo*; *Orange-crowned, Nashville, Yellow, Black-throated Gray* and *Townsend's Warbler*; *Savannah* and *Lincoln's Sparrow*; and *Western Tanager*. Some of these species breed in the park, and most of them are found in both spring and fall, but a few, such as the *Townsend's Solitaire* and *Nashville Warbler*, are seen almost exclusively in spring.

Water bird migration in Stanley Park is not as spectacular as it is on the Fraser delta, but you are more likely to see rare or unusual species like a *Yellow-billed Loon* or *Tufted Duck*. These are usually seen in early spring.

## Summer

Some species, such as the *Bald Eagle*, begin breeding as early as late February, but most breeding activity takes place from late May through July. The nesting seabird colony on the Prospect Point cliffs, just west of the Lions Gate Bridge, includes up to 40 pairs of *Pelagic Cormorants* and a dozen or so pairs of *Glaucous-winged Gulls* and *Pigeon Guillemots*. A few pairs of gulls usually nest on the concrete bases of the bridge towers. You can see the colony best from the seawall walk at its base. A few *Pelagic Cormorants* use this area as a roost throughout the year. Nesting species in Stanley Park including one or more pairs of *Bald Eagles* and a pair of *Common Ravens* have nested in the area for several years. At least one pair of *Barred Owls* inhabits the heavy forest near Beaver Lake.

Beaver Lake in Stanley Park. Bill Kinkaid

However, the dominant breeding species are *Canada Geese*, *Wood Ducks* (which use the nest boxes at Beaver Lake) and *Mallards*. In addition to the nesting geese, many non-breeding or post-breeding geese find safety in the park from late June to early July during their brief flightless period, when they moult their wing feathers.

In June and July, the Beaver Lake area is the best part of the park to see a large variety of birds, partly because its denser forest stands support species such as *Hammond's Flycatchers* and *Townsend's Warblers*. You may also find the *Hairy Woodpecker*; *Olive-sided* and *Pacific-slope Flycatcher*; *Red-breasted Nuthatch*; *Brown Creeper*; *Golden-crowned Kinglet*; *Cassin's Vireo*; *Orange-crowned, Black-throated Gray* and *Wilson's Warbler*; *Western Tanager*; and *Black-headed Grosbeak*. In the shrubbery around the lake, look for breeding *Willow Flycatchers, Yellow Warblers, Song Sparrows* and *Red-winged Blackbirds*. The lily-choked lake itself has breeding *Wood Ducks, Mallards, Virginia Rails* and, in some years, *Pied-billed Grebes*.

## Fall

The fall migration of land birds takes place mainly between mid-August and mid-October. Concentrations tend to be smaller than those in spring, in part because of the more stable fall weather. Most of the common land bird species in fall are the same as those listed for spring, but you have a better chance of seeing an out-of-range vagrant, perhaps because of the high percentage of inexperienced juvenile birds.

During August, migrating shorebirds begin to appear. Repeated visits to Ferguson Point and upper Coal Harbour at low tide, preferably before 10 a.m., may allow you to see *Greater* and *Lesser Yellowlegs*, *Least* and *Western Sandpipers* and possibly *Black-bellied Plovers* or *Phalaropes*.

The most interesting time to go birding is on a cold, clear day with brisk northwest winds following several overcast rainy days. Such weather triggers southward movements of many species, from ducks and birds of prey to sparrows. Northwest winds are especially favourable for observing southward-flying raptors. There is a fall migration route along the North Shore Mountains and some of these birds cross over into Vancouver via Stanley Park. Among the commoner species like the *Red-tailed, Sharp-shinned* and *Cooper's Hawk*, you may spot a *Turkey Vulture*

Black Oystercatcher with a catch at Third Beach in Stanley Park. Colin Clasen

or an *Osprey*. On a cold-front day in late September you may also find large numbers of *Yellow-rumped Warblers*, *American Pipits*, *Savannah Sparrows*, *Dark-eyed Juncos* and *Ruby-crowned Kinglets*, as well as late-departing individuals of several other warbler species. After a cold front in mid-October, you may find dozens of *Buffleheads*, a *Ring-necked Duck* or a small flock of *Hooded Mergansers* where there were none the day before.

Along English Bay and Burrard Inlet, look for unusual gulls and terns. Large flocks of *Bonaparte's Gulls* feed offshore from August through December. They are often joined from August through late October by *Common Terns*, which, unlike the *Bonaparte's Gull*, is not seen in spring. Small numbers of *Franklin's Gulls* are seen regularly with the *Bonaparte's Gull*, and rare species like *Heermann's* and *Sabine's Gulls* and *Caspian, Arctic* and *Forster's Terns* have been recorded. In September and October, off Siwash Rock and Ferguson Point, it is possible to see a *Parasitic Jaeger* harassing gulls and terns, in an effort to steal fish from them. A scan of English Bay might reveal a *Pigeon Guillemot*.

A Great Blue Heron soaring silently over a marsh. Virginia Hayes

## Great Blue Heron Colony

At the southwest corner of Stanley Park, next to the tennis courts, apartment buildings, parking lots and Beach Avenue, is the largest *Great Blue Heron* colony within the City of Vancouver. These large, majestic, non-migratory birds have been successfully nesting at this location since 2001. The number of nests varies from year to year, depending on variables such as weather conditions and predators like *Bald Eagles*, owls and raccoons. The Stanley Park Ecology Society (SPES) monitors this colony, and the full history of the colony can be read on their website (stanley-parkecology.ca).

The SPES website observes that in the 2015 nesting season, out of a total of 108 nests, there were 83 active nests, producing an estimated 175 fledglings. Since 2007, there has been an average of two successful fledglings per nest, with one nest in 2015 producing five successful fledglings.

*Written by Wayne Weber and Brian Kautesk.*
*Revised by Catherine J. Aitchison, 2001 and 2015.*

# 2. PACIFIC SPIRIT REGIONAL PARK

## INTRODUCTION

MOST OF THIS METRO VANCOUVER PARK IS FOREST, INCLUDING SOME of the oldest and most diverse second-growth stands in the Lower Mainland. The forest spreads across a gently rounded, undulating plateau bounded by steep cliffs and gullies with beaches and marsh below. In the early 1860s, the tip of the Point Grey Peninsula was reserved from settlement to defend the Crown colony from potential American or Russian invaders. The first timber leases were granted in

One of the many entrances to Pacific Spirit Regional Park. Colin Clasen

1865. The entire park has since been logged, much of it selectively. In 1923 the area became an endowment to the future University of British Columbia and several subdivisions were carved out of the forest. Some later subdivision attempts were halted after the land was cleared. The vegetation has since grown back into thick red alder and cottonwood stands. As the city surrounded the remaining woods, the forest became more popular for naturalists, horseback riders and walkers. Today the area is protected within Pacific Spirit Regional Park, and it contains many different vegetation associations, from abandoned pastureland to mature evergreen forest, beaches and bogs. The diversity of habitats supports numerous bird species.

## DIRECTIONS

Pacific Spirit Regional Park stretches across the tip of the Point Grey Peninsula, just north of the mouth of the Fraser River and west of Vancouver's downtown core. Formerly known as the University Endowment Lands, the park surrounds the University of British Columbia. Over 50 km of trails lead through a mosaic of good birding habitats within minutes of downtown Vancouver. It is easy to reach by car along 4th Avenue, 10th Avenue, 16th Avenue or SW Marine Drive.

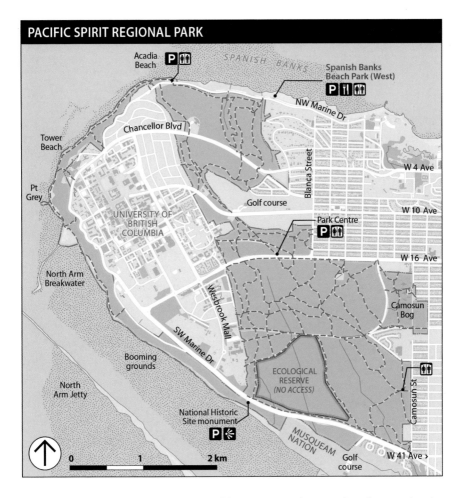

**PACIFIC SPIRIT REGIONAL PARK**

From downtown Vancouver, several buses run to the area, but they service the UBC campus rather than the park itself. Because of the size of the park, you should consult a good map to determine the area you want to reach and choose a bus route accordingly. Ask the driver for the stop nearest to the area you want to visit. For the most up-to-date bus information, check the TransLink website (translink.ca).

The Pacific Spirit Park Centre is located at 4915 West 16th Avenue on the north side of the road, 0.5 km west of Blanca Street. Maps of the many trails may be obtained here and there are washrooms and drinking water.

## BIRD SPECIES

Along Marine Drive, all the way around the point, from Spanish Banks past the campus and east again to Camosun Street, look for **Bald Eagles** perched on cedar snags. Several other roads cut through the park and many more trailheads await exploration at the ends of neighbourhood streets. Start your hike at the Pacific Spirit Park Centre or any one of several trails where they cross major roads.

## Coniferous Forest

The famous west coast evergreens flourish in the large area south of 16th Avenue, where the dense canopy dominated by Douglas-fir rustles with birdlife. You may get tired from peering up into the dark branches, but patience could pay off

with good observations of a *Brown Creeper*, *Golden-crowned Kinglet* and other, often unseen, species going about their business oblivious of your presence. The movements of hunting owls may also catch your eye as they search the open forest floor in the deep shade; the *Northern Saw-whet Owl* and *Great Horned Owl* have been sighted in the park and the *Barred Owl* is known to nest there. The power line along Imperial Trail cuts a welcome swath through the canopy, and the sunlit salmonberry layer beneath the lines is often busy with birdlife.

The cute and lovable Black–capped Chickadee is a year–round resident. Virginia Hayes

Salmonberry begins to bloom in early April some years. As soon as the large magenta blossoms appear, you may hear the zing of a foraging male *Rufous Hummingbird*. Later, as the air warms and the females arrive, watch for their bright courtship flights against the evergreen backdrop. This power line and others in the park are also good places to spot hunting owls at dusk, particularly in early fall. South of Imperial Trail, farther from the spine of the peninsula, more moisture in the soil encourages growth of western hemlock, western red cedar and Sitka spruce, resulting in a more diverse rainforest with a thicker deciduous understorey. The *Purple Finch*, *Pacific Wren* and *Pacific-slope Flycatcher* abound in summer. Where large trees have fallen, listen for the song of the *Black-throated Gray Warbler* in spring. In the more mixed areas of the forest, *Hutton's Vireo* calls in the clearings.

## Deciduous Forest

North of 16th Avenue, patches of coniferous and mixed forest can be found, but most of the area has been recently disturbed. Sunny patches of bitter cherry and fragrant black cottonwood interrupt large stands of red alder, while the ravines and steep slopes at the northern edge are full of bigleaf maples. Edges of subdivisions, ravines and clearings provide the best birding spots. The old pasture clearing called the Plains of Abraham at the north end of Pioneer Trail is a suntrap on spring mornings and provides a berry feast in the fall; it is often busy with many species of songbirds. The park is a wonderful place to hear the songs of the *Swainson's Thrush* starting in early May. Start from the trailhead kiosk on NW Marine Drive just west of the most western concession stand at Spanish Banks, where washrooms and parking are available.

The tiny Downy Woodpecker has a shrill, descending whinny call. Jim Martin

## Ocean Beach

The rocky beaches west of sandy Spanish Banks are one of the best places in the Vancouver area to view sea ducks. All three scoter species can be seen here from October to April, as well as the *Barrow's Goldeneye* and other divers. Watch for shorebirds, too, including *Black Oystercatchers*. Be sure to walk as far as the old searchlight towers, and check the breakwater at Wreck Beach for accidental species blown in from the sea. The city can seem very far away from this wild landscape of wind, waves and towering cliffs. Start from the Acadia trailhead at the park entrance sign on NW Marine Drive, where washrooms and parking are available, or hike down one of the steep trails to Wreck Beach from the campus. Be forewarned that Wreck Beach has clothing-optional status and sunbathers in a natural state can be encountered at any time.

## Booming Ground Marsh

The Wreck Beach breakwater protects the estuarine marsh to the south. Here, fresh water from the Fraser River's North Arm collects and logs are stored. The trail follows the base of the steep slope past secluded sunbathing areas. The *Marsh Wren* and other marsh species rustle among the cattails, and *Virginia Rails* have been spotted near the mouth of Booming Grounds Creek, close to the park boundary. Various duck and shorebird species can also be found in this increasingly rare habitat. Walk south from the busy beach area, or hike down from the historic monument parking lot on Marine Drive to the quieter marsh area below.

*Written by Sue-Ellen Fast, 2001. Updated by Adrian Grant Duff, 2015.*

# 3. JERICHO BEACH PARK

## INTRODUCTION

SITUATED ON ENGLISH BAY, JERICHO IS PROBABLY ONE OF THE BEST CITY parks for birding. At 47 ha, the park is less than one-sixth the size of Stanley Park, yet it can offer almost the same number of species. Many unusual and accidental species have been found here.

The park has had a checkered history and has been much affected by human activity. The name derives from Jerry's Cove, after Jeremiah Rogers, who established a base camp on the edge of the wilderness in the 1860s and set about felling the enormous trees that once grew here. A few stumps from this era can be found in the park. Later, picnickers came by barge from downtown Vancouver. The area then became part of a golf course for the Jericho Country Club.

In 1942 the Federal Department of National Defence bought most of the land, which was used as a seaplane base; concrete taxiways were constructed along with a ramp that jutted out into the bay. In 1973 the land was sold back to the city and landscaped to form the park as we see it today.

During fall migration, the south portion of the taxiway, with seedy grasses growing along the cracks in the concrete, used to bring in the *Horned Lark, Snow*

The west pond at Jericho Beach Park. Colin Clasen

*Bunting* and *Lapland Longspur*, but this area was grassed over in the 1990s. Until recently, a remnant of the northern taxiway remained as a large concrete wharf east of the Jericho Sailing Club, known as the Marginal Wharf. In 2011 the Vancouver Park Board demolished the wharf, and the area returned to natural beach and foreshore.

Ongoing work by the Jericho Stewardship Group (of which Nature Vancouver is a member) seeks to restore natural vegetation to the extent possible in a city park, especially to the west and south of the ponds.

Birding is good year-round, dropping off only in the summer months. Within the park's boundaries are woodland, meadow, freshwater marsh and ponds, scrub, flat grassy areas, sandy foreshore and a saltwater bay. The best time to visit is *very* early morning. Jericho Park has become more popular, so cyclists, joggers, dogs and water sports can interfere with birding, especially on weekends.

From Jericho Beach, depending on tides, you can walk west along Spanish Banks to the Point Grey headland, or east along rocky Bayswater Beach to Kitsilano Beach.

## DIRECTIONS

Jericho Park is located on the west side of Vancouver, north of West 4th Avenue between Wallace Street on the east and Discovery Street on the west. The park can

View north from Jericho Beach Park, over English Bay toward Cypress Mountain.
Bill Kinkaid

## JERICHO BEACH PARK

be entered anywhere along its perimeter, and cycling is permitted. No cars are allowed within the park; however, there is ample parking along West 4th Avenue and in pay parking lots on the western and eastern ends of the park. At the time of writing, the eastern parking lot is pay parking year-round and the western parking lot is pay parking May 1 to September 30.

There are a number of bus services that run east–west on West 4th Avenue, along the south boundary of the park. To get up-to-date and reliable bus information, check the TransLink website (translink.ca).

## BIRD SPECIES

From October through May, this is an excellent location for waterfowl; many of the common species can be found on the freshwater ponds or the bay. At the pond in winter, look for a **Eurasian Wigeon** amongst the **American Wigeon** and a few **Greater White-fronted Geese** amongst the **Canada Geese** in the fall. The **Ring-**

*necked Duck* has wintered here regularly in recent years, and the *Hooded Merganser* and *American Coot* are often present. However, the *Northern Pintail, Gadwall, Northern Shoveler, Green-winged Teal, Wood Duck, Common Merganser* and *Pied-billed Grebe* are found less frequently. *Cinnamon* and *Blue-winged Teal* may touch down on the ponds for a few days in spring. In the marsh and along pond margins, the *Virginia Rail* is encountered rarely in summer, and *Wilson's Snipe* can be found occasionally in March through May.

On the bay in winter, you will find the *Common Loon, Horned Grebe, Double-crested* and *Pelagic Cormorant, Surf Scoter, Common* and *Barrow's Goldeneye, Bufflehead,* and *Common* and *Red-breasted Merganser.* Species seen less often, including birds that tend to be farther from shore, are the *Red-throated* and *Pacific Loon, Western* and *Red-necked Grebe, White-winged Scoter, Lesser Scaup,* and occasionally *Pigeon Guillemot* and *Marbled Murrelet.* Common winter gulls include *Mew, Ring-billed* and, less commonly, *California, Thayer's* and *Herring. Bonaparte's Gull* is a regular in spring and fall, although usually well offshore. In summer, small flocks of *Caspian Terns* may forage offshore; the *Common Tern* and *Franklin's Gull* are seen rarely in fall.

Shorebirds are present irregularly during migration, scurrying along the beaches or foraging on exposed mud flats around the pond in the fall. You may find the *Western Sandpiper* and other peeps, *Dunlin, Killdeer, Long-billed Dowitcher* and overwintering *Sanderling. A Great Blue Heron* is a common sight at Jericho year-round, fishing for stickleback in the west pond, loafing in nearby trees

The White-crowned Sparrow sometimes repeats its melodic song for hours. Liron Gertsman

The year–round House Finch frequently visits backyard feeders. John Lowman

or wading inshore. The **Belted Kingfisher** also frequents the pond, while the **Red-winged Blackbird** is abundant here and nests in the marginal cattails. The **Common Yellowthroat** (summer) and **Marsh Wren** (year-round) are rare here. In summer, four species of swallow—**Barn**, **Violet-green**, **Tree** and **Northern Rough-winged**—hawk for insects over the ponds and adjacent grassy areas. On days with low cloud, **Black** and **Vaux's Swifts** are lucky sightings. The **Willow Flycatcher** sings from its namesake trees around the marsh.

The woodlands, small semi-wild meadows and shrubby areas of the park support a variety of passerines. The most common species are year-round residents: the **Black-capped Chickadee, Pacific Wren, American Goldfinch, Song Sparrow, Pine Siskin, Golden-crowned Kinglet, American Robin, Spotted Towhee, House Finch** and **Northern Flicker**. Slightly less common are the **Bushtit, Downy Woodpecker, Common Raven, Steller's Jay, Bewick's Wren, Brown Creeper, Red-breasted Nuthatch, Cedar Waxwing, White-crowned Sparrow, Purple Finch, House Sparrow, Pileated Woodpecker** and **Anna's Hummingbird**. Additional birds in winter include the **Fox Sparrow, Dark-eyed Junco** and **Varied Thrush**, and less commonly the **Ruby-crowned Kinglet** and **Hermit Thrush**. Mixed flocks of sparrows, including many **Golden-crowned**, forage along the edges of blackberry tangles. Summer additions include the *Warbling Vireo, Pacific-slope Flycatcher, Swainson's Thrush*, occasional *Black-headed Grosbeak*, and *Brown-headed Cowbird* (spring). Warblers include *Yellow, Wilson's* and *Common Yellowthroat*.

*Cooper's* and *Sharp-shinned Hawks* are the most common raptors, followed by *Merlin* and *Red-tailed Hawks*. The *Northern Goshawk* has overwintered here, feasting on wigeon. *Northern Harriers* and *Ospreys* are seen infrequently. Owls are scarce, although the *Barred* is possible. *Bald Eagles* are relatively easy to find: look for them overhead, perched on snags, or scavenging out on the beaches with the gulls at low tide.

Spring and fall bring many migrating birds to the park. In spring, watch for mixed flocks of small passerines as they move through the woods and in the trees near the ponds. These flocks may include warblers (*Orange-crowned, Yellow-rumped, Black-throated Gray, Townsend's*), *Hutton's Vireos, Western Wood-Pewees* and *Western Tanagers*, as well as other species mentioned above. Additional, less common species are always possible.

In the spring, the *Rufous Hummingbird* visits the early salmonberry flowers. In the fall, the *Band-tailed Pigeon* feeds on acorns from the oak trees south of the east pond. *Lincoln's* and *Savannah Sparrows* pass through the park and can be temporarily numerous in open grassy and weedy areas, while the *American Pipit* prefers the short-grass area north of the ponds.

About 34 species probably breed in the park: the *Canada Goose; Mallard; Pied-billed Grebe; Bald Eagle; American Coot; Rock Pigeon; Rufous* and *Anna's Hummingbird; Downy Woodpecker; Northern Flicker; Willow* and *Pacific-slope Flycatcher; Warbling Vireo; Northwestern Crow; Common Raven; Tree, Violet-green* and *Barn Swallow; Black-capped Chickadee; Bushtit; Pacific Wren; Swainson's Thrush; American Robin; European Starling; Cedar Waxwing; Yellow* and *Wilson's Warbler; Spotted Towhee, Song* and *White-crowned Sparrow; Red-winged Blackbird; Brown-headed Cowbird; House Finch;* and *American Goldfinch*.

The eBird website (ebird.org) lists 212 species that have been seen in Jericho Park over the past 10 years, although for 63 of these, there are fewer than about 10 sightings.

*Written and revised by Daphne Solecki, 2001.*
*Updated by Daphne Solecki, June Ryder and Adrian Grant-Duff, 2015.*

# 4. QUEEN ELIZABETH PARK

## INTRODUCTION

QUEEN ELIZABETH PARK IS LOCATED NEAR THE CENTRE OF THE CITY OF Vancouver on Little Mountain, one of the highest hills in the city. Atop the hill is the Bloedel Floral Conservatory, a popular Vancouver tourist attraction, which features a dome that houses a wide variety of tropical and desert flora and fauna, including an array of colourful birds. This area was a rock quarry in the early part of the last century. When the quarry ceased production, the area was eventually replanted and now some areas are dedicated to native plants and some to ornamental plants.

Queen Elizabeth Park's main quarry and the tall conifers beside it, which attract many birds. Colin Clasen

From the perimeter of the conservatory, you have a panoramic view of much of Vancouver and the surrounding municipalities. To the north the mighty Coastal Mountains—Cypress, Grouse and Seymour—dwarf the high-rises and office towers around English Bay. To the west the University of British Columbia and Pacific Spirit Park project out toward the Strait of Georgia, and on a clear day, you can see Vancouver Island. To the south are the vast floodplains of the lower Fraser River delta, and to the east Burnaby Mountain and Central Park rise out of the city and suburbs of Burnaby.

Since this guide was last published in 2001, the stunning views to the north and west have been made possible by many trees being topped and felled. This has unfortunately made these areas less valuable to wildlife. Certain gardening practices have also reduced the amount of wildlife-friendly habitat. Fortunately, there is still enough of the bird-friendly habitat to make it very worthwhile for birders to spend time here.

## DIRECTIONS

To reach the park from downtown Vancouver, drive south on Cambie Street to

33rd Avenue, turn left and proceed for about 160 m, and then turn left again into the parking lot. There is also a ring road that circles around the north side of the park and goes up to another parking lot that sits atop a major water storage reservoir. These are both pay parking lots, but free parking is also available along most adjacent streets. Check the regulations carefully before leaving your car.

Queen Elizabeth Park is also easily reached by bus from downtown Vancouver, or from many areas along 33rd and 16th Avenues, from 29th Avenue Station to UBC. If you plan on taking the Canada Line SkyTrain from either Richmond or Vancouver, you can get off at King Edward (25th) Avenue and walk south five blocks to the park, or take a bus to a stop at the northwest corner of the park. For the most up-to-date transit information, see the TransLink website (translink.ca).

If you are cycling, you will be pleased to know about both the Ontario Street cycling route and the 37th Avenue cycling route, along the east and south sides respectively.

**QUEEN ELIZABETH PARK**

## BIRD SPECIES

A stunning male Anna's Hummingbird. These birds come to feeders year–round. Michelle Lamberson

*Anna's Hummingbird* is abundant in the park year-round and can start breeding as early as late January, when you can spot the males displaying and, if you are lucky, see a female collecting lichen and spider webs for her nest. In March, *Anna's* is joined by the migratory *Rufous Hummingbird*, which also breeds in the park. *Yellow-rumped* and *Orange-crowned Warblers* start arriving in late March and early April, increasing in numbers until flocks of 50 or more birds at a time can be observed in late April and early May. They can be accompanied by any number of migrants including, but not limited to, the *Townsend's*, *Black-throated Gray* and *Mac-Gillivray's Warbler*; *Cassin's* and *Warbling Vireo*; *Lincoln's* and *Savannah Sparrow*; and *Pacific-slope Flycatcher*. At this time you can look for the rare, but regular, *Chipping Sparrow*, *Calliope Hummingbird* and *Nashville Warbler*.

As mid-May rolls around, the park sees a major switch in species composition. The majority of the flocks moving through are now composed almost entirely of *Wilson's Warbler*, which can swarm through the park in astonishing numbers. Joining these warblers come the *Willow Flycatcher*, *Yellow Warbler* and *Western Tanager*. Also in mid-May, the *Western Wood-Pewee* and *Olive-sided Flycatcher* can be seen hawking insects from the tops of trees and snags around the park. The *Swainson's Thrush* is commonly encountered at this time, as well as the *Black-headed Grosbeak* and the occasional *Lazuli Bunting*.

*Black* and *Vaux's Swifts* can be seen in late spring darting over the park in small flocks, and there is a chance of seeing any of the six commonly encountered swallow species in Vancouver at this time. Keeping your eyes up, you can see migrating *Caspian Terns*, *Greater White-fronted Geese* or *Common Loons*. May also brings large flocks of *Cedar Waxwings* and often even larger flocks of *Red Crossbills*. Once June rolls around, the park quietens down, but many species remain to breed, including the *Oregon Junco*, *Song Sparrow*, *Spotted Towhee*, *Yellow-rumped (Audubon's) Warbler*, *Cooper's Hawk*, *Northwestern Crow*, *Downy Woodpecker*, *Brown Creeper*, *Mallard*, *Gadwall*, *White-crowned Sparrow*, *Red-breasted Nuthatch* and *Black-capped Chickadee*. For these birds, the park offers a crucial urban refuge in which to lay eggs and raise their young, in an increasingly fragmented urban landscape. Once July and August bring summer heat to the park, the migration starts again, with many of the same species coming through in larger numbers, with the addition of their young of the year. In October keep your eyes out for *White-throated Sparrows*, which visit the park in small numbers every year.

In the winter you can find *Golden-crowned, White-crowned, Song* and *Fox Sparrows*, numerous duck species including *American* and *Eurasian Wigeons; Ring-necked Ducks; Hooded Mergansers; Gadwall* and *Buffleheads; Pacific* and *Bewick's Wrens; Golden-crowned* and *Ruby-crowned Kinglets; Great Blue Herons; Chestnut-backed* and *Black-capped Chickadees; Varied* and *Hermit Thrushes; American Robins*; and many other common winter Vancouver birds.

This park offers a great place to reliably find the *Ruby-crowned Kinglet* and *Hermit Thrush* in the winter. The slopes and open sight lines at this time of year make it an excellent spot to see raptors in the city. In addition to the resident *Cooper's Hawk*, the *Merlin, Peregrine Falcon, Sharp-shinned Hawk* and *Bald Eagle* are frequently observed.

Though most of the park is very good for birding, there are a few hot spots that you should be aware of if you are to bird the park productively. The most easterly portion of the park, near the intersection of Ontario Street and 33rd

Rufous Hummingbird female feeding chicks. Jim Martin

Avenue, boasts two connected ponds that can have waterfowl at any time of year. In the trees around these ponds, you can see any number of flycatchers and warblers in the springtime. On the west side of the pitch-and-putt, there is a lawn-bowling green that can be very good for spotting a *Townsend's Solitaire* in the winter and early spring. These birds also visit both quarries in the early spring. Other birds that can be spotted on the berry bushes in these three places in the winter are the **Pine Grosbeak** and **Bohemian Waxwing**. From the bowling green, there is a con-

crete path that leads north across the main road up to the Seasons In The Park Restaurant. In this area, there can be some very productive spring birding. Along here you can spot the **Hermit Thrush** in the winter, and in the spring and summer, the **Olive-sided Flycatcher** and other flycatchers, along with **Cassin's Vireo** and other vireos. This path leads along the base of the small quarry and along an exposed north-facing slope. This slope can be very good for morning birding during migration, as it heats up faster than many other spots in the park and can provide wonderful views of tanagers, warblers, vireos and grosbeaks catching insects in the morning sun. Along here keep your eyes and ears open for **Hutton's Vireo**, which breeds in the park and is present year-round. This trail ends in a T-intersection. Just before and on the other side of this junction is a

Male Rufous Hummingbird—migratory and more aggressive than the Anna's. John Lowman

wonderful place to look for **Barred Owls**, which often roost in these conifers and can be vocal on some spring evenings. In the shade of these trees, look for **Varied Thrush, Kinglets, Brown Creepers** and migrating **Townsend's Warblers**.

Farther west from this patch of conifers, you come to an area that is dense with salmonberry and various maples. This area, and all the way southwest to a grassy slope and a bench looking westward over Cambie Street, is an extremely productive location during migration. The vantage point provided by the bench can be invaluable, as on poor-weather days during the spring, the trees on the hillside below it can hold hundreds of songbirds. It is essential not to stray from the path around here, as the rocks and stumps in this area are home to Western Red-backed Salamanders. On early spring nights after a rainfall, one can walk along these trails and see dozens of these lung-less salamanders as they crawl out of the protection of stones and fern clumps to feed and breed. Step with care at all times of the year, as their rocky hideouts can be dangerously dislodged with a single footstep. Other non-birds that can be enjoyed in the park are crayfish, catfish, butterflies, dragon-flies, moths, coyotes, striped skunks, northern raccoons, bats and the occasional garter snake.

Queen Elizabeth Park provides a unique opportunity in Vancouver to see very large numbers of migrants at close range, and on good migration viewing days, one can encounter large numbers of birds almost anywhere in the park. Queen Elizabeth Park also helps us to appreciate the value of productive habitat for migratory birds and the wildlife that can exist in the middle of an urban area when habitat is present.

## WHEN TO VISIT

The time of day, season and weather play a major part in birding in Queen Elizabeth Park. The best time of the year for migrant songbirds, for which the park is famous, is from mid-April through late May and from early August through mid-October. The best time of day is early morning, although late afternoons can sometimes be productive. Don't be discouraged by a little rain, as drizzly overcast mornings are the ideal conditions for finding migrants. This is especially true on mornings following overnight rains, because birds migrating overnight can be brought down into the park in truly spectacular numbers from inclement weather, creating the legendary bird fallouts that birdwatchers dream about. With its central location, elevated topography and easy sight lines, Queen Elizabeth Park is perhaps unparal-leled in the city for the fallout birding opportunities it provides. After spring rains, the park can be absolutely dripping with tanagers, grosbeaks, warblers, flycatchers and vireos resting and refuelling for the next leg of their journey.

*Written by Dale Jensen, 2001.*
*Revised by Jeremiah Kennedy and Ian Thomas, 2015.*

# 5. FRASER RIVER PARK / MUSQUEAM MARSH NATURE PARK / BLENHEIM FLATS

## INTRODUCTION

In the southwest part of Vancouver, along the Fraser River from Angus Drive to the Musqueam First Nations Reserve, you will find a unique rural area of the city. The diversity of habitats fosters an exceptional array of bird species.

There are two large parks located here and three riverfront trails. Between these two major parks, there is also one small riverfront park, Derring Island Park, as well as two private golf courses and one public City of Vancouver golf course. Large parcels of private land, still in the Agricultural Land Reserve (ALR) and located in the community known today as Southlands, contain equestrian stables and paddocks as well as a major retail garden centre. These ALR lands historically were three large farms that provided milk, meat and vegetables for early Vancouver settlers.

As in most areas near rivers, dykes were built to channel the river and protect lowlands from flooding. The habitats include western red cedar and red alder. There are thickets of mixed woods, including cottonwoods and Lombardy poplars, along the horse trail, dyke areas, sloughs and horse pastures in the vicinity of Blenheim Flats and Musqueam Marsh Nature Park.

Fraser River Park is a relatively new park, running west along 75th Avenue on a narrow strip of tidal river edge. It provides access to the Fraser River in a setting that attempts to recreate the original natural riparian habitats. A small marsh and

Mouth of Musqueam Creek. Al Grass

Deering Island Park trail. Al Grass

tidal flats have been replanted with native vegetation. Thickets of blackberry, salmonberry, wild rose and snowberry provide food and shelter for passerines, and grasses and thistles have been planted to attract a variety of finches and sparrows. A boardwalk along the water's edge and a short pier make it easy to scan the river for water birds. Several clumps of tall cottonwoods often attract warblers in spring. Interpretive signs at intervals along the paths, and an interpretive court at the east end of the park, explain the history of the area and the many artifacts.

A small replacement marsh was planted at the west end of Derring Island Park to compensate for the loss of slough habitat during the construction of a housing development on Derring Island in the 1980s. Thickets of native riparian vegetation were re-established along portions of the river walkway. Southlands once had salmon streams, frog and salamander ponds and a large population of muskrats and river otters. Riverfront shipyards and upland housing developments have contributed to changing Southlands considerably over the years.

The park at the Angus Street Road entrance and parking areas make the park accessible to wheelchairs and visiting walkers.

Thickets of wild Nootka rose, salmonberry and snowberry, restored marsh grasses and big-headed sedge are found in the dredged river sand dunes. A wooden boardwalk along a portion of the tidal riverfront leads to an observation pier and a small sandy beach. This area is known for observing waterfowl and *Bald Eagle*.

Depending on your pace and diversions, these areas can be birded in a couple of hours, or you can take a full day. Fraser River Park and Heron Nature Trail in Musqueam Marsh Nature Park probably offer the best birding opportunities.

## DIRECTIONS

Car access to Fraser River Park is available via 75th Avenue west of Granville Street, or at the foot of Angus Drive turning south off SW Marine Drive. There are two small parking lots here with washrooms and picnic tables.

Blenheim Flats, a rural area of horse stables, paddocks and garden centres, is located near the foot of Blenheim Street, in the area known as Southlands. It is roughly bounded by SW Marine Drive, Blenheim Street, Macdonald Street and the North Arm of the Fraser River. There are golf courses to the east and west. Blenheim Flats is best birded on foot, walking along the relatively quiet residential streets and paying close attention to the pastures and shrubby areas.

Heron Nature Trail in Musqueam Marsh Nature Park begins at the foot of Alma Street (one block west of Dunbar Street) and ends at Crown Street. There are no facilities here, but there is limited street parking at the trailhead.

The local bus routes bring you within easy walking distance of these birding areas. Check the TransLink website (translink.ca) for specific details.

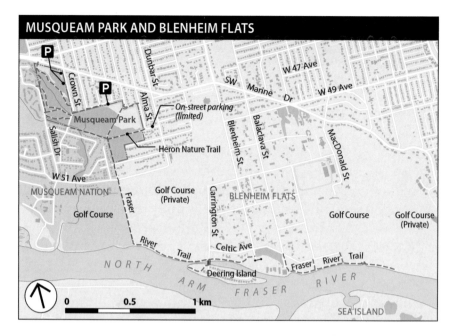

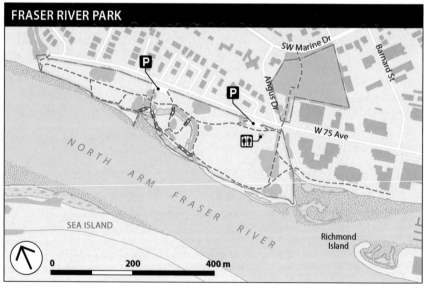

# BIRD SPECIES

Birding opportunities change with the season and habitat, but a good variety of species can always be found. The annual run of eulachon (a small herring-like fish) occurs during April. The calls of the *Bonaparte's Gull* and occasionally the *Common Tern* are a sure sign that eulachon are in the river. Other gulls, particularly the *Glaucous-winged*, are attracted in numbers. Look for *Mew*, *Ring-billed*, *Herring*, *Thayer's* and other gull species among the loafing flocks settled on the log booms. The *Caspian Tern* is seen in summer.

The *Double-crested Cormorant*, *Common Loon*, *Western Grebe* and other fish-eating species, including the *Common* and *Red-breasted Merganser*, are often seen on the river. Smaller numbers of these species can be seen through the winter months.

Many of Vancouver's common waterfowl species will be found frequenting the sloughs and side channels. *Mallard*, *Green-winged Teal*, *Greater Scaup* and *Great Blue Heron* abound. Vegetated shoreline and drainage channels may shelter a *Green Heron*. The *Killdeer* occurs in the more open areas, and the *Spotted Sandpiper* frequents the river edge in summer.

The Spotted Towhee has a wide repertoire of calls. Michelle Lamberson

The very eye-catching, thistle-loving American Goldfinch. John Gordon

Around the stables and in the horse paddocks, the **Brewer's** and **Red-winged Blackbird** and **Brown-headed Cowbird** are always present. Mixed flocks of these species will gather, especially in winter. The horse paddocks occasionally sport a **Short-eared Owl** or two, and **Barn Owls** reportedly reside in some of the stables. The **Ring-necked Pheasant** maintains a small population in this area. On the flats you may see raptors, including the **Red-tailed Hawk**, **Bald Eagle** and **Cooper's** and **Sharp-shinned Hawk**.

The Song Sparrow, our most common sparrow, responds quickly to pishing. Jim Martin

Musqueam Marsh Nature Park has long been known for its forest birds. The **Black-capped** and **Chestnut-backed Chickadee**, **Golden-crowned** and **Ruby-crowned Kinglet**, **Red Crossbill**, **Hutton's Vireo**, **Hammond's Flycatcher** and **Western Wood-Pewee** are regulars in spring. In the alder forest along the horse trail, the **Willow Flycatcher**, **Yellow Warbler** and other warblers and vireos are summer residents. In winter, flocks of **Pine Siskins** (occasionally with **American Goldfinches** and **Common Redpolls** mixed in), **Fox** and **Song Sparrows**, **Varied Thrushes**, **Dark-eyed Juncos** and **Spotted Towhees** frequent this habitat. The **Evening Grosbeak** is a regular visitor to this area in spring and autumn. Looking for **Northern Saw-whet** and **Great Horned Owls** in Musqueam Park can be particularly rewarding.

The horse trail, from near the west end of Heron Nature Trail toward the dyke, provides excellent birding during the spring migration period. The mixed forest/thicket habitats are excellent for warblers, sparrows and other small songbirds.

From June through July, **Black-headed Grosbeaks** and **Bullock's Orioles** are regular breeding species, but their numbers are very small. Tall birch thickets and Lombardy poplars are the places to look for these species.

In past years this area of Vancouver has turned up some "firsts." A **Western Scrub-Jay** appeared one fall and stayed for several weeks, and the **Black-and-white Warbler** has occasionally been found here.

*Written by Bill Merilees. Revised by Catherine J. Aitchison, 2001.*
*Revised by Terry Slack, Al Grass and Jude Grass, 2015.*

# 6. MAPLEWOOD CONSERVATION AREA

## INTRODUCTION

THE CONSERVATION AREA AT MAPLEWOOD FLATS IN NORTH VANCOUVER is operated by the Wild Bird Trust of British Columbia (WBT) and is the last undeveloped waterfront wetland on the north shore of Burrard Inlet. For over 20 years, public interest groups lobbied to preserve this prime site as a wildlife sanctuary. This is a non-profit, membership-based, provincial organization with charitable status, founded by Dr. Richard C. Beard and Patricia M. Banning-Lover in 1993. There are over 3 km of wheelchair accessible trails, memorial and resting benches, a viewing platform, an installed freshwater wetland with well and pumphouse, a covered area for picnics and a native vegetation nursery. The Corrigan Nature

Springtime beauty at the West Pond at Maplewood. John Lowman

House was dedicated in March 2015. The bird species list, which stood at 208 in 1993, increased to 246 by 2015.

Several conservation programs have been implemented:

**Purple Martin Nest Box Monitoring Program**: Nest boxes are provided for this blue-listed migratory bird, which spends our winters in Brazil.

**Anise Swallowtail Butterfly Restoration Project**: A critical mass of food plants is slowly being amassed to support reintroduction in the west tidal salt marsh.

**Killdeer Nesting Habitat**: This comprises an area of about 1,400 square m on the western boundary.

Other wildlife seen here includes coastal black-tailed deer, coyotes, northern river otters, beaver, mink, weasels, skunks, raccoons and squirrels. Black bears arrive in summer to feast on blackberries, and very occasional sightings of a bobcat and a cougar have been recorded. WBT's Big Sit is held in late spring, and the annual "Return of the Osprey" Festival is celebrated on the last weekend in July. Other regular events include a bird survey on the first Saturday of each month and a guided nature walk on the second Saturday of each month. All regular events are free and there is no gate admission to the site.

## DIRECTIONS

Maplewood Conservation Area is situated on the south side of the Dollarton Highway, east of the north end of the Ironworkers Memorial (Second Narrows) Bridge. Drive east from downtown Vancouver via Hastings Street, left (north) on Renfrew Street, then right (east) on McGill Street onto the bridge, which crosses Burrard Inlet to North Vancouver. Take the first exit (#23B, Dollarton Highway) and proceed for approximately 2 km, where a large blue WBT sign signals the

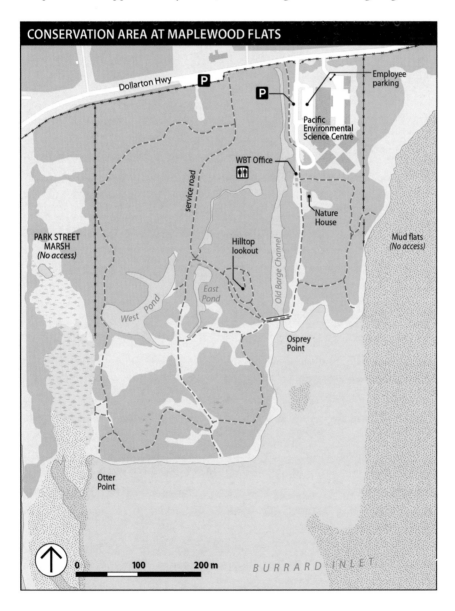

CONSERVATION AREA AT MAPLEWOOD FLATS

entrance at 2645 Dollarton Highway.

It can be reached by public transit from downtown Vancouver and there is a bus stop at the entrance. For current bus information, check the TransLink website (translink.ca).

The property is shared with Environment Canada's Pacific Environmental Science Centre. Visitors to the conservation area are requested not to use Environment Canada's employee parking during their office hours. There is ample free parking Monday to Friday after 5 p.m. and on weekends. At the time of writing, Environment Canada's gate, which previously automatically closed at 6 p.m. weekdays and 4 p.m. weekends, is no longer operational. In case this changes in the future, check with the WBT office.

## BIRD SPECIES

There are seven habitat types in the area, so the species to be expected are grouped by habitat. As of 2015, a total of 246 bird species had been recorded (up from 208 in 1993). The upland section of the conservation area is a rescued brown field site, which was created by humans for industrial and commercial uses. In the 1950s, 1960s and 1970s, truckloads of fill (asphalt, concrete, bricks and all types of soils) were dumped on the intertidal flats and salt marshes to a depth of 3 m to create an industrial site. As a result of the dumping of soils from gardens, up to 70 percent of the plants on the upland filled area are exotic species. Native bird species and people have added more exotic plant species.

### 1. Intertidal Flats

Flats to the south, west and east are most extensive on the eastern side, with mud, silts, gravel and cobblestones. There are a number of shell, shingle and sand bars. The flats have 37 groupings of old poles (called dolphins), which were used for log boom storage and sorting. The tidal flats are fully exposed only at low tide; at high tide the salt marsh fringe is also flooded. In winter this zone is a major feeding ground for flocks of *American Wigeons* (often with *Eurasian Wigeons*), *Green-winged Teals*, *Northern Pintails*, *Mew Gulls* and *Mallards*, with small groups of *Hooded* and *Common Mergansers*, *Greater Yellowlegs*, *Dunlins*, *Killdeers* and *Spotted Sandpipers*. At times the high-tide line attracts flocks of up to 20 *Red Crossbills*, which eat small shellfish, salt and other trace minerals. March through May brings small numbers of migrating *White-fronted* and *Cackling Geese*, *Trumpeter Swans* and various plovers and sandpipers. *Ring-billed*, *California* and *Mew Gulls* arrive in larger flocks. Autumn migration starting in July brings *Least*, *Western*, *Baird's*, *Pectoral*, *Stilt* and *Semipalmated Sandpiper*; *Dowitcher*, *Yellowleg* and *Phalarope* species; *Black-bellied* and *Semipalmated Plovers*; *Bonaparte's Gulls*; and *Common*

Adult male Purple Martin feeding a dragonfly to two chicks at Maplewood. John Lowman

*Terns*. Most of these species are generally gone by the end of September.

In summer, bachelor parties of **Harlequin Ducks** use the southeastern area, along with **Black Oystercatchers**. Breeding **Ospreys** returned to Burrard Inlet in 1991, with the first pair nesting at Maplewood in that year. Up to six pairs now nest along Burrard Inlet. While watching the **Osprey** hunt, keep a watch for visiting **Caspian Terns**.

In 1992, a nest box project brought breeding **Purple Martins** back to mainland BC for the first time in 22 years. The nest boxes were attached to the dolphin post clusters, which stand in the mud flats and are surrounded by salt water for much of the time. From a single nesting pair in 1994, the new colony grew to a record 77 nesting pairs in 2014, out of a total of 99 nest boxes. Most martins arrive in early May and depart at the end of August, with a few remaining in the first week of September. They are most easily observed in late July and August in good weather when they are hunting or in song flight over the area, or with a scope when they are perched around their nest boxes. They are very defensive of their breeding sites and have been observed in aerial pursuit and attack on **Cooper's Hawks**, **Merlins**, **Peregrine Falcons**, **Glaucous-winged Gulls** and **Northwestern Crows**. The **Ospreys** also get harassed but not to the same extent. McCartney Creek estuary at the very eastern end of the flats is a good place to see **American Dippers**, yellowlegs, dowitchers, plovers and sandpipers.

## 2. Deep Saltwater Basin

To the south of the filled upland area is a deep saltwater basin that holds water at low tide and provides a deep-water feeding zone for flocks of *Barrow's* and *Common Goldeneyes*, *Buffleheads* and small numbers of *Greater Scaups*, *Horned Grebes*, *Double-crested* and *Pelagic Cormorants*, *Red-breasted Mergansers*, *Common Loons*, *Harlequin Ducks* and *Surf Scoters* in winter. Unusual species in winter include the *Red-necked* and *Western Grebe*, *Red-throated Loon*, *Long-tailed Duck*, *Brandt's Cormorant*, *Marbled Murrelet* and *Common Murre* in ones or twos. Late summer may provide sightings of a *Common Tern* or *Parasitic Jaeger*.

## 3. Freshwater Marsh/Ponds System

With funding secured by Wild Bird Trust from government, industry and the public, an extensive freshwater marsh and ponds system with interconnecting creeks was excavated in the 60-year-old filled area in the western part of the site. The system was completed in the spring of 1997 and is now a breeding site for the *Wood Duck, Mallard, Hooded Merganser, Red-winged Blackbird, Sora*, and *Virginia Rail*. In spring and fall, the *Marsh Wren, Common Yellowthroat, Northern Shoveler, Ring-necked Duck, American Coot, Pied-billed Grebe, Cinnamon* and *Blue-winged Teal*, and *Green Heron* use the pond. In winter, a number of duck species, including the *Ring-necked Duck, Northern Shoveler, Hooded Merganser* and *American Coot*, are seen. On summer evenings, *Violet-green, Northern Rough-winged, Barn, Tree*

Wood Duck pair gliding in for a graceful landing. John Lowman

and *Cliff Swallows* feed over the pond, where *Purple Martins*, *Vaux's* and *Black Swifts* may join them when the weather is overcast. Directly to the west of the pond is a natural freshwater marsh/pond and salt marsh complex, which is a small example of the original shoreline habitat. It is best observed from Otter Point and the commercial area to the west of the conservation area. This marsh pond zone provides breeding habitat for the *Virginia Rail* and *Sora*, *Spotted Sandpiper*, *Green Heron*, *Bewick's Wren*, *Purple Finch*, *Spotted Towhee* and duck species. From autumn through spring, the complex is used by duck species, *Wilson's Snipe*, *Killdeer* and *Great Blue Heron*.

## 4. Western and Eastern Salt Marshes

These remnant salt marshes can attract migrating *Townsend's Solitaires*; *Western Meadowlarks*; *Western Bluebirds*; *Eastern* and *Western Kingbirds*; *American Kestrels*; *Short-eared Owls*; *Northern Pygmy-Owls*; *Northern Harriers*; *Northern Shrikes*; *Savannah*, *White-* and *Golden-crowned Sparrows*; *Purple Finches*; and *American Pipits*. Unusual species to watch for are the *Snow Bunting* and *Lapland Longspur*.

## 5. Open Rough Meadow

This area of 60-year-old filled-in mud flats is now habitat for *White-crowned*, *Golden-crowned*, *Savannah* and *Lincoln's Sparrows* and *American Goldfinches*, as well as the preceding species to be looked for on the salt marshes. This meadow is habitat for Townsend's vole, which is a food item for the *Northern Pygmy-Owl*, *Northern Shrike*, *American Kestrel*, *Short-eared Owl*, *Rough-legged Hawk* and *Northern Harrier*, all of which hunt the meadow when migrating through this area.

## 6. Black Cottonwood, Red Alder, Eastern Coniferous Forest

The northwest and northeast portions of the site have deciduous (northwest) and mixed coniferous-deciduous (northeast) riparian forest of approximately 60 to 80 years of age. In spring and autumn, these trees are feeding habitat for migrating woodpecker, warbler, vireo, flycatcher, tanager and thrush species. In summer, look for the *Black-headed Grosbeak*, *Swainson's Thrush*, *Downy* and *Hairy Woodpecker* and *Warbling*, *Cassin's* and *Red-eyed Vireo*. In winter, the *Red-breasted Sapsucker*, *Brown Creeper*, *Hermit Thrush*, *Pacific* and *Bewick's Wren* may be seen with the flocks of kinglets and chickadees. Groups of *Varied Thrushes*, *Spotted Towhees*, *Song* and *Fox Sparrows* forage in the leaf litter. In the eastern mixed coniferous (Sitka spruce, western red cedar, Douglas-fir and western hemlock) and deciduous forest, the *Chestnut-backed Chickadee*, *Red-breasted Nuthatch*, *Red Crossbill*, *Pileated Woodpecker* and *Steller's Jay* can be added to the winter mix of species. In summer, look for the active *Bald Eagle* nest and the two to four active *Great Blue Heron* nests in this forest.

Wintertime beauty at the West Pond at Maplewood. John Lowman

## 7. Himalayan Blackberry, Red Alder, Pacific Crab Apple Shrub Zone

Much of the eastern area and scattered zones throughout the rest of the site are covered by a mixed-species shrub and small tree habitat, which includes some old red alder and black cottonwood. The shrub zone, while dominated by Himalayan blackberry, has mixed through it 14 native species and 8 exotic species of berry-bearing shrubs and small tree species. Of these, only European holly, the Himalayan cotoneaster species, European hawthorn and the native Pacific crab apple keep their berries well into winter, when bird species need them most. This area and other parts of the site, such as the west berm, have been planted with over 1,600 trees and shrubs of more than 130 species in the past 40 years. This has increased biodiversity on the site and created an arboretum. The species mix includes Garry oak, ponderosa pine and incense cedar, all species that are adapted to hot, dry summers.

In summer, look for the *Cedar Waxwing, Black-headed Grosbeak, Western Wood-Pewee, Bushtit, Spotted Towhee, Rufous Hummingbird, Yellow* and *Wilson's Warbler* and *Purple Finch* (this species has a strong affinity for Pacific crab apple berries). In winter, flocks of *Pine Siskins* (watch for *Common Redpolls*), *Purple* and *House Finches, American Goldfinches* and *Varied Thrushes* feed on the blackberry, alder and other seeds and berries. The *Pacific* and *Bewick's Wren*, *Fox* and *Song Sparrow*, *Spotted Towhee*, *Hermit Thrush*, *Downy Woodpecker* and *Ruby-crowned* and *Golden-crowned Kinglet* also use these shrub thickets. Watch for *Hutton's Vireos* and *Band-tailed Pigeons*, which are not common birds now.

## Raptors and Owls

The *Cooper's* and *Red-tailed Hawk*, *Merlin*, *Peregrine Falcon*, *Barred* and *Great Horned Owl* can be expected at any time of year. The *Northern Harrier*; *Sharpshinned* and *Rough-legged Hawk*; *Gyrfalcon*; *Northern Goshawk*; *Northern Pygmy-*, *Northern Saw-whet* and *Short-eared Owl* are autumn through late winter migrants. The *Turkey Vulture* and *Osprey* are late spring to October visitors.

## Common West Coast Birds

Common species of birds to watch for include the *Harlequin Duck* (summer through winter), *Surf Scoter* (winter), *Barrow's Goldeneye* (winter), *Pelagic Cormorant* (all year), *Bald Eagle* (all year), *Black Oystercatcher* (late summer through late winter), *Glaucous-winged Gull* (all year), *Rufous Hummingbird* (summer), *Red-breasted Sapsucker* (winter), *Steller's Jay* (autumn and winter), *Northwestern Crow* (all year), *Purple Martin* (summer), *Bushtit* (all year), *Bewick's Wren* (all year), *Pacific Wren* (all year), *Varied Thrush* (winter), *Black-throated Gray Warbler* (spring and late summer) and *Spotted Towhee* (all year).

The *Great Blue Heron*, *Belted Kingfisher*, *Common Loon*, *Glaucous-winged Gull* and *Killdeer* are year-round residents. There have been some decreases of species at the site in the past 50 years, such as the *Black Turnstone*, *Dunlin*, scoter species, *Gadwall*, *Savannah Sparrow* and *Cliff Swallow*. However, the *Eurasian Collared-Dove* is now in the area and the *American Redstart* is expanding its breeding range into the site.

*Written and updated by Kevin M. Bell and Patricia M. Banning-Lover, WBT President/ Co-Founder, 2015.*

# 7. LIGHTHOUSE PARK / KLOOTCHMAN PARK

## LIGHTHOUSE PARK — INTRODUCTION

LIGHTHOUSE PARK IS LOCATED IN WEST VANCOUVER, A SHORT DRIVE from downtown Vancouver. Point Atkinson, the rocky headland on the southern tip of the park, was named after Thomas Atkinson, a Royal Navy captain, by Captain George Vancouver while he was engaged in survey work on the southern British Columbia coast in 1792.

In 1873–74, the first lighthouse was built to protect ships sailing to logging camps and sawmills on the shores of Burrard Inlet. The stone base of this old wooden tower is still visible to the west of the present lighthouse. In 1881 the 75 ha section of Crown land to the north of the lighthouse was granted to the Dominion government for a lighthouse reserve. In 1910 the reserve was leased to North Vancouver and then leased to West Vancouver upon its incorporation in 1912.

Looking west from Lighthouse Park. David Cook

Today's Lighthouse Park has remained relatively undisturbed. It contains a remarkable range of natural conditions and varied environments. Approximately two-thirds of the park's perimeter is shoreline, consisting of coves, rocky headlands, high granite cliffs and a group of small rocky islands to the northwest of the park. Trees and shrubs, such as arbutus, shore pine and salal, thrive here. The interior of the park is punctuated by high, rounded granite outcrops, up to almost 120 m above sea level. Between them are valleys and narrow draws where deeper soil supports a magnificent coniferous forest. The largest trees are Douglas-fir, some over 400 years old, 60 m high and 2 m in diameter. Other tree species include western hemlock and western red cedar, with lesser numbers of bigleaf maple and red alder. The shaded forest floor is covered with red huckleberry, sword fern, western hemlock seedlings and thickets of salmonberry as well as colonies of Oregon grape, deer fern and various mosses.

A ubiquitous resident in Lighthouse Park is the Douglas squirrel, a tiny, golden-brown creature often mistaken by visitors for a chipmunk. Douglas squirrels are the only west coast native species. The best location to view shorebirds in this area is actually outside Lighthouse Park, in another small park just to the west. This is Klootchman Park (described below), which consists mainly of a trail with a steep set of staircases leading down through the forest from the top of the cliff to Indian Bluff, a rocky lookout facing the Grebe Islets (about 15 minutes' walk). Try to visit on a low tide, which exposes feeding sites on the islets, and use a scope to obtain the best views.

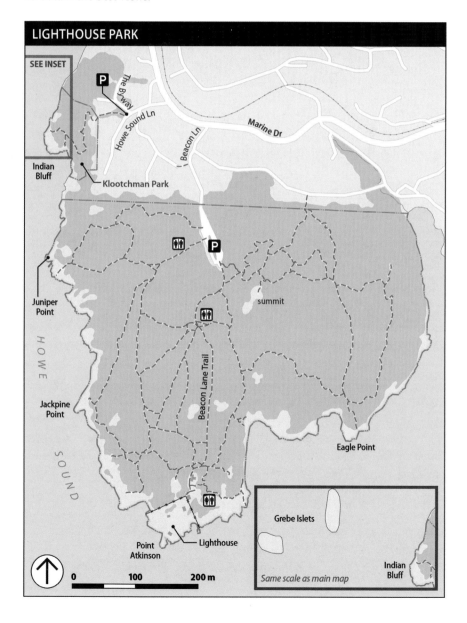

## DIRECTIONS

To reach Lighthouse Park from Vancouver, drive north over the Lions Gate Bridge and take the exit to West Vancouver. The first traffic light is at the intersection of Marine Drive and Taylor Way. Go straight through this intersection and follow Marine Drive west for 10.3 km to Beacon Lane (watch carefully for the small Lighthouse Park sign on your left). Turn left on Beacon Lane and follow it for 0.3 km to the park gate and parking area. Alternatively, you can take the Ironworkers Memorial (Second Narrows) Bridge north from East Vancouver or Burnaby to North Vancouver. Continue west on the Upper Levels Highway (Highway 1) to the Taylor Way exit (#13), then turn left on Taylor Way, drive south to the intersection with Marine Drive, turn right and proceed as above.

Lighthouse Park is easy to reach by bus from downtown Vancouver, using the City of West Vancouver's public Blue Bus. Ask the driver to let you off at the stop closest to the park entrance. For the most up-to-date Blue Bus information, please see the *Public Transit* section of this guide for their website and phone number.

## BIRD SPECIES

Over 150 bird species have been recorded in the park. There are opportunities for viewing both sea and land birds, but because of the rugged terrain, visitors must be prepared and alert. Sturdy footwear will allow you to explore the many steep, rocky trails, while common sense will keep you a safe distance from steep cliffs.

Lush ground cover in the interior of the park is a favourite haunt of the *Song Sparrow*, *Spotted Towhee*, *Dark-eyed Junco* and *Pacific Wren*. As you walk the trails, listen for *Red-breasted Nuthatches*, *Bushtits*, *Varied Thrushes* and *Hutton's Vireos* (most vocal from February to April), *Cassin's Vireos* and *Warbling Vireos*. The three large open areas (the parking lot, the area near the outdoor theatre and along the service road) are good locations from which to search the forest canopy for the *Band-tailed Pigeon*, *Purple Finch*, *Evening Grosbeak*, *Pine Siskin* and *Red Crossbill*. Early spring arrivals include *Violet-green Swallow*, *Tree Swallow* and *Rufous Hummingbird* (March), while species such as the *Western Tanager*, *Black-headed Grosbeak*, *Barn Swallow* and *Swainson's Thrush* arrive later in May.

Four species of flycatchers summer in the park. *Hammond's* and *Pacific-slope Flycatchers* prefer the deep forest, *Western Wood-Pewees* prefer slightly more open areas and *Olive-sided Flycatchers* will often be found high on a conifer snag. The *Common Raven*, *Northwestern Crow* and *Steller's Jay* are the resident corvid species. The *Brown Creeper*, *Chestnut-backed Chickadee* and *Golden-crowned Kinglet* are park residents that form mixed flocks with the occasional wintering *Ruby-*

Pileated Woodpecker, our largest woodpecker, excavates rectangular holes. John Gordon

*crowned Kinglet*. Breeding warblers include *Townsend's* and *Black-throated Gray* high in the trees, while *Wilson's, Orange-crowned* and *MacGillivray's* are found in the understorey. The *Yellow-rumped Warbler* occurs only as a transient. Check the snags in the park, as they provide foraging and breeding sites for the *Downy, Hairy* and *Pileated Woodpecker, Northern Flicker* and *Red-breasted Sapsucker*. The park offers the opportunity to view a few birds of prey, such as the *Bald Eagle, Red-tailed Hawk* and *Cooper's Hawk*. Owls are rare, but the most likely to appear are the *Barred Owl* and *Northern Pygmy-Owl*.

The cliffs and rock bluffs of the park provide many excellent sites to scan for birds on the water. The *Common Loon* is abundant in winter. The *Red-throated* and

*Pacific Loon* also winter here, but they occur in lesser numbers. Of the gulls that can be seen in the park, the *Glaucous-winged Gull* is a year-round resident. There are *Mew* (some summering birds), *Thayer's* and a few *Herring Gulls* present in the winter. Look for the *Bonaparte's Gull* from April to November and *Common Tern* (uncommon) during the spring and fall migrations. Alcids can also be found in the offshore waters. The *Pigeon Guillemot* and *Marbled Murrelet* are park residents. In winter, the *Common Murre* and *Rhinoceros Auklet* can occasionally be seen.

## KLOOTCHMAN PARK — DIRECTIONS

To reach Klootchman Park from Lighthouse Park, return to Marine Drive and turn left. The first left is Howe Sound Lane, leading to Klootchman Park. The trail to Klootchman Park begins just past The Byway on your right. Parking is very limited here; be sure you don't park in a driveway or private parking space.

## BIRD SPECIES

This is probably the best place in the Vancouver area to view the *Marbled Murrelet*. Often in pairs, murrelets can be seen offshore during the winter. They are best viewed using a scope, as they can be distant. Less common are the *Rhinoceros Auklet* and *Common Murre*. The *Ancient Murrelet* has not yet been reported but could appear, particularly in late autumn. The *Black Oystercatcher* is a resident of the Grebe Islets and is joined in winter by numbers of *Surfbirds*, *Black Turnstones* and (rarely) *Rock Sandpipers*. Three species of grebe can be seen in the winter: *Western*, *Red-necked* and *Horned*. *Double-crested* and *Pelagic Cormorants* are resident, while *Brandt's Cormorant* occurs only in small numbers in winter. *Harlequin Ducks* and *Surf Scoters* can usually be seen year-round (smaller numbers in the summer) and are joined in winter by *Greater Scaups*, *Buffleheads*, *Barrow's* and *Common Goldeneyes*, *Common Loons*, *Pacific Loons* (uncommon), *Red-throated Loons* (uncommon), *White-winged Scoters* (uncommon), *Black Scoters* (rare), *Common* and *Red-breasted Mergansers*. As you walk down the trail, forest birds similar to those found at Lighthouse Park are sometimes active. These include *Red-breasted Sapsucker*, *Pacific Wren*, *Varied Thrush*, *Chestnut-backed Chickadee* and *Anna's Hummingbird*, amongst others.

*Written by Danny Tyson, 2001.*
*Updated by Derek Killby, Rob Lyske and Quentin Brown, 2015.*

# 8. AMBLESIDE PARK

## INTRODUCTION

AMBLESIDE PARK IS A SMALL, URBAN WATERFRONT PARK IN WEST Vancouver, across the Lions Gate Bridge from downtown Vancouver. It faces Stanley Park across the waters of the First Narrows of Burrard Inlet. With the right weather conditions, Ambleside Park can be an excellent place to see migrant birds. The park contains many different habitats, including a golf course surrounded by ornamental plantings, a rocky foreshore, a tidal river mouth and mixed second-growth woodland. A marshy area to the north of the railway tracks has been recently restored. These varied habitats can be host to many migrant species. The park is used heavily by the public and is very popular with dog walkers; therefore, an early morning start is advised.

The tranquil pond at Ambleside Park. Colin Clasen

## DIRECTIONS

To reach Ambleside Park from Vancouver, drive north over the Lions Gate Bridge and take the exit to West Vancouver. This exit will lead you to a traffic light at Marine Drive and Taylor Way. Continue west on Marine Drive past Park Royal Shopping Centre. Turn left (south) on 13th Street, cross the railway tracks and turn left (east) again into Ambleside Park. Leave your car in the farthest east parking lot. Directly opposite the parking lot is the Ambleside Pond.

Alternatively, you can take the Ironworkers Memorial (Second Narrows) Bridge north from East Vancouver or Burnaby to North Vancouver. Continue west on the Upper Levels Highway (Highway 1 West) to the Taylor Way exit (#13), then turn left (south) on Taylor Way. Turn right (west) on Marine Drive, then left (south) on 13th Street and left (east) into Ambleside Park.

By bus, it takes less than 15 minutes to reach Ambleside Park from downtown

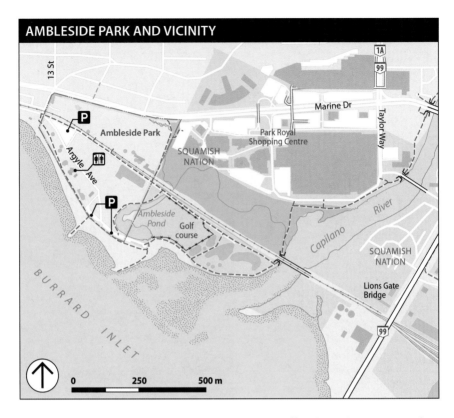

Vancouver, using the West Vancouver Blue Bus. Get off at the 13th Street stop, then walk south across Marine Drive and the railway tracks toward the water, and you will enter the park. To access the most up-to-date information on schedules and routes, please see the *Public Transit* section of this guide for the website and phone number.

## BIRD SPECIES

The Ambleside Pond should be checked from September to May for the ***Ring-necked Duck*** among the ***Greater*** and ***Lesser Scaup***. Other waterfowl usually present are the ***Mallard***, ***Common Goldeneye***, ***Bufflehead*** and the occasional ***Hooded Merganser*** or ***Pied-billed Grebe***. ***American Wigeon*** frequents the grass playing fields near the pond and is often accompanied by one or two ***Eurasian Wigeon***. ***Canvasback*** and ***Tufted Duck*** are rare possibilities.

Songbirds are attracted to the ornamental plantings surrounding the pond and rough areas to the east. These sites can sometimes be alive with migrant passerines, although they are normally quiet. Common residents include the ***Bushtit***, ***Northwestern Crow***, ***House Finch***, ***Red-winged Blackbird***, ***Pacific Wren***, ***Black-capped***

*Chickadee* and *White-crowned* and *Song Sparrow. Golden-crowned Sparrow, Dark-eyed Junco, Fox Sparrow, Golden-crowned* and *Ruby-crowned Kinglet* join in the winter. You may also encounter a *Red Crossbill* or *Pine Siskin* in winter, but sightings are sporadic.

Springtime migrants include the *Cedar Waxwing, Black-headed Grosbeak* and *Yellow-rumped, Wilson's, Yellow, Black-throated Gray, Townsend* and *MacGillivray's Warbler*. These birds can also be seen in the fall, along with the chance of uncommon migrants. In recent years, *Swamp Sparrows, Harris's Sparrows* and *Palm Warblers* have been recorded. There is always the possibility of a "mega" sighting. A *Painted Redstart* delighted a number of birders here. To date, it remains the only Vancouver record.

The newly named Spirit Trail running alongside the railway hosts *Red-winged Blackbirds*, nesting *Bald Eagles, Pileated* and *Downy Woodpeckers* as well as the occasional *Cooper's* and *Sharp-shinned Hawks*.

After checking the pond, walk south to a small rocky spit that juts out into Burrard Inlet. From fall through spring (October to March) large numbers of *Surf Scoters* and *Barrow's Goldeneyes* congregate, with lesser numbers of *Long-tailed Ducks* and *White-winged* and *Black Scoters* (rare) mixed in. Other birds present on the water include the *Common* and *Red-throated Loon; Red-necked, Horned* and *Western Grebe; Double-crested* and *Pelagic Cormorant;* and occasional *Brandt's Cormorant, Harlequin Duck, Red-breasted Merganser* and *Pigeon Guillemot*. The *Marbled Murrelet* is sometimes seen but is rare.

During low tides, gravel bars are exposed and can be viewed from the spit. Check the flocks of *Glaucous-winged* and *Mew Gulls* for *Thayer's, Herring, Western*

An American Robin feeding on hawthorn berries. Jim Martin

(rare) and *Glaucous Gulls* (rare) in the winter, and *California Gulls* and *Bonaparte's Gulls* in the spring and fall.

Follow the shoreline east from here to reach the Capilano River. This can be a good spot to see the *Great Blue Heron, Common Merganser, Gadwall* (winter), *Bald Eagle*, more roosting gulls, *Belted Kingfisher* (usually around the railway bridge) and *Northern Rough-winged Swallow* (summer). Sometimes an *American Dipper* can also be found wintering in the lower stretch of the river.

*Written and revised by Danny Tyson, 2001.*
*Updated by Derek Killby, Rob Lyske and Quentin Brown, 2015.*

# 9. LONSDALE QUAY / KINGS MILL WALK PARK

LONSDALE QUAY AND KINGS MILL WALK PARK ARE LOCATED ONLY ABOUT 1.5 km apart on the waterfront of the City of North Vancouver and therefore can both be conveniently visited in a couple of hours.

## LONSDALE QUAY – INTRODUCTION

Lonsdale Quay, with SeaBus arriving. Colin Clasen

Lonsdale Quay is a waterfront area at the south foot of Lonsdale Avenue in North Vancouver. It is the northern terminus for the SeaBus from downtown Vancouver and has many shops and restaurants. At the time of writing, the surrounding area is undergoing a large redevelopment. Once home to large, bustling shipyards that reached their heyday during the Second World War, building many ships for the Canadian Navy, the area is now becoming a hub for restaurants, housing and historical displays. One goal of the redevelopment has been to open access to the public to view Burrard Inlet and the always interesting and busy Port of Vancouver.

## DIRECTIONS

To reach Lonsdale Quay by car from Vancouver, cross the Lion's Gate Bridge and take the North Vancouver exit. Follow Marine Drive east for 4 km until you reach the intersection with Keith Road heading up to the left and 3rd Street heading to the right. Take 3rd Street to Forbes Avenue and follow Forbes to the right. At the bottom is West Esplanade. Continue two blocks east to Lonsdale Quay.

From the eastern parts of Vancouver and the Lower Mainland, cross the Ironworkers Memorial (Second Narrows) Bridge and take the Main Street exit (#23A). Continue west along the Low Level Road for 3 km, which will bring you right to Lonsdale Quay. You may also continue along Highway 1 and take the Lonsdale Avenue exit (#18), turn south and continue to the foot of Lonsdale and Lonsdale Quay. Pay and street parking is available.

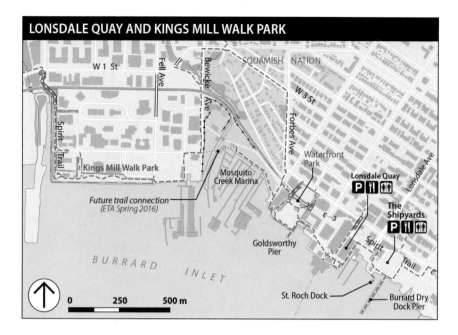

To reach Lonsdale Quay via public transit, the best option from downtown Vancouver is to cross the harbour using the SeaBus. For other transit options, check current schedules on the TransLink website (translink.ca). The #231 bus travels between Lonsdale Quay and Kings Mill Walk Park.

## BIRD SPECIES

Birds seen at Lonsdale Quay will overwhelmingly be seabirds. The SeaBus terminal building is a good spot to view the **Pelagic** and **Double-crested Cormorant**, along with an occasional **Brandt's Cormorant**. To the east of the Quay, there is a large pier that extends out 200 m into Burrard Inlet. Formerly part of Wallace Shipyards, it is now part of the improved access to the waterfront and is the best location for viewing the birds in the harbour.

Under the pier, there are large square openings that are home to nesting *Pigeon Guillemots*. Close-up views from the pier are a real treat, and views into the openings under the pier can be had from a smaller pier to the west.

Around the landing areas and viewing areas of the Quay, it is easy to see *Rock Pigeons*, *House Sparrows* and *Song Sparrows*. *Canada Geese* are nearly year-round residents and can be seen nesting on some of the barges and structures of the harbour. In winter, there are many species to be seen in the inlet. The ***Common*** and ***Barrow's Goldeneye*** and ***Horned Grebe*** are winter residents. The rarer ***Red-necked Grebe*** and some ***Western Grebe*** are possible, particularly in spring and fall migration. Scaup, mostly ***Greater Scaup***, are seen offshore.

A Double–crested Cormorant drying its wings. John Lowman

Gulls are always present, with *Glaucous-winged* being the most abundant. *Mew* and *Bonaparte's Gulls* can often be seen feeding in the harbour. The *Ring-billed Gull* is rarer. The *Surf Scoter* is regularly seen in the fall and winter. Keep an eye out for the *White-winged* and (far rarer) *Black Scoter*. The *Common Merganser* and *Common Loon* are slightly less frequent.

While many of the water birds leave in spring, the Quay still is good for many spring and summer birds. The *Violet-green Swallow*, *White-crowned Sparrow*, *House Finch*, *Bushtit*, *Ruby-crowned Kinglet*, *Yellow-rumped Warbler*, *American Robin* and *Northern Flicker* can be seen, especially 125 m to the west of Lonsdale Quay in the greener Waterfront Park (follow Chadwick Court) and close to the eastern edge of the Squamish First Nation and Mosquito Creek Marina.

## KINGS MILL WALK PARK – INTRODUCTION

Kings Mill Walk Park is a waterfront park in North Vancouver, at the south foot of Fell Avenue, south of the Northshore Auto Mall. Located about 1.5 km west of Lonsdale Quay, it has views of the inner harbour, Canada Place and Stanley Park. It has a diverse range of birds, which is surprising considering its location. Surrounded by the auto mall and business parks to the north, an active ship-yard to the west, a busy working marina to the east and the very busy Vancouver harbour, this park can produce many seabird species, shorebirds and a wide range of songbirds.

## DIRECTIONS

It can be easily reached by car. From downtown Vancouver, drive north over the Lions Gate Bridge and take the North Vancouver exit. Continue east on Marine Drive for 4 km to Fell Avenue, turn right (south) and follow Fell Avenue to the waterfront. From Burnaby and eastern parts of the Lower Mainland, take the Ironworkers Memorial Bridge north and take the Main Street exit (#23A). Continue west for 4 km via either 3rd Street or the new Low Level Road. Upon reaching Fell Avenue, turn left (south) and

The oceanfront walk at Kings Mill Walk Park.
Colin Clasen

continue to the waterfront. Alternatively, after crossing the Ironworkers Memorial Bridge, continue west along Highway 1 for about 5 km and take the Lonsdale Avenue exit (#18). Go south on Lonsdale Avenue and turn right (west) on 3rd Street. Continue west, turn left (south) on Fell Avenue and continue to the waterfront.

To reach Kings Mill Walk Park via public transit, the best option from downtown Vancouver is to cross the harbour using the SeaBus. From the SeaBus terminal at Lonsdale Quay, take the #231 bus to Kings Mill Walk Park. For other transit options, please consult the TransLink website (translink.ca).

## BIRD SPECIES

The small bay in front of the parking area has a range of species. The *Common* and *Barrow's Goldeneye*; *Bufflehead*; *Common*, *Red-breasted* and *Hooded Merganser*; *Pelagic* and *Double-crested Cormorant*, often perched on logs next to Mosquito Creek Marina, are common fall and winter residents. Gulls are resident year-round, with *Glaucous-winged* being the most common. The *Mew Gull* can be seen in good numbers in the fall and winter, before its northward breeding migration in the spring. Be sure to scan the gulls for any *California*, *Herring*, *Bonaparte's* or *Ring-billed* that occasionally show up. The *Common Loon*, *Horned Grebe*, less commonly *Red-necked* and *Western Grebe* are winter residents. Flocks of *Canada Geese* should be watched for a *Cackling* or *Snow Goose*. A *Bald Eagle* may be seen soaring overhead (keep an eye out for a *Turkey Vulture* or *Red-tailed Hawk*), with the North Shore Mountains providing a breathtaking backdrop.

Walking west (toward the shipyard), you can follow the shoreline, which often

Pigeon Guillemots are seabirds that "fly" underwater searching for food. John Lowman

produces a few shorebirds. **Black Turnstone**, **Greater Yellowlegs** and the occasional **Spotted Sandpiper** are present, particularly in fall and winter. At the west end of the park, you reach the mouth of Mackay Creek.

From April to September, be sure and look toward the shipyard and spot the **Osprey** nest on top of a tall structure, slightly north from where the shoreline meets the creek. This creek is currently undergoing a habitat restoration program. This area now hosts breeding **Killdeers**, which can be easily viewed with binoculars from the trail that runs north, up the east side of the creek. The creek will have **Mallards**, **American Wigeons** in fall and winter (watch for a **Eurasian Wigeon**), **Hooded Mergansers** and **Buffleheads** (also in winter).

The wooded trail along the creek hosts many songbirds, depending on the time of year. **Song**, **Fox**, **White-crowned** and **Golden-crowned Sparrows** and **Spotted Towhees** are reliably seen. **House** and **Purple Finches** can be spotted in the trees. While this park is not home to large numbers of flycatchers or warblers, always keep an eye out for the "rarity."

*Written by Derek Killby, 2015.*

# 10. MOUNT SEYMOUR PROVINCIAL PARK

## INTRODUCTION

MOUNT SEYMOUR PROVINCIAL PARK IN NORTH VANCOUVER AND CYPRESS Provincial Park in West Vancouver provide the most accessible subalpine birding in the Vancouver area. Mount Seymour Provincial Park is a 3,508 ha mountain wilderness bounded on the east by Indian Arm, on the south by the municipality of North Vancouver, on the west by the Seymour River and the Greater Vancouver Water District watershed and on the north by the Coast Mountains. The park includes most of Mount Seymour and nearby Mount Elsay and Mount Bishop, all of which are over 1,400 m high.

Pond and picnic tables by upper parking lot on Mount Seymour. Al Grass

Much of the original coastal hemlock forest, which is found at elevations below 1,000 m, was logged in the 1920s. The resultant second-growth forest is a mixture of deciduous (mostly red alder) and coniferous (mostly western hemlock) trees. At elevations above 1,000 m, characteristic plants of the coastal subalpine forest predominate. No logging took place in this higher area, so there are significant areas of old-growth mountain hemlock and yellow-cedar. The trees and associated shrubs, copperbush and white rhododendron tend to grow in "islands" separated by shrubs such as red heather and blueberry.

Sitka mountain-ash berries are an important food for birds in the subalpine zone. This area contains a number of water-related habitats, including bog vegetation fringing Goldie and Flower lakes. Open water is limited mainly to the larger lakes, such as Goldie Lake and, in the backcountry, Elsay Lake, which has been stocked with trout.

Ski runs in the park are covered with sparse pioneer vegetation, such as saxifrage and partridgefoot. This habitat is a factor of some importance to bird species such as *Sooty Grouse*, which roost in nearby trees but feed along the forest edges and ski slopes in summer and fall.

## MOUNT SEYMOUR PROVINCIAL PARK (CENTRAL SECTION)

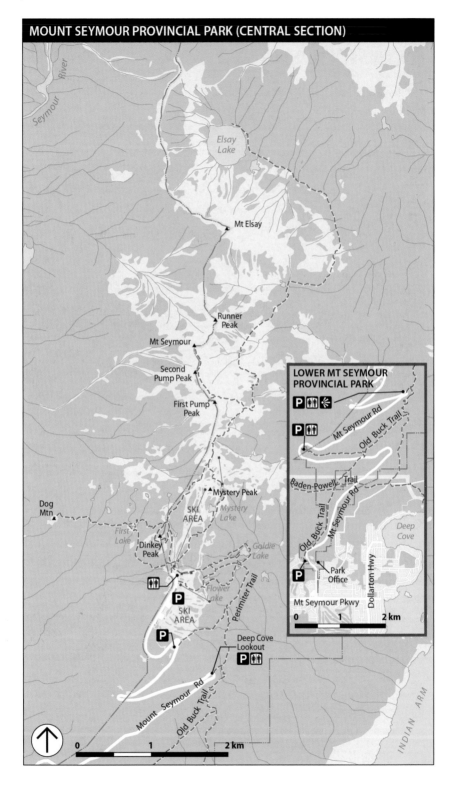

## DIRECTIONS

There is no public transit to Mount Seymour. To reach Mount Seymour from downtown Vancouver, drive east via Hastings or McGill streets to the Ironworkers Memorial (Second Narrows) Bridge, which crosses Burrard Inlet to North Vancouver. Take the Mount Seymour exit (#22B) that leads you to the right and onto Mount Seymour Parkway. Continue for about 7 km to Mount Seymour Road. Turn left and continue ahead. A sign directs you to the park office near the entrance, where maps and other information are available Monday to Friday during normal business hours. It is 10 km, via a paved road, from the park entrance at 100 m elevation to the topmost parking area at 1,000 m. At 850 m elevation, Deep Cove Lookout provides a scenic viewpoint. A network of hiking trails begins at the upper parking lots. Two suggested routes for birders are Goldie Lake with its associated ponds and bog vegetation (1 to 1.5 hours return) and Mystery Peak, including Mystery Lake (about 2 hours return and an elevation change of 450 m). For maps and more information, check this website: www.env.gov.bc.ca/bcparks/explore/parkpgs/mt_seymour.

The weather can change very rapidly on a mountaintop. Be prepared by taking warm clothing and/or rain gear with you. Wear good hiking boots and stay on the trails.

## BIRD SPECIES

About 126 species, of which 14 are accidentals, have been recorded in Mount Seymour Provincial Park. The park checklist indicates that occurrences of particular species are markedly seasonal and keyed to altitude. An updated checklist will no doubt add more species.

Most of the park's specialty birds are subalpine species. *Sooty Grouse* are seen at all elevations, commonly along the roadsides. A good time to see them is spring (May and June), when they are hooting. Hens with broods are often seen in the summer. *Sooty Grouse*, which live high up in trees, migrate to higher altitudes in winter. Tracks in the snow are a good clue to their presence. The *Rock* and *White-tailed Ptarmigan* are recent regular additions to the park species list. Mount Seymour is now *the* place to find these birds in winter, especially in the valleys between Mystery Peak and Second Pump Peak. Look for *Gray-crowned Rosy-Finches* in winter (November to March) in the subalpine regions. Flocks can be seen along roadsides, feeding on seeds.

Species typical of the lower coastal hemlock forest in summer are the *Swainson's Thrush*, *Black-headed Grosbeak*, *Warbling Vireo* and *Western Tanager*. The common resident birds include the *Pacific Wren*, *Varied Thrush* and *Chestnut-backed Chickadee*. In the mountain hemlock regions, common summer residents include *Hermit Thrush* and *Vaux's Swift*.

Bird species of lower elevations may be seen to have higher-elevation counterparts. For example, the *Black-throated Gray Warbler* of the lower slopes tends to be replaced by *Townsend's Warbler* at higher elevations. The *Swainson's Thrush* of lower slopes is replaced by *Hermit Thrush* in subalpine areas.

The *Northern Pygmy-Owl* is a park resident, but the best time to look for this species is in winter. Numbers vary from year to year. Look along roadsides and trail sides, where they often perch in the open. They feed on small birds such as kinglets and chickadees. The *Three-toed Woodpecker* is probably a resident in the subalpine area. Goldie Lake and Mystery Lake trails offer good possibilities to see them, and along the way you may also find a *Mountain Chickadee*. You might find the *Pine Grosbeak*, another winter subalpine resident, at Mystery Peak. A *Gray Jay* will probably find *you* if you eat your lunch in the

Mount Seymour is probably the most reliable location to see the always-curious Gray Jay. Colin Clasen

park! The *Chestnut-backed Chickadee* is generally distributed throughout the park. Both *Black* and *Vaux's Swifts* are summer residents here. Good places to see swifts are at Deep Cove Lookout on the main highway and at Mystery Peak. They are often present in good numbers when there is a low cloud ceiling.

Both *Red* and *White-winged Crossbills* occur throughout the park; the former are more regular in occurrence and numbers. Mystery Peak is a good place to find both species.

Be on the lookout during migration times, especially in the fall, for raptors such as accipiters, *Red-tailed* and *Rough-legged Hawks* and falcons. A fairly easy hike to Dog Mountain will bring you to a good, open lookout for a hawk watch.

*Written by Al Grass, 2001. Revised by Al and Jude Grass, 2015.*

# 11. CYPRESS PROVINCIAL PARK

## INTRODUCTION

CYPRESS PROVINCIAL PARK IN WEST VANCOUVER AND MOUNT SEYMOUR Provincial Park in North Vancouver provide the most accessible subalpine birding in the Vancouver area. Cypress Provincial Park, established in 1975 and now almost 3,000 ha in size, forms part of the North Shore Mountains, the scenic backdrop to Vancouver. An excellent paved road climbs through western hemlock and Douglas-fir forests, eventually reaching more level terrain near the headwaters of Cypress Creek at an elevation of 1,000 m. At this point you are in the lower reaches of the coastal subalpine forest, known to biologists as the Mountain Hemlock Zone. This zone is famous for its huge accumulations of snow in winter and subsequent late snowmelt in spring—and often early summer! Characteristic trees are mountain hemlock, yellow-cedar, amabilis fir and western white pine.

View from Hollyburn Ridge in Cypress Provincial Park.
Nancy Prober

Plants such as red heather, blueberry, huckleberry, false azalea, white rhododendron and copperbush dominate the understorey. A number of small lakes and fens add to the natural diversity, and much of the remaining forest is beautiful old growth, with many large trees and snags. Views are excellent from several places in the park, especially for the more adventurous birders who climb one of the three peaks. Large clear-cut areas detract greatly from the scenic beauty but provide summer habitat for *Sooty Grouse*.

## DIRECTIONS

There is no public transit to Cypress Park. From downtown Vancouver, drive west on Georgia Street and cross the Lions Gate Bridge, following signs to West Vancouver. At the first traffic light, bear right onto Taylor Way, then up the hill about 1 km

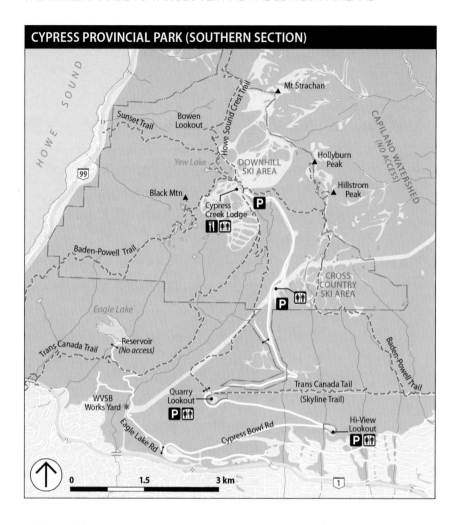

## CYPRESS PROVINCIAL PARK (SOUTHERN SECTION)

HOWE SOUND

Mt Strachan

Sunset Trail

Bowen Lookout

Howe Sound Crest Trail

CAPILANO WATERSHED (NO ACCESS)

99

Yew Lake

DOWNHILL SKI AREA

Hollyburn Peak

Black Mtn

Hillstrom Peak

P

Cypress Creek Lodge

Baden-Powell Trail

CROSS COUNTRY SKI AREA

P

Eagle Lake

Trans Canada Trail

Reservoir (No access)

Baden-Powell Trail

Quarry Lookout

Trans Canada Tail (Skyline Trail)

WVSB Works Yard

P

Hi-View Lookout

P

Eagle Lake Rd

Cypress Bowl Rd

0    1.5    3 km

1

and turn left (west) onto the Upper Levels Highway (Highway 1) and continue about 5 km to the Cypress Provincial Park exit (#8). Watch out for cyclists, as the road to Cypress is a popular cycling route. The road starts at 300 m elevation; it climbs gently at first to a tight corner, then more steeply to a second switchback at Hi-View Lookout. This is about 5.3 km from the highway at an elevation of 525 m. After a stop here, continue up the hill around two more switchback corners, past the cross-country ski area, until you reach the end of the road at the Cypress Bowl downhill ski area. The ski operations are owned and operated by Cypress Bowl Recreations Ltd., who also provide cafeteria service most of the year. Washrooms are located in the cafeteria building at the main parking lot. You have several options once you reach the parking area; indeed, there is a myriad of trails in this park.

The Yew Lake Trail, an easy 1.5 km loop, makes a good starting point. Starting at the bases of both chairlifts, this trail follows Cypress Creek through open forest to Yew Lake. At a small fen system near the lake, a boardwalk trail leads north into a patch of forest and then out onto a logging road in a burn area. A short walk to the northwest here provides a good view of Howe Sound and excellent birding, especially during fall migration.

The Howe Sound Crest Trail starts at the same point as the Yew Lake Trail, but branches off to the right (north) just past the Mount Strachan chairlift, climbing the ridge quickly and eventually leading (after a long and strenuous hike) to the Lions, perhaps Vancouver's most scenic mountains. Only experienced hikers with a good map should attempt the hike to the Lions; the trail is not maintained for the length of the ridge.

A section of the Baden-Powell Trail leads from the parking lot up the slopes of Black Mountain (1,217 m), where another loop trail winds around some small subalpine lakes. Another popular hike is up Hollyburn Mountain (1,325 m), which can be reached from the cross-country ski area.

## BIRD SPECIES

Cypress is best visited from May through October. The first stop can be to park across from the West Vancouver Works yard and walk along Eagle Lake Access Road. Throughout May and June, many songbirds can be seen and heard, including the *Swainson's Thrush*; *Warbling Vireo*; *Orange-crowned*, *Yellow*, *Black-throated Gray*, *Townsend's* and *MacGillivray's Warbler*; *Western Tanager*; *Black-headed Grosbeak*; and *Cedar Waxwing*. Continuing along the main road, make the HiView Lookout your next stop. It not only offers a magnificent vista of Vancouver (on a clear day, Vancouver Island, the Gulf Islands and the North Cascade Mountains can also be seen), but is also a great place to do some treetop birding. This viewpoint affords birders the luxury of being able to look down on tall cedars and hemlocks below. *Northwestern Crow*, *Steller's Jay*, *Pileated Woodpecker* and *Orange-crowned*, *Black-throated Gray*, *Townsend's*, *Wilson's* and *MacGillivray's Warbler* can sometimes be seen. The *Rufous Hummingbird* (April through June) often perches atop the trees as well and offers fabulous views of its sparkling colours. In addition, the *Willow Flycatcher* (June), *Swainson's Thrush*, *Warbling Vireo*, *Black-headed Grosbeak* and *Western Tanager* are all possible. *Bald Eagles* and *Turkey Vultures* often sail by. Also watch for *Band-tailed Pigeons*, a species that is declining in numbers in the Vancouver area.

Next stop up the road is Quarry Lookout (Cypress Park Picnic Area). Although there are fewer birds than the previous lookout and limited views, it is still worth a visit. In the fall, the *American Pipit* has used the grassy area and there is always the chance to glimpse a *Northern Pygmy-Owl*.

As you continue higher up the road, watch for **Sooty Grouse** on the roadsides, especially early in the morning. The deep, hooting calls of the males can be heard anywhere along the road in spring, but they become more numerous at higher elevations. The stretch of road near the cross-country ski area is prime **Red-breasted Sapsucker** habitat. They love the thin-barked hemlocks for drilling sap-wells. In May and early June, listen for their drum rolls, which, like all sapsucker tattoos, start out fast and end very slowly. Later in the summer, their nests can sometimes be found by listening for the incessant begging calls of the young.

The road ends at the downhill ski area. With the higher elevation, there are changes in the birdlife. Now **Swainson's Thrush** is less common, replaced by the beautiful song of the **Hermit Thrush**. The **Olive-sided Flycatcher** is also present with its distinctive song. A slow circuit of the Yew Lake Trail on a May or June morning will yield these, along with **Sooty Grouse** (at least the sound, if not the sight); the **Vaux's Swift**; **Red-breasted Sapsucker**; **Gray Jay**; **Steller's Jay**; **Common Raven**; **Rufous Hummingbird**; **Chestnut-backed Chickadee**; **Varied Thrush**; **Orange-crowned**, **MacGillivray's**, **Townsend's** and **Wilson's Warbler**; **Red Crossbill**; **Brown Creeper**; **White-crowned Sparrow**; the **Oregon** form of **Dark-eyed Junco**; and more. Try whistling like a **Northern Pygmy-Owl** here (or anywhere in the Cypress Bowl area); you will at least attract mobbing passerines, if not the diminutive owl itself.

A side trip to the burn area northeast of Yew Lake is often worth taking, especially in August and September, when raptor migration brings **Sharp-shinned**, **Cooper's** and **Red-tailed Hawks**; **Northern Harriers**; **American Kestrels**; and perhaps other species using the updrafts on the mountain slopes and cutting through the Cypress Creek Valley shortcut to the rest of the North Shore mountain ridges.

Sooty Grouse can often be approached very close. John Lowman

Continuing to the Bowen Island Lookout will provide gorgeous views of Howe Sound, along with **Gray Jay**, always looking for a handout! A longer hike up the Howe Sound Crest Trail could yield similar species to those found at the downhill ski area. One exception, the extremely rare (for Vancouver) **Three-toed Woodpecker**, has been recorded on this trail. Should you be lucky enough to see one, please report it on the Nature Vancouver website (naturevancouver.ca), click on "Birding

The brightly coloured Townsend's Warbler breeds on local mountains. Colin Clasen

Section" then go to "Report a Rare, Unusual or Interesting Bird Sighting," and follow the instructions.

Winter and early spring have their charms here, but you will usually have to stick to the roads if you do not want to don your skis or snowshoes to enter the forests. As well, the winter forests are rather silent, except for a few chattering flocks of **Chestnut-backed Chickadees**, **Pine Siskins** and **Golden-crowned Kinglets** or the croak of a **Common Raven** overhead. However, winter is the best time of year to see a **Gray Jay**, and a **Northern Pygmy-Owl** or **Red-breasted Sapsucker** may occasionally be seen.

*Written by Dick Cannings, 2001. Updated by Quentin Brown with assistance from Derek Killby and Rob Lyske, 2015.*

# 12. GEORGE C. REIFEL MIGRATORY BIRD SANCTUARY AND VICINITY

## GEORGE C. REIFEL MIGRATORY BIRD SANCTUARY — INTRODUCTION

THE GEORGE C. REIFEL MIGRATORY BIRD SANCTUARY IS SITUATED AT THE mouth of the South Arm of the Fraser River, less than an hour's drive from the City of Vancouver. It is 9 km west of Ladner on Westham Island in Delta. The non-profit British Columbia Waterfowl Society maintains and runs the sanctuary and encourages appreciation of wetland wildlife habitat in the Fraser River estuary.

The sanctuary is named after George C. Reifel, who purchased the north end of Westham Island in 1927. By 1929 most of the dyking and reclamation work was completed and he built the family home. Initially, grain was grown on the farm, but in World War II his son, George H. Reifel, grew much-needed sugar beet to seed, an important commodity during the war years. The farm has been part of the Westham Island farming community, where a wide variety of crops, including potatoes, corn, grain, cabbage, strawberries and raspberries, are all grown on prime agricultural land.

Largely as a result of the efforts of conservationists Barry Leach and Fred Auger, the BC Waterfowl Society was formed. The society leased land from the Reifel family to manage as a bird sanctuary. Ducks Unlimited Canada created a network of ponds and dykes and water control structures, and the wetlands were then enhanced for waterfowl nesting and loafing as well as public viewing. The provincial government reserved additional intertidal foreshore, bringing the total sanctuary area to 344 ha. The federal government bought the Reifel farm in 1973,

Observation tower and north end of the West Field at Reifel. Jim Martin

and the sanctuary's lands were donated at the same time. With federal ownership, it was then possible to formally declare the lands as the Alaksen National Wildlife Area and the George C. Reifel Migratory Bird Sanctuary. The BC Waterfowl Society now manages the public use area of the sanctuary under an agreement with Environment Canada's Canadian Wildlife Service.

The sanctuary is situated on the Fraser River estuary and much of it is below the high-tide line. Without the protective dykes, it would flood during every high tide, as would many parts of Westham Island. A network of dykes, trails and a two-storey observation tower provide wonderful vantage points overlooking the wetlands. All of the waterway and ponds are controlled to maximize bird use. Some areas are year-round wetlands, some are kept shallowly flooded for shorebirds in summer and fall, and others are maintained as deep water for diving ducks and fish-eating birds. Most of the ponds are slightly brackish in summer, as water is brought in from the Strait of Georgia when needed during hot weather months, but rainwater is the primary source of water for most of the year. The large slough areas in the Alaksen National Wildlife Area, which are viewable from the east side of the sanctuary, are all freshwater former river channels.

The 1 km driveway into the sanctuary parking lot is bordered by alder, blackberry, hawthorns, Pacific crab apples and a few coniferous species. The central area has a lot of shrub cover, along with Douglas-fir and black cottonwood trees. The outer west dyke is more open, with sparse vegetation. An extensive cattail marsh stretches to the west toward the Strait of Georgia. The highest tides in this area reach 4.8 m (16 ft), while the lows go down to 1.2 m (4 ft).

## DIRECTIONS

There is no public transit to the Reifel Migratory Bird Sanctuary. From Vancouver, take Highway 99 (Oak Street) south. Once out of the George Massey Tunnel, take the second exit (#28, Highway 17A South), keep in the right lane, and turn right (west) onto Ladner Trunk Road, which will take you through Ladner and will turn into 47A Avenue and then into River Road, well on your way to the sanctuary. For a more scenic route, take the first exit after the tunnel instead of the second one. This is the "back way" to Ladner, which will take you past the entrance to Ladner Harbour Park (detailed later in this section). As you continue west into Ladner, turn left at the stop sign at Elliot Street, right onto 47A Avenue three blocks later (at the traffic lights) and then onto River Road.

After only a few minutes' drive, 47A Avenue becomes River Road West. Follow it for 2.9 km and then turn right to cross the Westham Island Bridge. (There is a Reifel Migratory Bird Sanctuary sign at this corner.) Follow Westham Island Road for 4.8 km until you arrive at 5191 Robertson Road, where the road widens and

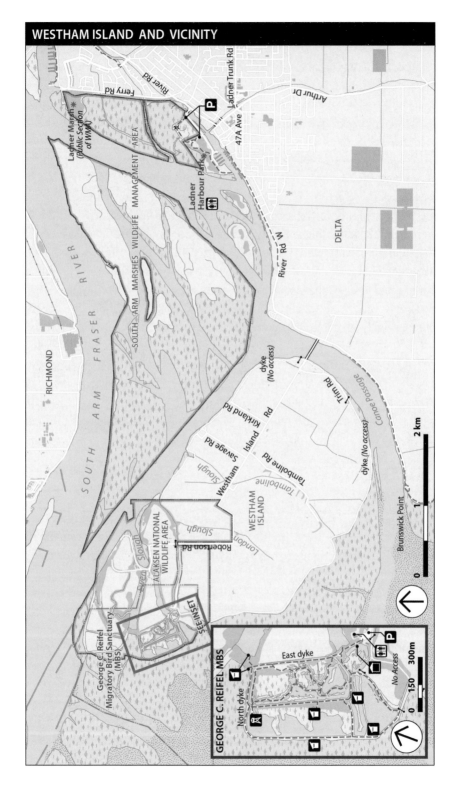

WESTHAM ISLAND AND VICINITY

there are two sets of gates. Take the left-hand driveway through black gates and follow it for 1 km to the parking lot. The entrance to the trails starts at the Gift Shop.

The sanctuary is wheelchair-accessible and has an outdoor picnic area and public washrooms. The Warming Hut is available for sheltered lunch breaks during cold weather, and the Gift Shop sells a variety of items, from chocolate bars to binoculars. A collection of over 400 stuffed birds is housed in the Lecture Hall and can be viewed on Sunday mornings, or as part of booked programs. Guided tours are offered to pre-booked birding or school groups of fifteen or more people. A guided drop-in tour is also offered to the public every Sunday morning at 10 a.m. The sanctuary is open every day from 9 a.m. to 4 p.m. (no entry allowed after 4 p.m.). There is a small admission ($5 for adults and $3 for seniors and children). Frequent visitors can purchase an annual pass ($25 each or $50 per family).

## BIRD SPECIES

A list of birds seen in the sanctuary during the past week is always posted on the Gift Shop window, and a "bird sightings log book" is located at the side of the building. For a general monthly update, check the website (reifelbirdsanctuary. com), and for up-to-date information on particular species or to purchase field guides, inquire at the Gift Shop.

To date, 290 bird species have been recorded for the sanctuary. In winter, waterfowl and raptors are at their best. Large flocks of **Lesser Snow Geese** arrive mid-October

One of the huge flocks of Lesser Snow Geese that arrive annually. John Gordon

from Wrangel Island, Russia, and can be found offshore at low tide and often in farm fields at high tide. Many wintering ducks and shorebirds follow the same pattern of being out in the intertidal areas at low tide and flying in at high tide.

Over 24 duck species have been recorded here. The *Hooded* and *Common Merganser* are found throughout the winter, as are the *Lesser Scaup*, *Bufflehead* and *Ring-necked Duck*. A few *Eurasian Wigeons* can sometimes be seen in winter on the sloughs and fields, feeding with the flocks of *American Wigeons*. Large flocks of *Trumpeter Swans* and a few *Tundra Swans* feed and roost offshore, as well as on Westham Island and the Delta farmland.

The *Wood Duck* is common throughout the year, and many nest boxes have been installed for this species along the trails. In summer, *Cinnamon* and *Blue-winged Teal* are present, as are large numbers of *Gadwalls*, which, after the *Mallard* and *Wood Duck*, is the most common breeding duck. The *Northern Pintail*, *American Wigeon* and *Northern Shoveler,* although common from fall to spring, are very scarce in summer. Most waterfowl nests hatch in May and June and most waterfowl enter an eclipse plumage and flightless period between June and September. Large flocks of *Canada Geese* moult in the area in late summer and congregate offshore, with as many as 2,000 seen off Westham Island.

Peak migration times at the sanctuary are April through May and August through October. In April there is an influx of fish-eating birds at the river mouth and offshore feeding on eulachon (an oily herring-like fish). Loons, mergansers

**Sandhill Crane pair on nest with egg at Reifel, where they breed annually.** Michelle Lamberson

and cormorants gather offshore to feed before moving north to breeding areas. *Bald Eagles*, *Double-crested Cormorants* and many gulls are also present but are quite hard to identify due to their distance offshore.

The sanctuary has recorded sightings of 41 species of shorebirds. Shorebirds are eager to get north in the spring. *Dunlins*, *Western Sandpipers*, *Black-bellied Plovers* and dowitchers pass through in April. Some can be seen resting and feeding in the West Field at high tide, offering a closer look at their plumage. The first *Western Sandpipers* of the fall start coming south in late June, followed by *Least Sandpipers* and a few *Semipalmated Sandpipers*. Later, in July and August, large numbers of *Greater* and *Lesser Yellowlegs*, along with *Long* and *Short-billed Dowitchers*, also start to move south. Other shorebird species here range from an accidental *Spotted Redshank* or *Wood Sandpiper* to the more regular but uncommon *Ruff*, *Sharp-tailed*, *Baird's* and *Solitary Sandpiper*.

Long–billed Dowitchers frequently chatter when feeding in a group. Virginia Hayes

Passerines follow a similar pattern of arrival at the sanctuary. Although warblers, flycatchers and other passerines start a little later in May, they do not return until August. The winter sparrows, such as *White-crowned*, *Golden-crowned*, *Fox* and *Song*, can be found along the East Dyke. Lucky observers may occasionally find a *Lincoln's*, *White-throated*, *Harris's* or *Swamp Sparrow* along any of the trails; though, a traditional spot to find the *Swamp Sparrow* is on the dyke trail near the observation tower.

*Black-crowned Night-Heron*, a bird that is hard to find in the Vancouver area, has wintered at Fuller Slough for several decades now. It often perches on the fallen trees on the sunny side of the slough, or over closer to the museum building. A *Green Heron* might also be seen in the sanctuary in July or August.

Many birds of prey can be seen at the sanctuary. The *Red-tailed* and *Cooper's Hawk*, *Bald Eagle*, *Northern Harrier*, *Great Horned* and *Barn Owl* all breed in the area. The *Rough-legged Hawk*, *Gyrfalcon* and *Snowy Owl* are rare winter visitors from the north. The *Peregrine Falcon*, *Merlin*, *Sharp-shinned Hawk* and *Northern Saw-whet Owl* are seen regularly throughout the winter, the latter drawing significant visitor numbers because of their tendency to roost low in the trees along the trails. The *Turkey Vulture* and *American Kestrel* are seen as they pass through and rarely stay more than a few days. The first *Black-shouldered Kite* in Canada was seen here in April 1990.

# WESTHAM ISLAND

Between Ladner and the Reifel Bird Sanctuary, there are a few interesting hot spots to check. Along River Road, watch for **Mourning Doves** and **Eurasian Collared-Doves**. After crossing the bridge onto Westham Island, park safely on the right side of the road and walk back on the bridge to check the Canoe Pass river channel. In fall and winter, shorebirds, dabbling ducks, diving ducks such as **Common** and **Barrow's Goldeneyes**, and **Red-necked**, **Western** and **Horned Grebes** can often be seen here. A **Bald Eagle** nest has been active on the River Road side of the bridge for years. Remember to be considerate of other drivers on this narrow, single-lane bridge and do not park to birdwatch on the bridge itself.

All of the lands on Westham Island are private property, including the dykes. Please do not trespass. Upon crossing the bridge, the main Westham Island Road leads eventually to the sanctuary, but it is sometimes worth exploring some of the paved side roads. Trim Road, the first road on the left, ends where private dykes begin along the seaward side of the island. There are good views of Canoe Pass and Brunswick Point along the road. At low tide, a mud flat is exposed, which holds a good number of gulls in winter, staging flocks of **Canada Geese** in late summer, and shorebirds during migration. **Bald Eagles** and **Red-tailed Hawks** are common along farm roads like this, and there is always a chance of a **Peregrine Falcon**, **Merlin** or **Kestrel** hunting the seaward marshes and farm fields during migration months.

Reifel is the only reliable location in BC for seeing the Black–crowned Night–Heron. Jim Martin

Tamboline Road is approximately 1.4 km farther along Westham Island Road on the left. Its mix of roadside ditches, marsh channels, trees and hedgerows often holds wintering **Wilson's Snipes** and abundant flocks of **Golden-crowned Sparrows**, plus **White-crowned** and **Fox Sparrows** during spring migration. Spring and fall warblers can be surprisingly abundant, and a diversity of summer waterfowl, including all three teal, frequents the quiet waterways. The junction of Tamboline Road and Westham Island Road is a good location to watch for **Barn Owls** at dusk. Unusual species such as the **Yellow-headed Blackbird** or **Harris's Sparrow** are sometimes seen in this area.

Marsh Wren singing at the Reifel Bird Sanctuary where many breed annually. Colin Clasen

In fall and winter, the fields of Westham Island can be teeming with wildfowl, but due to the hunting activities, the birds tend not to be present during the daytime. Outside of the hunting season, however, or in areas closed to hunting, such as the fields near the entrance to Reifel Bird Sanctuary, the views can be spectacular. In the fall, flocks of up to 25,000 *Snow Geese* can be on farm fields on certain days, as can hundreds of *Trumpeter Swans*, a few *Ring-necked Pheasants*, a few dozen *Sandhill Cranes* and thousands of dabbling ducks. The *American Wigeon*, *Mallard* and *Northern Pintail* are abundant species, but in winter-ponded fields, *Northern Shoveler* and *Green-winged Teal* can also be seen foraging through the soft mud. In some years, a surprising number of *Eurasian Wigeons* can be seen in with grazing flocks of *American Wigeons* in grass cover. In February 1989, for example, 100 were observed. In the spring, migrant flocks of *Cackling Geese*, *Greater White-fronted* and *Canada Geese* can also be seen on fields. Sloughs are worth pausing at, as they provide good, close views of both *Hooded* and *Common Mergansers* fishing.

## LADNER HARBOUR PARK AND SOUTH ARM MARSHES WILDLIFE MANAGEMENT AREA

If you take the first exit south of the tunnel off Highway 99 onto the "back road" into Ladner, you are on part of River Road. For the first part you are following along a shady slough on the right (Green Slough), then marinas just before Ladner. While passing through this area, you may want to stop to investigate trails in

Ladner Marsh, the decommissioned sewage lagoon, Delta's Ladner Harbour Park, or even some of the nearby trails through subdivisions that are close to Green Slough, including part of Canada's Millennium Trail.

To access Ladner Harbour Park, turn right off River Road onto McNeeley's Way and the park is about 400 m on the right. This municipal park has parking, picnic facilities, washrooms, many views of the harbour, and trails through the floodplain forests along the Fraser River.

Most of the islands in the South Arm Marshes Wildlife Management Area are managed under agreements and not open to the public. To explore the Ladner Marsh component, however, turn right (north) from River Road onto Ferry Road, which ends at Captain's Cove Marina. Just before the marina, on the left, there is a walking trail and boardwalk through cottonwood forests and floodplain marshes. It ends at a covered viewing tower overlooking the river. To the south, Ladner's old sewage lagoon now takes the form of a natural basin, with a top trail around the north end overlooking the tidal floodplain marshes of Ladner Marsh.

The mix of tidal marshes, riparian shrubs and floodplain forests, quiet shady backwater sloughs off the Fraser River (such as Green Slough) and the main channel of the Fraser River as it passes by Ladner makes this a very interesting general area for birders. Woodland areas attract a broad spectrum of passerines in spring and summer, including the *Bewick's Wren*, *Black-headed Grosbeak*, *Yellow Warbler*, *Common Yellowthroat* and *Western Tanager*. In May and September, you may be able to spot numerous migrants, such as *Cassin's*, *Warbling* and *Red-eyed Vireos*; and *Nashville*, *Townsend's* and *Yellow-rumped Warblers*.

In summer, this is a good spot to see *Cliff*, *Barn*, *Violet-green* and *Tree Swallows*. The *Rufous Hummingbird* is also common in summer. Marsh areas are good spots to check for the *Virginia Rail*, *Sora*, *Marsh Wren* and raptors, such as the *Short-eared Owl*. In winter, expect *Bald Eagles* in the trees along the river and carefully check flocks of chickadees and kinglets for an occasional wintering warbler. *Common Yellowthroats*, *Orange-crowned* and *Yellow-rumped Warblers* usually turn up here every Christmas Bird Count.

*Written by John Ireland and Robin Owen. Revised by John Ireland, 2001.*
*Updated by Kathleen Fry and Varri Raffan, 2015.*

# 13. TSAWWASSEN FERRY JETTY / BRUNSWICK POINT

## TSAWWASSEN FERRY JETTY — INTRODUCTION

THE TSAWWASSEN FERRY TERMINAL AND 3-KM-LONG CAUSEWAY WERE built in the 1960s. Ferries sail from here to Swartz Bay (for Victoria), Duke Point (for Nanaimo) and destinations on the Gulf Islands. In a later terminal expansion, a Habitat Compensation Area was built on the north side, with the goal of replacing valuable fish habitat. This area has come to be known by local birders as the Compensation Lagoon. It provides very good high-tide roosting for many shorebirds, terns and gulls.

The point of land immediately south of Canoe Pass, the most southerly arm of the Fraser River and south of Westham Island, is known to Vancouver birders by the unofficial name of Brunswick Point. It is an easy walk (about 1.5 hours) along the dyke from Brunswick Point to Roberts Bank, with good birding along the way.

Looking south along the Tsawwassen ferry jetty toward the ferry terminal. Bill Kinkaid

Roberts Bank forms the shallow water around Brunswick Point, which contains an extensive cattail marsh. The farmlands above the high-tide level are protected by a system of dykes. Potatoes and other mixed vegetables and cereals are grown in the fields, which are surrounded by drainage ditches and, in some places, hedgerows.

The Roberts Bank causeway should be avoided. It contains a bulk coal loading facility on the north side and a burgeoning container terminal on the other side, intent on further expansion. This area is patrolled by rail company police and Port of Vancouver security guards, and it is made very clear that birders and the general public are not allowed access.

## DIRECTIONS

To reach the ferry terminal from downtown Vancouver by car, take Highway 99 (Oak Street) south, and 1.4 km after exiting the George Massey Tunnel, turn right

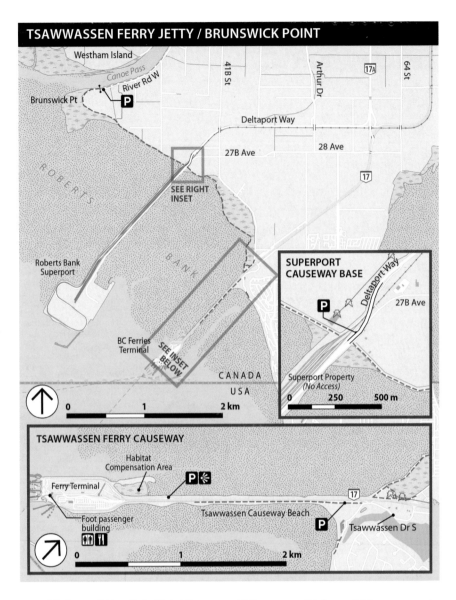

onto Highway 17A at Exit #28. After several kilometres, Highway 17A merges onto Highway 17, which continues on to the ferry terminal. From Highway 99 it is 10.3 km to the base of the jetty. A gravel road runs along the south side of the jetty and it is potholed and rough, but useable. As you approach the jetty, look for the access at a traffic light just before the base of the jetty. Or drive down the jetty for 2.4 km and look for a tiny parking lot (10 cars only) on your right. This gives access to the Compensation Lagoon. By public transit from downtown Vancouver, take the Canada Line SkyTrain to Bridgeport Station in Richmond and then take a bus to the base of the ferry jetty or the ferry terminal. Allow at least 1.5 hours travel time. For up-to-date SkyTrain and bus information, please consult the TransLink website (translink.ca).

**Note:** The ferry jetty runs almost exactly in a northeast/southwest direction, so the side closet to the community of Tsawwassen is referred to as either the south or east side, and the side closest to the coal terminal is referred to as either the north or west side, depending on personal preference.

## BIRD SPECIES

Jaegers and terns are common offshore in late summer, and numerous cormorants roost on the outer rocky breakwater. Loons, grebes, *Brants* and a large assortment of diving ducks frequent the bay in the winter. The south side outer end is a reliable site to find a small number of *Harlequin Ducks*. Sometimes *Snow Buntings* can be seen along the gravel road from November to March. Search the rocky shoreline for *Black Oystercatchers*, *Black Turnstones*, *Surfbirds* and even a *Rock Sandpiper*, which comes as a rare winter visitor. There is often a roost of gulls at the shoreline beyond the end of the gravel road; *Bonaparte's* and *Franklin's Gulls* have been found here.

Birding at the Compensation Lagoon is very tide dependent, being best on a rising or low high tide. Although this marsh area is fairly new, it is gaining a reputation as a good place to see shorebirds at migration time, and even to find some rarities. It seems to be particularly attractive to the larger, longer-legged

A typical "cloud" of Dunlin between the Tsawwassen ferry jetty and the Roberts Bank coal terminal. Michelle Lamberson

shorebirds, such as the **Black-bellied Plover**, and both **Marbled Godwit** and **Willet** have been observed. The **Black Oystercatcher** breeds here, and in summer there can be hundreds of non-breeding **Caspian Terns** loafing in the area. Both **Ruddy** and **Black Turnstone** are also seen. Check the flocks of **Bonaparte's Gulls** for more unusual species.

At the base of the jetty, the trees on the bluffs contain over 100 **Great Blue Heron** nests at time of writing, and in the spring, it is interesting to watch the interaction between the **Great Blue Herons** and **Bald Eagles**, both intent on finding a quick meal. These trees and the shrubby habitat on both sides of the road contain the usual local sparrow and finch species.

**Note:** *For information about birding from the ferries themselves, see the separate "Birding from BC Ferries" section.*

## BRUNSWICK POINT – DIRECTIONS

To reach Brunswick Point, follow the directions to the Reifel Migratory Bird Sanctuary, but do not turn right onto Westham Island. Instead, follow River Road West for 2.5 km to its end, where you can park on the roadside and walk along the dyke. Please respect the parking signs and keep farm gateways clear. It is about a 1.5-hour, easy walk on the dyke from Brunswick Point to Roberts Bank. You will have salt marsh, farmland and open water to search for birds. There is no public transit that would get you to this site. There are also no toilet facilities or other services here. For these you will have to drive back into the community of Ladner.

Looking west over the wide salt marsh at Brunswick Point, part of the Roberts Bank Wildlife Management Area. Ron Long

View north from Brunswick Point across Canoe Pas
Bill Kinkaid

Tundra Swan—much scarcer than its cousin, the Trumpeter Swan. Jim Martin

## BIRD SPECIES

This is an excellent birding spot from at least September through May, when large numbers of waterfowl are present. The main attractions are swans and *Snow Geese*. Up to 400 swans, mainly *Trumpeter*, concentrate here and at the Reifel Migratory Bird Sanctuary from November to March. Up to 10,000 *Snow Geese* can be seen from October to April, although the geese are much less predictable. Thousands of dabbling ducks, often including several *Eurasian Wigeons*, feed in the marshes and mud flats around the point. The waterfowl are best seen at high tide, when they are forced closer to the dyke. Flocks of up to 10,000 *Dunlins* can be seen feeding on the flats or flying by in dense masses. Canoe Pass, the arm of the Fraser River between Brunswick Point and Westham Island to the north, usually has rather few birds, but the *Western Grebe, Double-crested Cormorant, Bufflehead* and *Common* and *Red-breasted Merganser* may be seen.

The farm fields inside the dyke are excellent for birds of prey, including many *Red-tailed* and *Rough-legged Hawks, Northern Harriers* and *Bald Eagles*. *Peregrine Falcon* and *Merlin* are often seen, and in some winters a *Gyrfalcon* or *Prairie Falcon* may be present. Scan the fields and treetops often as you walk along the dyke.

Some of the most interesting birds can be found in the shrubs and dense weed patches just outside the dyke. This is a regular spot in winter for **American Tree Sparrows**, and there are several records of **Swamp Sparrow**, also in winter. A **Short-eared Owl** may burst out of the shrubbery, and in an irruption year, it's possible to see **Snowy Owl** along the dyke or perching on a log out in the marsh. **Marsh Wren** is a resident but is most easily found in spring and summer, when it is very vocal on territory. Occasionally, you will be rewarded with the sight of an **American Bittern** flying low over the marsh.

The Brunswick Point area can produce some interesting birds during spring and fall migration. Especially worth checking are the shrubby thickets and tall poplars near the west end of West River Road. The brush can hide a variety of sparrows and warblers, including **Lincoln's Sparrow** and even a rare **White-throated Sparrow**. Occasionally, a **Long-eared Owl** or **Barn Owl** conceals itself in the densest brush. **Horned Lark**, **Lapland Longspur** and **Snow Bunting** are sometimes seen along the dyke in early spring or late fall. Spectacular concentrations of **Western Sandpiper**, with smaller numbers of other shorebirds, can be seen on the point in spring and fall (especially in the last week of April), and small flocks of the locally rare **Greater White-fronted Geese** occasionally stop on the point in late April or early May. Possibly the nicest time to visit Brunswick Point is on an evening in late April or early May, on a rising tide just before sunset. Sit on a log, watch the sunset over the Strait of Georgia and listen for the booming of an **American Bittern** or the calls of **Virginia Rail** or **Sora**.

## ROBERTS BANK

Although we have stressed that the Roberts Bank causeway should be avoided, there is some good shorebird habitat at intermediate tide levels on both sides *at the base*. At present this can be viewed without having to use the road. Park underneath the Deltaport Way overpass and check the shoreline on both sides.

*Note: If the railway tracks have trains on them, do not attempt to cross. The unit coal trains are computer controlled for unloading and move without warning. Container trains are also shunted backward and forward without warning. This shoreline may become inaccessible in the future and the whole area closed to the general public, as there is a container storage facility and an industrial park in the planning.*

*Written by Gerry Ansell. Revised by Richard Swanston and Catherine J. Aitchison, 2001. Additional information from Brian Self, 2015.*

# 14. POINT ROBERTS, WASHINGTON

## INTRODUCTION

ALTHOUGH IN WASHINGTON STATE IN THE UNITED STATES, POINT Roberts is nonetheless included in this guide, because it is a favourite location among Vancouver birders for seabird watching. The area consists of the tip of a peninsula, which stretches southwards at the west end of Boundary Bay. The northern portion of the peninsula contains the suburban community of Tsawwassen. The southern portion is Point Roberts, which is only about 12 square km in size, on the south side of the 49th parallel international boundary. The area has the look and feel of a seaside resort community, with much of the oceanfront property built up with both permanent and seasonal residences. However, there is still plenty of accessible beach. The high bluffs at Lily Point on the southeast tip of the peninsula provide two good lookout points for scanning the ocean and western Boundary Bay. Lighthouse Marine Park, on the southwest tip of the peninsula,

The round-rock-covered shoreline of Lighthouse Marine Park at the southwest corner of Point Roberts, looking south toward the Gulf Islands.
Ken Klimko

provides some of the very best seabird watching in the Vancouver area, as it protrudes into the Strait of Georgia. Seabirds tend to fly "around the corner" here, in and out of Boundary Bay, and a spotting scope can be extremely worthwhile in fall and winter. There is also plenty of good woodland birding, making a trip to Point Roberts doubly rewarding.

## DIRECTIONS

To reach Point Roberts from downtown Vancouver, take Highway 99 (Oak Street) south over the Oak Street Bridge, and 1.4 km after exiting the George Massey Tunnel, turn right onto Highway 17A South at Exit #28. After about 4 km, Highway 17A merges onto Highway 17 and continues toward Tsawwassen and the ferry terminal. Turn left at the traffic lights at 56th Street and travel straight for 4.5 km until

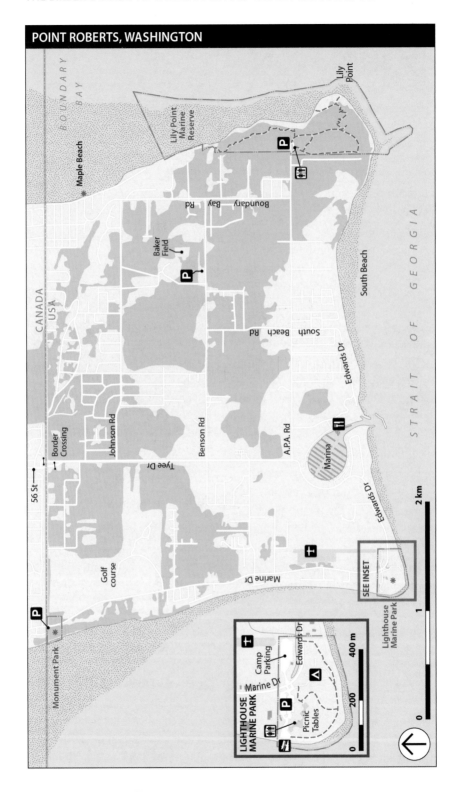

POINT ROBERTS, WASHINGTON

you come to the border crossing between Canada and the USA. At the border, all necessary travel documents for entering the USA will need to be shown. The border crossing is open 24 hours and has a Nexus Lane open during the day.

Once you cross the international boundary, continue south (straight) for approximately 3.5 km to APA Road. Turn left (east) and continue for 2.5 km to the end of APA, until you arrive at Lily Point Marine Reserve, a park of about 111 ha. There is a gravelled public parking lot with restrooms that are open year-round.

The forested upland is the second highest elevation (about 70 m) in Point Roberts and has a public trail system running through the park, with one trail containing stairs that lead down to the beach below.

## BIRD SPECIES

*Bald Eagles* nest here and the ethereal song of the many *Varied Thrushes* in the late winter can be enchanting, although winter birding in the upland forest can be very quiet. During spring migration, many songbirds can be detected along the trail network, and a lucky birder may stumble upon a mini-fallout of migrating warbler flocks feeding in the tops of the big leaf maples. *Red-breasted Sapsucker, Downy Woodpecker, Northern Flicker, Black-capped* and *Chestnut-backed Chickadee, Bewick's* and *Pacific Wren, Brown Creeper, Black-headed Grosbeak,* kinglets and finches are seen in appropriate seasons. This is a very good location for *Hutton's Vireo* all year, but mainly from February through May, when it is singing on territory. At other times of the year, watch for it in mixed-species flocks with chickadees or kinglets. Scan the skies for a *Red-tailed, Sharp-shinned* or *Cooper's Hawk,* especially during migration. A lucky birder may discover a migrating flock of *Vaux's Swift* or stumble upon a *Pileated Woodpecker*. Listen and watch for flocks of *Red Crossbills*. The early spring blossoms of the salmonberry and flowering current will draw the attention of the returning and migrating *Rufous Hummingbird,* while *Anna's Hummingbird* is now a year-round resident that is commonly found visiting feeders in many neighbourhoods. There is a fair chance of hearing the *Barred* and *Great Horned Owl* late in the evening or during an early morning visit.

Bring your spotting scope to the lookout at the top edge of the glacially deposited sand cliffs to scan Boundary Bay, where you may get distant looks at loons, grebes, goldeneyes, scoters and gulls. A walk down to the beach will of course provide much closer viewing conditions, with the added benefit of walking through the shoreline growth, which may yield its treasure of sparrows and finches. *Belted Kingfishers* are known to have nested in their nest burrows constructed in these sand cliffs. Remnants of the Alaska Packers Association cannery can still be seen here.

Return to the parking area by taking the round trip trail north to Cedar Point

Black Turnstones blend in well with the rocky shorelines they inhabit. Liron Gertsman

Avenue and returning down Boundary Bay Avenue, or by taking the south trail behind the residences along Claire Lane. Each of these options will take close to an hour, depending on the number of stops made by the observer.

Another birding walk can be made behind the Point Roberts volunteer fire hall. Leaving the Lily Point parking area, drive back toward Tyee Drive along APA Road, turning right onto Boundary Bay Road at the stop sign. Head up Boundary Bay Road to Benson and turn left. Continue until you reach the signed entrance to the Baker Community Field, just before the fire hall, and turn right into the gravel parking area by the skateboard park. This tiny parking lot has been good for *Townsend's* and *Black-throated Gray Warbler* in season. You can also park in the paved parking lot in front of the fire hall.

Take the trail from the parking area to Baker Field. In season this grass sports field is good for swallows, robins, sparrows and finches. Walk the perimeter of the field to benefit from observing both the field and forest edges. You will find a trail across the field at the northwest corner. This trail borders an old fill site with young growth and can be productive for flycatchers in season. In all seasons, watch overhead for raptors, especially during the fall months. The late arriving *Swainson's Thrush* can be heard uttering its "whit" calls from the vegetation around the water tanks and communication tower. This is the highest point of the peninsula at approximately 72 m. Exit this area by means of the gravel road back to the fire hall parking area.

You can take a quick road trip of the point from the Baker Field parking area.

Exit the park and turn right onto Benson Road, and then left onto South Beach Road about 0.5 km down the road. Continue on South Beach Road past the stop sign at APA Road to the bottom of the hill at the beach. You may park in the restaurant parking lot (a good place for dinner) or in the grass field across the street. Scanning this extensive view of the Strait of Georgia may produce good numbers of all three species of scoter and loons during the fall and winter. Take a close look along the water's edge for *Sanderling* flocks.

Returning to the road, turn west along Edwards Drive instead of heading back up South Beach Road. After approximately 0.5 km, you will arrive at an open grass field at the corner of Largaud Drive and Edwards Drive. Park off to the side of the road and scan this field and the trees across the field for roosting raptors. The *Red-tailed Hawk*, *Northern Harrier* and *Bald Eagle* can be seen here. The large cottonwood at the side of the road has contained an active *Bald Eagle* nest for a few years. Historically, this field and adjacent fields were prime areas for viewing *Barn Owl* coursing these fields near the northern edge of its North American range. While parked here, take a brief walk down the gravel lane that leads to the beach. Scanning the beach from here is likely to produce *Sanderlings* and more sea ducks during fall and winter months. The water toward the rock breakwater can be productive for the *Harlequin Duck*. During the summer, be sure to take a few minutes and check the open water for possible passing orca (killer whale) pods.

Continue driving west along Edwards Drive for a short distance until you travel through a series of short bends in the road, checking the overhead utility lines for *Eurasian Collared-Dove*, a recent permanent resident in Point Roberts. Pull into the marina restaurant parking lot. Restaurant hours vary seasonally, but it is sometimes open for lunch and dinner. A walk along the edge of the marina channel and grass field can produce a number of species. *Western Meadowlarks*, *American Pipits*, *Snow Buntings* and sparrows have all been seen here, and a *Mountain Bluebird* was once spotted. The marina channel may offer good looks at *Common Loons*, *Buffleheads*, *Belted Kingfishers*, both species of goldeneye and maybe a *Horned Grebe* or two. As you approach the marina breakwater, be on the watch for the many beautiful *Harlequin Ducks* hauled out onto the beach in winter in the quiet bay. Be sure to scan the rock breakwater for the *Black Turnstone*. Albeit very uncommon, the *Ruddy Turnstone* and *Wandering Tattler* have been recorded on this breakwater. With luck, a *Black Oystercatcher* and the odd *Surfbird* can be seen in front of the townhouses.

Leave the parking area and turn left onto Simundson Drive and then left again at APA Road. Continue down APA Road to Tyee and turn left. The road now becomes Marina Drive and soon becomes Edwards Drive. Keep a look up for a migrating *Turkey Vulture* in the fall. Turn right onto Ocean View Court to scan the pond for staging wintering ducks and geese. *American Wigeon* flocks should be carefully scanned for a *Eurasian Wigeon*. *Hooded Merganser*, *Mallard*, *Gadwall*, *Scaup* and *Bufflehead* are all common here in the winter, and a brief walk to the shore of the pond may kick up *Wilson's Snipe* and *Western Meadowlark*. In the fall, this area can produce *American Kestrel*.

At the end of this road are weedy fields bordered by blackberry hedgerows. By walking along the hedgerows, you can find *Spotted Towhee* and *Fox, Song, Golden-crowned, White-crowned* and occasionally *Lincoln's Sparrow* (frequent during migration). The weedy fields have *American Goldfinch, House Finch* and *Savannah Sparrow* (plentiful in spring, rare in winter). *Northern Shrike* (winter) and raptors occasionally frequent this area.

Return to Edwards Drive and turn right. Shortly, turn left into the parking area for Lighthouse Marine Park. Overnight camping sites are available in the park and there are year-round restroom facilities here also.

Lighthouse Marine Park is the crown jewel of birding locations in Point Roberts and attracts birders year-round. It is not uncommon to meet other birders standing behind their scopes at the southwest corner of the park by the light tower, scanning the Strait of Georgia. The depth of the water rapidly drops to 130 m in a very short distance. This single corner of land may be the best location in the Vancouver Checklist Area for seabirds and the most reliable for good viewing of alcids. One of the allures of the park is the potential for the uncommon to rare species that have been seen here.

A visit to the park in season can produce *Common Murre, Pigeon Guillemot, Marbled Murrelet, Ancient Murrelet* and *Rhinoceros Auklet*. Four species of loon have been reported here (although *Yellow-billed Loon* is extremely rare), and the passage of hundreds of *Pacific Loon* in the fall and spring is not soon to be forgotten. Wintering *Brant* can also number in the hundreds. Migrating flocks of *Bonaparte's Gull* and *Common Tern* use these waters for feeding in the fall and attract *Parasitic Jaeger*, with the very rare report of *Long-tailed* and *Pomarine Jaeger* in the mix. These migrating flocks have contained such rarities as *Little Gull, Sabine's Gull, Franklin's Gull* and *Black-legged Kittiwake*. Such is the fun of a late summer and fall visit to the park. This is also a favourite location of local birders for *Heermann's Gull* in October. *Brown Pelican* has also been rarely reported from here.

Shorebirds that can be seen along the beach include *Black Turnstone, Sanderling* and *Black Oystercatcher*. Occasionally, *Dunlin, Black-bellied Plover* and *Surfbird* may show up, and rarely, *Ruddy Turnstone* and *Rock Sandpiper*. *Wandering Tattler* has been reported from here but is not to be expected. The sighting of rare gulls, shorebirds and passerines is just part of the attraction of visiting this park.

From mid-October to late February, sea ducks can be found in large numbers: *Greater Scaup; Long-tailed Duck; Black, Surf* and *White-winged Scoter; Bufflehead; Harlequin Duck;* and *Red-breasted Merganser*. *Double-crested, Brandt's* and *Pelagic*

*Cormorant* are all commonly seen, with *Brandt's* being seen in the fall and winter months. Also seen flying overhead, usually in the early morning, are *Snow Geese* and occasionally a *Trumpeter Swan*, also in the fall and winter.

Lighthouse Marine Park is also a well-known viewing location to see passing pods of orca, primarily in the spring and summer months. You may also see other marine mammals, with harbour seals, harbour porpoise and sea lions being the most likely.

From Lighthouse Marine Park, turn left onto Edwards Drive, which becomes Marine Drive as it swings north. Follow it for approximately 2 km to the four-way stop at Gulf Road. Turn left and park at the Reef Pub and Restaurant to scan the gulls and cormorants roosting on the pylons.

To leave Point Roberts and return to the border crossing, drive east on Gulf Road, turn left on Tyee Drive and continue to the border.

Killdeer are known for their broken–wing display to lure predators away. Peter Candido

For those with additional time, Point Roberts has two other public parks with similar birding opportunities. Monument Park is at the very northwest corner of Point Roberts (Roosevelt Way and Marine Drive), where a fairly steep path with switchbacks leads to the beach. Expect similar species to those at Lily Point. The second park, Maple Beach Park (with eight public parking spots), is at the northeast corner of Point Roberts (Roosevelt Way and Bay View Drive). During summer months, the tide exposes the huge intertidal sand flats of Boundary Bay during the day, so it is full of sun-loving beachgoers and is not conducive to good birding. However, during the winter, when daytime tides cover the sand flats, this same bay supports a large variety of sea ducks as well as other marine-loving birds.

This peninsula is diminutive in size, but it offers productive marine and terrestrial habitats. There are many records of rare or accidental species, making it an allure for visitors and locals alike.

*Written by Thomas Plath. Updated by Ken Klimko and Kyle Elliott, 2001.*
*Updated by Ken Klimko and reviewed by Brian Self, 2015.*

# 15. BOUNDARY BAY REGIONAL PARK: WEST SECTION

## INTRODUCTION

THIS SMALL AREA BORDERS THE WESTERN PERIMETER OF BOUNDARY BAY. Because of the historical development of the area, combining agriculture, early settlers' cabins and more recently, rural development, there is an interesting diversity of habitat. It is possible for new birders to observe many species of birds at relatively close range, and the experienced birder has an opportunity to chase down some rare species. The communities of Beach Grove and Centennial Beach still retain many of the old coniferous and deciduous trees combined with native brush and garden habitat. During the spring and fall migrations and the entire winter season, a walk along some of the older side streets will produce most of the West Coast sparrows, warblers, finches and other common land birds.

View north from Centennial Beach at Boundary Bay Regional Park. Ron Long

Beach Grove Park and the adjacent woodlots create an active all-season corner worthy of a little time, with **Barn Owls** and **Great Horned Owls** nesting here on a regular basis. The old black cottonwood stand adjacent to the beach is also a winter resting place and roost for numerous **Bald Eagles**. The short drive south from the foot of 12th Avenue to the community of Centennial Beach passes through farmland with some good hedgerows and brushy stands of trees. The 12th Avenue Dyke Trail from the foot of 12th Avenue, with limited parking facilities, is the main attraction for local birders. This 1 to 3 km walk begins in a treed and grassy area, opening up in only 50 m to a shallow intertidal lagoon (12th Avenue Lagoon) on the left and rough grass farmland on the right, interspersed with drainage ditches and small stands of alder and birch trees. In the first decade of the 2000s, a second lagoon has formed 200 m to the south and has become an attraction for shorebirds. The open bay, with its huge expanse of intertidal mud flats and sandbars, supports good eelgrass meadows that are critical to wintering **Brant**, as well as the spring herring spawn and its associated feeding birds. Birding along the shoreline and the bay is dependent on tidal conditions (see the **Tides** section of this book). Inside the dyke, the habitat quickly becomes a combination of old grasses and marshes. It eventually opens up at its southern extremity into an interesting savannah marsh habitat divided into mini-ecosystems by the old sand berms running parallel to the foreshore. Trails crisscross this habitat, making it easy to search for birds.

At the southern end of this area, Centennial Beach abuts the border with the United States at Point Roberts. The intertidal beaches, with their ever-changing sandbars on a receding tide, make an ideal resting and preening area for many shorebirds and gulls during the spring and fall migrations, always with the possibility of something unusual dropping in from the nearby open waters off Point Roberts.

Approximately one-third of the total area between Boundary Bay Road and the beach is a Metro Vancouver park, which includes the dyke and beach. Viewing platforms have been built at the lagoon and in several other places.

## DIRECTIONS

To reach Beach Grove from downtown Vancouver, take Highway 99 (Oak Street) south, and 1.4 km after exiting the George Massey Tunnel, turn right onto Highway 17A at Exit #28, heading toward Tsawwassen. Highway 17A merges into Highway 17 after several kilometres. In 7.7 km turn left (south) at the lights onto 56th Street (Tsawwassen/Point Roberts turnoff), and left again in 1.2 km at the 16th Avenue light, driving to the T-intersection with Beach Grove Road, where another left turn will lead to Beach Grove Park and the school. Park in the small parking lot (which belongs to the local park) and walk along some of the old back streets and through the Beach Grove Park woodlot area. Note that this park is an off-leash dog area.

To drive directly to the 12th Avenue Dyke Trail and 12th Avenue Lagoon, continue south on 56th Street to 12th Avenue (2 km south of Highway 17) and turn left at the traffic lights. Follow 12th Avenue for 0.7 km past the golf course to the small parking lot at the foot of the avenue. To reach the farmland and Centennial Beach, turn right on Boundary Bay Road at the foot of 12th Avenue and continue for 1.6 km, turning left into Boundary Bay Park (Centennial Beach). From the parking lot, you can walk to the beach or the open savannah habitat to the north. It is possible to walk along the beach, the dyke or the trails inside the dyke between the two parking lots at 12th Avenue and Centennial Beach. There are also several public paths to the shoreline between the houses of Beach Grove and Centennial Beach communities.

Allow at least 1.5 hours travel time by public transport from downtown Vancouver, first via the Canada Line SkyTrain to Bridgeport Station, then by bus to

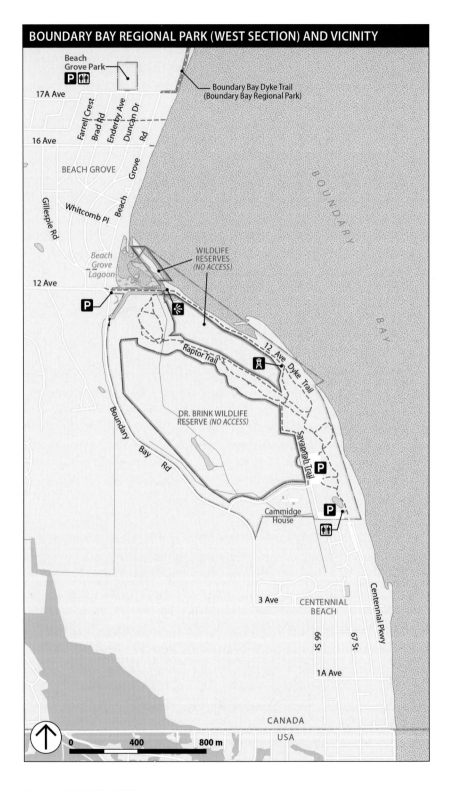

BOUNDARY BAY REGIONAL PARK (WEST SECTION) AND VICINITY

Beach Grove Park

Boundary Bay Dyke Trail
(Boundary Bay Regional Park)

17A Ave

Farrell Crest
Brad Rd
Enderby Ave
Duncan Dr
Rd

16 Ave

BEACH GROVE

Beach Grove

Gillespie Rd

Whitcomb Pl

Beach
Grove
Lagoon

WILDLIFE
RESERVES
(NO ACCESS)

12 Ave

Raptor Trail

12 Ave Dyke Trail

DR. BRINK WILDLIFE
RESERVE (NO ACCESS)

Boundary Bay Rd

Savannah Trail

Cammidge
House

BOUNDARY

BAY

3 Ave

CENTENNIAL
BEACH

Centennial Pkwy

66 St
67 St

1A Ave

CANADA

USA

0          400          800 m

either 16th Avenue or 12th Avenue in Tsawwassen. For current transit information, check the TransLink website (translink.ca). You can then walk a few blocks to the sites listed.

## BIRD SPECIES

Over 210 species of birds have been recorded in this relatively small area. Walking along the dyke has the advantage of permitting close observation of many ducks, gulls, shorebirds and some pelagic species under ideal conditions. The high tide brings the water right up to the dyke and slowly fills the lagoons. Winter populations of ducks in the bay exceed 70,000, with up to 18 species of mixed dabbling and diving ducks. Other winter residents include 50,000 *Dunlins* and several hundred *Sanderlings*. Add 3 loon species, 4 grebe species, 3 cormorant species and at least 6 gull species, and a winter dyke walk can be exciting.

Among the ducks and pelagic species arriving in early September and resident into April and May, the highlights to be looked for are the *Eared Grebe*, *Tufted Duck*, *Eurasian Teal* and high numbers of *Eurasian Wigeon* (up to 23 individuals have been counted from this location).

This is a favoured preening area and resting beach for *Brant*, although very few winter in the bay. The wintering counts are improving, with in excess of 200 birds seen at this location in late winter. Watch for the subspecies *Gray-bellied Brant* among the flocks. The tidal effects on the bay create ideal feeding conditions for the non-migratory *Great Blue Heron* population, and recent fall and winter counts from the 12th Avenue dyke have reached 235 birds. The *Bald Eagle* winters locally and scavenges the tide lines of the bay, feeding mainly on ducks and other water birds. Some 68 individuals have been seen here at one time, perched on drift logs or just standing on the beach, sometimes in small groups.

Over 20 raptor species are known to use the bay area, primarily over the winter. The dyke walk at 12th Avenue passes through typical raptor habitat and is a good location to observe the *Peregrine Falcon* and *Merlin* as they hunt over the salt water and fields. A *Prairie Falcon, Gyrfalcon* or *Northern Goshawk* may also appear as a rare winter bird. An early morning or late evening walk may bring the most success in locating a *Barn Owl*, which probably comes from the nesting location at Beach Grove Park.

An occasional *Western Sandpiper* or a more unusual wintering *Least Sandpiper* might be found with the wintering flocks of *Dunlins* that move with the tide along this beach. The fall shorebird migration becomes apparent as early as the first week of July, when adult *Western Sandpipers* begin to appear in the lagoon. In some years, there is literally no clear break between the spring and fall shorebird migrations in this area. July, August and September are the active months for fall migrants, with the numbers peaking in late August. Over the years, 50 shorebird species have been identified around the bay; the Beach Grove area should therefore produce up to 25 species annually. This gives observers the opportunity to study this rather difficult group of birds from relatively close range, as they do not all follow the tide line each day. A few individuals usually remain resting and feeding in the small pools below the dyke.

*Western* and *Least Sandpiper* are the most common shorebirds, but all three phalaropes and three species of plovers have been seen inside the lagoon. *Greater* and *Lesser Yellowlegs*, *Dowitchers* and *Killdeers* make up the species of larger shorebirds commonly seen during fall migration, but an occasional *Stilt Sandpiper*, *Ruff*, or *Hudsonian Godwit* might also be seen. Spring shorebird migration, from early April until mid-May, may not be as spectacular, but most of the same species of birds can be seen in their more colourful breeding plumages.

The shallow lagoon and the long, sloping shoreline outside the sandbar, seen from the viewing platform, are excellent resting and preening areas for up to 9 species of gulls throughout the year. Several *Franklin's Gulls* may be present during August and September. Up to 30 *Caspian Terns*, including some very young birds, have been seen since 1987 and are a new breeding tern species for the province. These terns are also regular summer residents in this location. A few *Common Terns* pass through as spring migrants, and flocks of up to 150 may be seen in September, either feeding or resting on the shoreline.

Inside the dyke the summer birding is quiet, with the predominant birds being the *Savannah Sparrow*. *Cinnamon Teal*, *Mallard*, *Gadwall* and *Blue-winged Teal* all nest here, and single pairs of *Northern Harrier* and *Cooper's Hawk* have nested here. The marsh is home to a good population of *Marsh Wren*, a few *Common Yellowthroat* and *Red-winged Blackbird* and a possible *Sora*. Winter birders should look for an occasional *Swamp Sparrow* and small flocks of *Western Meadowlarks*.

Beach Grove Park seems to have good peak days during spring and fall migrations in May and September, when relatively large numbers of insectivorous species may bunch up in this isolated woodlot. Species that may be found include *Lincoln's Sparrow* and a good representation of warblers, with an occasional kingbird and *Bullock's Oriole*.

There are eleven months of excellent birding opportunities in the Boundary Bay area. June is the month of least activity.

*Written by Allen Poynter. Revised by Catherine J. Aitchison, 2001.*
*Updated by Brian Self, 2015.*

# 16. BOUNDARY BAY: 64TH STREET TO 112TH STREET

## INTRODUCTION

BOUNDARY BAY, WITH ITS MANY BIRDING SITES, IS ONE OF THE BEST places to see shorebirds and winter raptors in western Canada. At least 47 species of shorebirds, over 30 of them occurring regularly, have been seen in and around Boundary Bay over the years. Mega-rarities that have been recorded here over the years include the *Snowy Plover*, *Lesser Sand-Plover*, *Far-eastern Curlew*,

Bar-tailed Godwit, Red-necked and *Little Stint* and *White-rumped Sandpiper*. It also contains much of Canada's best wintering raptor habitat (all five North American falcons have occurred here), large standing gull roosts and huge numbers of wintering waterfowl and other water birds. Its numerous hedgerows, woodlots, sloughs and fallow fields shelter and feed many migrant, wintering and res-ident songbirds. Rare passerine

View of the Boundary Bay Dyke Trail and extensive salt marsh, looking east from 72nd Street. Ron Long

species that have been recorded here include the *Ash-throated Flycatcher*, *Sage Thrasher*, *Tropical Kingbird*, *Palm Warbler*, *Bobolink* and *Smith's Longspur*. Around the farmlands, the *Eurasian Collared-Dove* first began to show up here around 2008 and have now become widespread and common. At least 75 percent of the species in the Vancouver Checklist Area, many of them vagrants, have been seen in the Boundary Bay area.

Boundary Bay is a large, shallow tidal bay, about 16 km wide from east to west and bordered by a dyke along its entire length. On top of the dyke is the wide, flat, gravelled and well-maintained Boundary Bay Dyke Trail. The dyke is open to public access, except for the easternmost segment between Mud Bay Park and the Nicomekl River estuary. At low tide the sand and mud flats extend up to 2 km south of the dyke, opening large feeding and roosting areas for waterfowl, gulls and shorebirds. The remnant salt marsh forms a fringe between the high-water mark and the dyke. There are fairly extensive eelgrass beds at several locations offshore. As a general birding destination, Boundary Bay offers many excellent birding locations, from Blackie Spit at the eastern end of the Bay to the 12th Avenue Lagoon and Centennial Beach at the western end. (These latter two sites are treated separately, in Section 15 of this guide.) This section focuses on the northern segment of Boundary Bay.

The entire length of the bay has been dyked to prevent high-tide damage to the adjacent farmland. Because the resulting agricultural lands surrounding the bay are fairly homogeneous, a list of species for any one of the numbered streets giving access to the bay could, with little modification, stand for all. Although the area is mostly agricultural, there has been considerable commercial intrusion in recent years. Several extremely large greenhouse complexes have been erected, a highly controversial golf course was developed on 72nd Street, and several very large private dwellings have appeared. In 2014 the new Highway 17 South Fraser Perimeter Road was opened, displacing a wide swath of prime habitat. All these have been sited on rough field terrain that comprised some of the best raptor foraging areas. In addition to these recent developments, there is also the Boundary Bay Airport and the smaller private Delta Air Park at the south end of 104th Street. The Orphaned Wild Life (O.W.L.) Rehabilitation Centre for raptors (eagles, falcons, hawks and owls) is also on 72nd Street. Since this guide was last revised in 2001, there has been gradual and continual loss of prime habitat: more greenhouses, major expansion and development at and around the Boundary Bay Airport (most recently the addition of Boundary Bay Industrial Park) and conversion of rough fields to intense cultivation.

The area of Boundary Bay described here has experienced a significant increase in the number of wildlife-viewing visitors. This is largely due to the switch from film to digital imaging, which has resulted in an almost exponential growth of photographers whose prime subject happens to be birds, and especially large birds of prey. It is gratifying to see so many taking up an interest in the wild world, but at the same time, the best interests of the birds must always come first, by keeping a respectful distance. For more details, please see the "Area of Special Concern: Boundary Bay from 64th Street to 112th Street" subsection of the *Birding and Bird Photography Etiquette* section.

## DIRECTIONS

General access to the Boundary Bay area is from Highway 99. If you are approaching from the north, take Exit #23, which leads to a traffic light at Ladner Trunk Road and 80th Street. From here, turn right to access lower numbered streets, left to access higher numbers. If you are approaching from the south, take Exit #20 to Ladner Trunk Road. Just after exiting, turn left at the traffic light onto Ladner Trunk Road and go over the overpass to another light. To reach 96th Street and

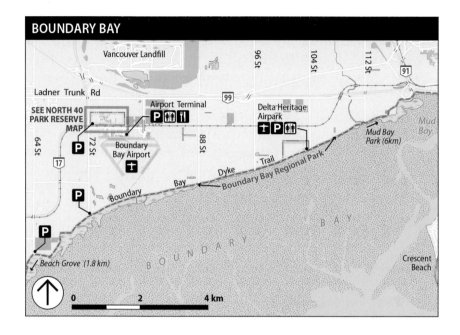

higher-numbered streets, turn left here onto Hornby Drive. To reach lower-num-
bered streets, go straight through the traffic light onto Ladner Trunk Road. (Both
Ladner Trunk Road and Hornby Drive run east–west, paralleling Highway 99 on
its south side.)

Ladner Trunk Road, between Highway 17A and Highway 91, used to also be
called Highway 10, but it was removed from the provincial highway system in
2003. Highway 10 now officially starts eastward from Highway 91. (This is only
mentioned for clarification, because you'll still hear some birders refer to Ladner
Trunk Road as Highway 10.)

Private vehicles are not permitted on the dykes; you must walk, cycle or ride a
horse. Parking in this entire area is limited and is provided only at the south ends
of 64th, 72nd and 104th streets. The parking at 104th Street is in the parking lot of
the Delta Air Park, which has a portable toilet.

## BIRD SPECIES

### 64th Street

Turn south off Ladner Trunk Road and drive through the housing development
for 0.8 km. South of this is agricultural land. To the left are several sets of power
lines and poles that **Red-tailed Hawks** and **Northern Harriers** use for roosting and
hunting perches. In winter and migration, you can find the **Peregrine Falcon** and
sometimes the **Rough-legged Hawk**. All five falcon species use this area in winter

or in migration, but the *Prairie Falcon* is extremely rare. The *Barn Owl* used to be relatively common throughout the area; it has been declining in recent years but can still be found, mainly at dusk.

In spring and fall migrations, both *Pacific* and *American Golden-Plovers*, in small numbers, and an *American Pipit* may use these fields. Wintering waterfowl use them as grazing lands, and shorebird flocks displaced by the bay's high tides await lower water, sometimes in very large standing roosts. Fields used for roosting change from year to year, and also from season to season, so specific locations are not provided here. At the 3.8 km mark, an overpass above the railway and Deltaport Way offers an elevated perch from which to scan the surrounding fields, fence posts and hedgerows for a *Northern Shrike* and other raptors. The ditches along the tracks often contain waterfowl at any time of the year, but in spring and summer *Blue-winged* and *Cinnamon Teals* may be present. Another 0.6 km leads to a large commercial greenhouse on the left, where winter flocks of *Red-winged* and *Brewer's Blackbirds* and *European Starlings* may occasionally harbour a *Yellow-headed Blackbird* or an

Lesser Yellowlegs—the daintier version of the Greater Yellowlegs. Ron Long

even rarer *Rusty Blackbird* (see also 96th and 112th streets), with a handful of overwintering *Brown-headed Cowbirds*. At the south end of the road, check the hedgerows on both sides for mixed flocks of wintering and migrant sparrows. The *Golden-crowned* and *White-crowned Sparrow* are relatively common migrants and this is a reliable location to find the *Savannah* and *Lincoln's Sparrow* in the winter, when they are scarce in the region. The *Vesper*, *American Tree*, *White-throated* and *Harris's Sparrow* are regular winter rarities in habitat such as this throughout the Vancouver Checklist Area.

On the foreshore on an average winter day, you can see flocks of tens of thousands of *Dunlins*, sometimes mixed with a small proportion of *Sanderlings*. During high tides, murmurations of these little sandpipers can be observed coursing over the mud flats—a truly outstanding wildlife spectacle. A thorough search may turn up one or two wintering *Western Sandpipers*. Huge numbers of *American Wigeons* and *Green-winged Teals*, with smaller numbers of *Northern Pintails* and *Mallards*, will also be here. The *Eurasian Wigeon* is regularly seen in these flocks and seems to be increasing in numbers. *Short-eared Owls* sometimes quarter the foreshore with the more common *Northern Harrier*, while *Red-tailed* and less common *Rough-legged Hawk* circle overhead. The *Bald Eagle* is surprisingly numerous, usually standing along the waterline. The *Peregrine Falcon* regularly hunts along the foreshore, and there is the possibility of a *Gyrfalcon* appearing here. A *Prairie Falcon* has been observed here in a few winters, but this may well have been a single individual. In spring and fall, there are large flocks of *Black-bellied Plovers* and *Western Sandpipers* along the foreshore, usually tide-displaced from feeding areas at the eastern end of the bay. *Northern Shrike* is regular from October in small numbers. Examine any thickets along the dyke for wintering and migrant passerines.

Note: *The salt marsh is fragile. Please stay on the obvious trails.*

## 36th Avenue

This east–west road connects 64th and 72nd streets, 1.5 km south of Ladner Trunk Road. Along its south side, the ploughed fields offer good habitat for the *Black-bellied Plover* and *Golden-Plover*, *American Pipit*, *Lapland Longspur* and more rarely, *Snow Bunting*. Gull flocks occasionally use these fields as standing roosts.

## 72nd Street

Immediately south of Ladner Trunk Road, the new (2014) South Fraser Perimeter Road/Highway 17 has displaced what used to be excellent gull roost fields and hawthorn hedgerows. Most of the action now takes place on the west side of 72nd Street and south of the railway, where there is a large composting facility and turf farm with extensive fields of short grass. These fields are used by large roosts of gulls sated from feeding in the composting facility and the Vancouver Landfill, a few kilometres away on the north side of Highway 99. (The landfill management does not allow birding within the landfill.) The roosts mainly contain *Glaucous-winged*, *Mew* and *Thayer's Gulls*, with *Herring* and *California Gulls* in small numbers. *Western* and *Glaucous Gulls* are rare but fairly regular; *Slaty-backed* and *Iceland Gulls* are possible. The *Ring-billed Gull* has become an abundant summer bird. These fields, extending south to the railway tracks, are also good raptor habitat. The dense rows of hawthorn trees adjacent to the road provide sheltered roosts and abundant food for fruit-eating species. Occasionally, a *Long-eared Owl* can be found here on winter days.

The turf farm's extensive fields of short grass provide Vancouver's best site for the *Buff-breasted Sandpiper*, which may pass through in August and September, but not every year. In addition, both species of *Golden-Plover* and *Baird's Sandpiper* and potentially many other vagrant species may turn up. In recent years this has also become one of the best places to find gull congregations and *Bald Eagles*.

Short–eared Owls are often seen at the Boundary Bay salt marsh. Jim Martin

Please keep in mind that this is private land and must be scanned from the roadside.

In winter, check the irrigation machinery for perched raptors, including the *Snowy Owl*. South of the railway on the left side is the ever-expanding Boundary Bay Airport. Just south of the airport on the left is the turnoff to the Orphaned Wild Life (O.W.L.) Rehabilitation Centre, which is well worth a visit; it specializes in raptors, and there are a number of non-releasable raptors on public display.

Some 2.4 km south of Ladner Trunk Road, at the intersection of 72nd Street and 36th Avenue (on the left), is the Benson Home, a heritage farmhouse. Its gardens, fruit trees and surrounding hedgerows offer cover for flocks of wintering songbirds. In the next kilometre, in a field to the right, a large radio/microwave tower provides a good raptor perch. At the end of the road are hedgerows that may contain many wintering and migrant passerines.

On the foreshore marsh and along the waterline, you can scan roosting shorebird and waterfowl flocks. About 1.5 km east along the dyke is a thicket, which has harboured wintering *Yellow-rumped Warblers* with the more usual sparrows. Wintering *Western Meadowlarks* and sometimes *Sandhill Cranes* use the fields in this vicinity. *Snowy Owls* can be found throughout the Fraser delta in irruption years, and the foreshore near the south end of 72nd Street is often the most likely place to find this species.

## Boundary Bay Airport Access Road

Approaching from the north, turn left (east) off 72nd Street onto Churchill Road, and in a few hundred metres on the right (south) side, you'll see the entrance road to the airport terminal. There are washrooms and a convenient restaurant open to the public in the airport terminal. The brushy strip between Churchill Road and the railway provides excellent cover and food for wintering songbirds, including *Northern Shrike*. North of the railway is the North 40 Park Reserve, which is covered next.

## North 40 Park Reserve

The North 40 Park Reserve can be found on the east side of 72nd Street. It encompasses 40 acres (16.2 ha) of land, hence the name. The park has an interesting history, since it was the site of a World War II airfield and as many as 4,000 personnel lived here. There are some excellent photographs from this era placed around the park and well worth looking at. After the war it became the Vancouver Wireless Station, which operated from 1949 to 1971 and monitored Soviet Union communications in the Arctic through the Cold War period. The road layout is still in evidence from these eras, although all of the buildings have long since been removed.

Directions to the North 40 Park Reserve from downtown Vancouver: Take Highway 99 South to the George Massey Tunnel and 1.4 km after exiting the tunnel on the south side, turn right onto Highway 17A (Exit #28). In 2.2 km turn left at the traffic lights onto Ladner Trunk Road East. In 2.4 km turn right at the traffic lights onto 72nd Street, and the entrance to the North 40 is in 0.7 km on the left and poorly signposted. If you cross a railroad line, you have driven 100 m past the entrance. Walk the paved road east from the parking lot. Throughout its war years and later, the site was well planted with trees, and the houses built to accommodate families had gardens. Their legacy stands today in the form of hawthorns, rose bushes, a copse of birch trees, sycamores, large weeping willows and a row of oaks, now over 75 years old. The large deciduous trees with the pale leaves at the northern perimeter are balsam and white poplar, habitat that attracts a decent bird population. This grassland and shrubby cover is characteristic of former Delta habitat that is now rapidly disappearing.

Because of its close proximity to the Vancouver Landfill site across Highway 99, the reserve is a common site for *Bald Eagles* from November to mid-summer and *Red-tailed Hawk* year-round. There have been a pair of *Cooper's Hawks* nesting on the southern edge, and winter will bring the occasional *Rough-legged Hawk* crossing the park. The more common gull species are well represented, again because of the nearby landfill site. The park sits between it and the waters of Boundary Bay.

The park had been an overwintering home to five species of owl, but since the Delta Municipality designated it an off-leash dog park, the number of people using it has increased dramatically and owls have become much harder to find. A diligent search of the larger trees may still produce surprises though.

Spring migration brings in up to five species of flycatchers: the *Olive-sided*, *Western Wood-Pewee*, *Willow*, *Hammond's* and *Pacific-slope Flycatcher*. Two of the five species of swallow nest here, as do *Bushtits*. Three species of wren can be found and all likely nest in the park. Eight species of warbler have visited the park, with two of them known to nest here. The regulars are the *Orange-crowned*, *Common Yellowthroat*, *Yellow-rumped* (Audubon and Myrtle varieties) and *Wilson's*. The *Townsend's* and *Black-throated Gray Warbler* are spring migrants, and

Beautiful image of a Barn Owl in hunting mode. John Gordon

*MacGillivray's Warbler* is a fall visitor. Sparrows are well represented, with *Savannah* (a summer breeder), *Fox* and *Golden-crowned* and *Dark-eyed Junco* (winter residents), *Song* and *White-crowned Sparrow* year-round, although the latter in steadily decreasing numbers. One of the star attractions in the early 2000s has been the presence of male *Lazuli Bunting*, a bird that is not common anywhere in our area. The repeated presence of *Bullock's Orioles* through the summer months indicates they nest here too.

The park can be a noisy and busy place on weekends. Boundary Bay Airport houses many small single- or twin-engine private planes and there is a growing helicopter presence too. If you can schedule your visit for a mid-week day, this is a worthwhile site to bird. It has a good historical background to interest most people too.

## 96th Street

The high-tide line moves progressively closer to the dyke, squeezing the foreshore salt marsh into an increasingly narrow fringe toward 112th Street and making closer views of shorebirds and waterfowl possible. Half a kilometre south from Hornby Drive on 96th Street is Cambridge Stables on the left, where large, wintering blackbird and starling flocks gather, joined by the occasional *Yellow-headed Blackbird* and a few *Brown-headed Cowbirds*. The *Rusty Blackbird* has wintered here. On the right, a row of dense conifers offers owl roost possibilities, and *Bald Eagles* often perch at the top of large Douglas-fir trees, where they are visible for many kilometres. On the dyke, about midway between 88th and 96th streets, there is a large and opulent private residence referred to by local birders as "the

Mansion." A small lagoon here, the outflow channel of a pumping station, provides one of the very best shorebird sites in the Vancouver area. Some of the interesting birds seen here include the **Green Heron**; **Stilt**, **White-rumped** and **Sharp-tailed Sandpiper**; **Ruff**; **Bar-tailed** and **Marbled Godwit**; and **Red Knot**.

Remember that there is no parking at either 88th or 96th streets, necessitating a walk or cycle of about 5 km return from the Delta Air Park on 104th Street.

## 104th Street

From the corner of Hornby Drive, large conifers and gardens on either side provide good cover for songbirds and perches for raptors. A small woodlot and hedgerows at the end of the road often conceal the usual mixed flock of sparrows and, in migration, other passerines, such as warblers. The waterline can be very close to the dyke at this point, making it a good location from which to scan waterfowl flocks and large groups of shorebirds displaced from their feeding areas to the east by rising tides.

Parking at the foot of 104th Street provides a central location to access the shorebird flocks, which move across the mud flats between 96th and 112th streets. Large flocks can frequent different areas of the bay on a daily basis depending on tide state and falcon disturbance. A scan from the foot of 104th Street will usually reveal the flock and help determine whether to walk east toward 112th Street or west toward 96th Street.

Knowing the tide state is essential in observing shorebirds at Boundary Bay. During a low tide, there is an endless expanse of mud flats, and shorebirds scatter over a large area, often well away from the dyke. Conversely, very high tides displace shorebird flocks after the water reaches the dyke, forcing them to roost in nearby fields or among foreshore vegetation toward the west end of the bay. The ideal (rising or falling) tide height for viewing shorebirds at Boundary Bay is approximately 3.7 m (12 ft). At this height, the rising tide pushes shorebirds close to the dyke but still leaves some exposed mud flats for feeding. It is advisable to arrive at least 1 hour before the tide reaches 3.7 m to allow sufficient time to walk from the parking lot at the foot of 104th Street and position yourself in an area where birds are being concentrated by the rising tide. It is also worth noting that tides rise and fall at different rates, which will dictate the amount of time available for viewing shorebirds at an ideal distance.

Spring migration is generally rushed and presents a lower diversity. It ramps up by mid-April and during peak migration, toward the end of the month, the **Dunlin** and **Western Sandpiper** form mixed flocks that number in the tens of thousands. **Black-bellied Plovers** also pass through in large numbers. Among these flocks, the **Semipalmated Plover**, **Whimbrel**, **Least Sandpiper** and **Short-billed Dowitcher** can be found in smaller numbers. **Red Knot** is scarce in spring, but a few generally turn up in mid-May. By late May, the big flocks of shorebirds have largely passed through on to their northerly breeding grounds.

For shorebirds, fall migration begins as early as late June. Adult shorebirds dominate the migration until about early August, when juveniles, embarked on their very first southbound migration, begin to outnumber them. Of the *Calidrid* sandpipers, **Western Sandpiper** is the most abundant species, and **Least Sandpiper** is also numerous. *Semipalmated Sandpiper* peaks in July and has largely passed through by late August. **Baird's Sandpiper** can be found during August and September; look for this bird close to the dyke among the dry seaweed. **Pectoral Sandpiper** also often forages near the dyke but tends to move through a bit later in September and October. These flocks should be checked for **Buff-breasted Sandpiper** (late August/early September) and **Sharp-tailed Sandpiper** (September/October), which turn up some years.

Large flocks of **Black-bellied Plover** are present throughout the fall, peaking in late September, and smaller numbers remain to overwinter. Among these flocks there are usually a few **Short-billed Dowitchers** (July to September), **Red Knots** (August to October) and **American Golden-Plovers** (September/October). *Pacific Golden-Plovers* (September/October) and **Ruddy Turnstones** (August) pass through in very small numbers. Some years, a **Bar-tailed Godwit** or **Hudsonian Godwit** will turn up and associate with these flocks.

## 112th Street

There is no parking at the south end of 112th Street. One can walk or cycle from 104th, or walk from the corner of 112th and Hornby. In winter the horse barns at this corner attract hordes of blackbirds and **European Starlings**, along with **Eurasian Collared-Doves** and the potential of a **Rusty** or **Yellow-headed Blackbird**. Occasionally, a **Cattle Egret** has shown up in the nearby fields in October and November, but it has not been found in recent years.

A short distance to the right (west), along the dyke, is a modern pumphouse and drainage outflow. The grating over the outflow is sometimes the fishing perch of a **Green Heron**. Many shorebirds use this area, except at high tide: **Least**, **Western** and **Semipalmated Sandpipers** on the rocks, algal mats and floating debris bordering the channel; **Greater** and **Lesser Yellowlegs**, and sometimes **Solitary Sandpipers**, on the muddy shores of the channel; **Black-bellied** and **Semipalmated Plovers**, farther out toward the tide line. Loons, grebes and diving ducks frequently come up the channel almost to the dyke. On the dyke to the east, walk around a low metal gate and scan the narrow, sandy bars projecting seawards (east) from the foreshore for several hundred metres. This general area is another productive place to look for migrating shorebirds; expect the same species and conditions as described for 104th Street. Accidentals recorded here include the **Snowy Plover**, **Little** and

*Red-necked Stint*, Vancouver's only *Lesser Sand-Plover*, and Canada's first and only *Far Eastern Curlew*. Large concentrations of gulls, shorebirds and waterfowl also gather here, joined in summer by *Caspian Terns*.

Water birds found here in summer include the *Common Loon, Mallard, Gadwall*, and *White-winged* and *Surf Scoter*. Winter brings sometimes-large numbers of *Common* and *Red-throated Loons* with small numbers of *Pacific Loons* (far more numerous off Point Roberts to the southwest). *Horned, Western* and *Red-necked Grebes*, huge numbers of *American Wigeons, Northern Pintails, Green-winged Teals* and *Mallards* may be inshore, as well as great rafts of all three scoter species. The *Long-tailed Duck, Common* and *Redbreasted Merganser* and both scaup species can also be found here. *Pelagic* and *Double-crested Cormorants* are common. *Brants* feed in small numbers on eelgrass beds here, though their main staging area is farther west, off Beach Grove and Roberts Bank.

The Ring–billed Gull inhabits many of the local shorelines. Colin Clasen

One of the best places on Boundary Bay to view these large gatherings is the head of a large grassy spit almost 1 km east of 112th Street. Take a trail that diverges diagonally right across the marsh toward the spit. From here you have an unobstructed view of Mud Bay, the main feeding ground. The enormous mass of Mount Baker looming in the distance on the usually clear days provides an awesome backdrop to the scene. Where there are shorebirds, there are falcons to hunt them. Search the foreshore and the dead trees at the seaward edge of the woodlot just north of the grassy spit for perched falcons. Sometimes a *Sharp-shinned* and *Cooper's Hawk* or roosting *Great Horned* and *Barn Owl* also use this woodlot, and it sometimes harbours good numbers of migrating passerines in spring. Transient *Ospreys* are regular here, especially in fall.

Eastward from the woodlot, the dyke passes some dense bramble patches that provide excellent cover for wintering passerines. Farther on, the dyke runs very close to Highway 99, and raptors often perch in the scattered tall trees along this stretch.

*For further reading:* A Nature Guide to Boundary Bay *by Anne Murray. This is the only comprehensive guide to the birds, animals and plants of the Boundary Bay area, including the Fraser River estuary and Burns Bog.*

*Written by Michael Price. Updated by Carlo Giovanella and Ilya Povalyaev, 2015.*
*North 40 Park Reserve subsection written by Brian Self, 2015.*

# 17. SERPENTINE WILDLIFE MANAGEMENT AREA (SERPENTINE FEN)

## INTRODUCTION

SERPENTINE FEN IS SITUATED IN SOUTH SURREY BETWEEN THE SERPENTINE River on the north and the Nicomekl River on the south. It is bordered by Highway 99 on the west and Highway 99A/King George Boulevard on the east. The fen covers an area of 106 ha, which includes 80 ha of dyked freshwater marsh and 4 ha of undyked salt marsh. The remainder is mostly hay fields and brushy patches.

One of three viewing towers at Serpentine Fen. Bill Kinkaid

The provincial government owns the present area, which was cut off from surrounding farms when the freeway was constructed. The province manages the fen, and over the years it has been used by Douglas College for farming, for various research schemes and by the White Rock and Surrey Naturalists Society for educational tours. Ducks Unlimited (Canada) have their office on the property and have made considerable changes to drainage patterns and excavated large ponds for waterfowl. The dykes have been widened and changes to the area are ongoing

The vegetation consists mostly of small trees and bushes, which are plentiful, especially around the parking lot and down the lane, which was 44th Avenue. Many of these plantings were done by the White Rock and Surrey Naturalists Society. Blackberries, elderberries, Pacific crab apples and mountain-ash berries all provide good food for birds. Some ponds have large patches of cattails. Fruit trees can be found near the Ducks Unlimited building.

There is a public trail network along most principal dykes and three viewing towers with good views of marsh and river habitats and fields. The trails are flat, providing very easy walking. Mammals to be seen include muskrats, coyotes and rabbits. Harbour seals can be found in the tidal Serpentine River.

# DIRECTIONS

From Vancouver, take Highway 99 (Oak Street) south through the George Massey Tunnel and continue on as the highway curves to the east, turning off at the sign for White Rock (Exit #10). Almost immediately, turn left onto Highway 99A North (King George Highway). Keep in the left lane and follow King George Highway north for approximately 2.4 km and turn left at 44th Avenue (a small country lane) beside Art Knapp Plantland. Follow this dirt lane to the parking lot on the left. There are picnic tables here, but no toilet facilities anywhere at the fen. About 400 m north of 44th Avenue, there is also a small parking area on the west side of King George Blvd., where it crosses the Serpentine River.

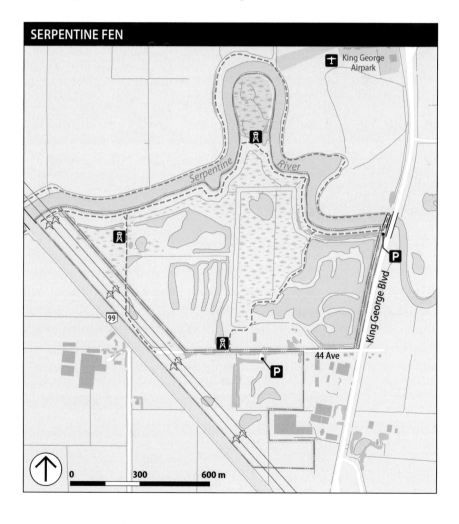

# BIRD SPECIES

Much of the birding at the fen depends on water levels, as in a dry summer, local farmers use the Serpentine River for irrigation.

Scopes are recommended, as you can't get close to most ponds. Over 175 species have been recorded in the immediate area of the fen. Of these, about 50 are listed as rare, casual or accidental.

Northern Pintail with the diagnostic white line arching up its neck. John Lowman

If you start your walk by going left (west) from the 44th Avenue parking lot down the lane, there are swallow boxes along the way and *Tree*, *Violet-green* and *Barn Swallows* are plentiful over the ponds and on the wires. The bushes and trees along the lane are good for the *Northern Flicker* and *Downy* and *Hairy Woodpecker*; *Steller's Jay*; *Black-capped Chickadee*; *Bushtit*; *Bewick's Wren*; *American Robin*; *Song*, *White-crowned* and *Golden-crowned Sparrow*; *Spotted Towhee*; *Ruby-crowned Kinglet*; *House* and *Purple Finch*; and *Red-winged* and *Brewer's Blackbird*. All can be seen almost all year-round. The *Willow Flycatcher*; *Cedar Waxwing*; *Orange-crowned, Yellow, Yellow-rumped* and *Wilson's Warbler*; *Brown-headed Cowbird*; and *Rufous Hummingbird* are more common in spring and summer. In fall and winter, look for the *Northern Shrike* and *Evening Grosbeak*. At the end of the lane, the trail turns north. Look up here to see what the power line towers have to offer. The *Red-tailed Hawk* is present year-round. A *Bald Eagle* nest, active for several years, is visible on a power line tower northwest of the viewing tower. *American Kestrels* may be here in spring and fall; and *Peregrine Falcons, Sharp-shinned, Cooper's* and *Rough-legged Hawks* can be found in winter. The *Northern Harrier* is common all year over the fields, and the *Bald Eagle* is seen frequently.

The ponds to the west of the trail sometimes have *Blue-winged* and *Cinnamon Teal* in the spring and summer. Climb the viewing tower here for a good overview of ponds to the west and east. The *Great Blue Heron* is common all year and the *Ring-necked Pheasant* is sometimes seen. *Canada Geese, Green-winged Teal,*

*Mallards*, *Northern Pintails*, *Northern Shovelers*, *American Wigeons* and *American Coots* are present most of the year. A *Glaucous-winged Gull* can always be seen, while *Ring-billed*, *Bonaparte's* and *Mew Gulls* are common seasonally. *Short-eared Owls* are a possibility, but they are uncommon now, as are the *Barn Owls* that once lived in the collapsed barn.

From the viewing tower, turn east along the Serpentine River dyke, keeping an eye out for birds on the river, especially when the tide is in. The Tynehead Hatchery in north Surrey releases salmon fry into the Serpentine River and is a destination for returning salmon.

The *Common Loon* and *Western* and *Horned Grebe* are seen in the fall and winter, and *Double-crested Cormorant* is present year-round. *Common Merganser*, *Bufflehead*, *Common Goldeneye* and *Ruddy Duck* appear at times. *Belted Kingfisher* patrols the river. When there is enough mud around the ponds, search the shorelines for shorebirds, keeping an eye out for something unusual, as this is where most of the rarities in the fen occur. In total, 32 shorebird species have been observed at the fen. *Greater Yellowlegs* and *Killdeer* are frequent except in winter. The *American Avocet*, *Black-necked Stilt* and *Ruff* have visited occasionally in the past.

Climb the next tower for a look around, and in spring try the bushes along the inside of the dyke for warblers and other migrants. After following the dyke almost to the highway, you will notice a small footbridge over the ditch to the south. Follow this trail, which gives a good view of the large pond to the east. Nest boxes for swallows can be seen around the pond edges. In the cattails, look and listen for the many *Marsh Wrens* and *Common Yellowthroats*. The *Savannah Sparrow* likes this area too. Secretive birds such as the *American Bittern* and *Sora Rail* have been spotted here.

There is just one more tower to climb before reaching the parking lot and completing the circuit. If you still want more, check the bushes down the lane to the east. Sometimes the old orchard near the Ducks Unlimited building is good for warblers and woodpeckers.

Other species seen here include the *Pied-billed Grebe*, *Wood Duck*, *Eurasian Wigeon*, *Lesser Scaup*, *Ring-necked Duck*, *Hooded* and *Red-breasted Merganser*, *Wilson's Snipe*, *Vaux's Swift*, *Common Raven*, *Anna's Hummingbird*, *Chestnut-backed Chickadee*, *Golden-crowned Kinglet*, *Fox Sparrow*, *Black-headed Grosbeak*, *Pine Siskin*, *American Goldfinch* and *Eurasian Collared-Dove*.

*Written and revised by the late Jack Williams, 2001. Updated by Liz Walker, 2015.*

# 18. BLACKIE SPIT / WHITE ROCK WATERFRONT / KWOMAIS POINT

BLACKIE SPIT (AT THE EXTREME NORTH END OF CRESCENT BEACH) AND the City of White Rock are situated about 30 km south of downtown Vancouver on the Semiahmoo (sem-ee-AH-moo) Peninsula, in the southwest part of Surrey.

The peninsula is bounded by the Nicomekl River on the north side, Mud Bay and Boundary Bay on the west side and Semiahmoo Bay on the south side. Most of the land on the peninsula has been developed for residential use.

Captain George Vancouver anchored his ship *Discovery* in 1792 near where the mouth of the Little Campbell River empties into Semiahmoo Bay. A large boulder, a relic of the Ice Age on White Rock's East Beach, was used as a navigational aid. The rock, limed white with guano, eventually gave the city its name. The rock's white appearance is now maintained with paint.

European settlement began in the mid-1800s. By 1910 White Rock was being promoted as a resort area because of its mild climate and sandy beaches. A cottage community sprang up along the Semiahmoo Bay waterfront. Today, White Rock city encompasses almost 8 square km and is surrounded by the southern portion of Surrey.

Looking north toward the tip of Blackie Spit, on its east side, with the Nicomekl River coming in from the right. Bill Kinkaid

## BLACKIE SPIT – INTRODUCTION

Blackie Spit was settled by Walter Blackie in 1871. He farmed the land on which the community of Crescent Beach is now situated. Today, Blackie Spit refers to the sandy point jutting into Mud Bay (the shallow northeastern part of Boundary Bay) at the mouth of the Nicomekl River, and the adjacent undeveloped land.

The vegetation consists of various salt- and sand-tolerant grasses, shrubs such as red elderberry, common snowberry, Indian-plum and Nootka rose, along with introduced Himalayan blackberry and Scotch broom. Trees include Pacific crab apple, Pacific willow, paper birch, black cottonwood, saskatoon, black hawthorn and introduced English hawthorn. Glasswort thrives in the saltwater marsh areas.

A sandy area on the north side of Farm Slough (the Rene Savigny Environmentally Sensitive Area) is bordered on its north side by an interesting stand of small trees that comprise an extensive clone of an introduced winged elm.

## DIRECTIONS

To reach Blackie Spit by car from Vancouver, take Highway 99 (Oak Street) south. After passing through Richmond and the George Massey Tunnel, the highway curves eastward and passes close to the north shore of Mud Bay. Take the White Rock/Crescent Beach exit (#10) and bear right, following the signs to Crescent Beach. You will now be on Crescent Road. After about 5 km, Crescent Road descends a hill and crosses a railway track. At a V-intersection just beyond the tracks, bear right onto Sullivan Street. Turn right again onto McBride Avenue (the

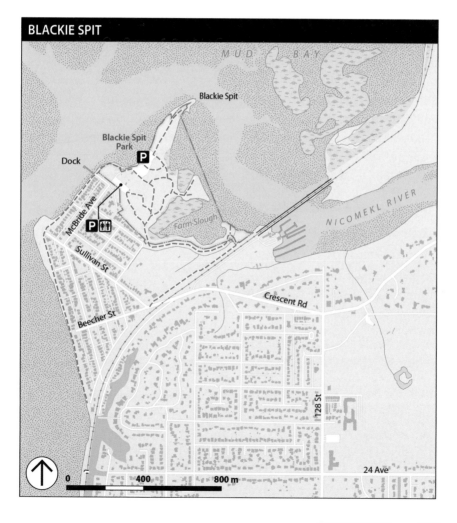

last street before the beach) and follow it to the end to reach the Blackie Spit parking area. The gate is open from about 8 a.m. to dusk. If you arrive before 8 a.m., park outside and walk in.

Blackie Spit can also be reached from downtown Vancouver by taking the Canada Line to Bridgeport Station in Richmond and transferring to the Crescent Beach bus, which provides service to Sullivan Street and McBride Avenue. Check the Translink website (translink.ca) for current transit information.

Washroom facilities are located at the far end of the parking lot, near the swimming pool and tennis courts.

## BIRD SPECIES

Almost 200 species have been recorded in the Blackie Spit/Crescent Beach area. Birding is best during migration periods and in winter, although rarities can show up in any season. Midsummer is the quietest period, when *Barn*, *Violet-green* and *Tree Swallow*; *White-crowned Sparrow*; *House Finch*; *Northwestern Crow*; *European Starling*; *Red-winged Blackbird*; and *House Sparrow* are the most numerous species. The *Eurasian Collared-Dove* has recently become part of the resident avifauna. It is wise to check tide levels (see the *Tides* section) before your trip to Blackie Spit. Tide levels are very important when looking for water birds and shorebirds, which predominate in this area. Make sure you arrive at least 1 hour (2 hours is even better) before high tide for optimum viewing. At low tide, any water birds present will likely be too far out to be seen adequately, if at all. Explore the centre of Blackie

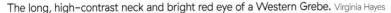

The long, high-contrast neck and bright red eye of a Western Grebe. Virginia Hayes

Spit, as well as both shorelines. *Savannah Sparrow* is a common breeder here and may be found in the grasses from April through September.

A few transient *Lapland Longspurs* and *Horned Larks* (September and October) and *Snow Buntings* (November and December) are sometimes seen. Watch for large flocks of shorebirds such as *Dunlins*, *Sanderlings* and *Black-bellied Plovers* from fall through late spring. Offshore, the *Common Loon* may be seen at any season, although it is most abundant from fall through spring. In winter, the *Red-throated Loon* is uncommon, and *Yellow-billed Loon* is possible but extremely rare. *Horned*, *Red-necked* and *Western Grebes* are likely to be found from fall through spring. Off the west side of the spit, diving ducks are usually abundant from fall through spring. Look for the *Bufflehead*, *Common Goldeneye*, *Surf Scoter*, *Greater Scaup* (sometimes in very large rafts), along with smaller numbers of *Long-tailed Ducks*, *Barrow's Goldeneyes* and *Common* and *Red-breasted Mergansers*. You may spot a few *Canvasbacks* and *White-winged* and *Black Scoters*.

The saltwater marsh across the Nicomekl River estuary opposite Blackie Spit is used by loafing gulls, *Great Blue Herons*, resident *Canada Geese* and sometimes *Bald Eagles*. At times it may teem with shorebirds. Harbour seals haul out regularly on certain islets. There is no public access to that area, but it is viewable by telescope from Blackie Spit. **Caution:** *Do not attempt to cross on the railway trestle.*

The shallow, sheltered waters off the east side of the spit are attractive to wintering dabbling ducks; the *Northern Pintail*, *Green-winged Teal*, *Mallard* and *American Wigeon* are abundant from fall through spring. The *Eurasian Wigeon* has become fairly common here, and it is not unusual to find a dozen or more. The *Double-crested Cormorant* rests on the pilings. Gulls like to loaf in the marshy area along the east side of the spit; look for the *Glaucous-winged* and *Ring-billed Gull* all year and *Mew* and *Thayer's* in winter. From late summer into fall, be alert for the possibility of a *Franklin's Gull* among the flocks of *Bonaparte's Gulls*. Transient *California Gulls* appear in small numbers in spring and fall. Watch and listen for the *Caspian Tern* (May to September) and possibly *Common Tern* (May and August through September).

If peaceful flocks of feeding or resting ducks, shorebirds, gulls or terns suddenly erupt into flight, the reason for the disturbance may be the approach of a raptor. Look for a *Bald Eagle*; *Northern Harrier*, *Sharp-shinned*, *Cooper's* or *Red-tailed Hawk*; *Peregrine Falcon*; or *Merlin*.

A short distance south and east of the spit is a small tidal pond surrounded by shrubs and trees that attract (in any season) the *Dark-eyed Junco*, *White-crowned* and *Song Sparrow*, *Black-capped Chickadee* and *Spotted Towhee*, with *Golden-crowned Sparrow* and *Purple Finch* in winter. Transient warblers may include *Orange-crowned*, *Yellow-rumped* and *Wilson's*. At low tide, it is possible to continue walking along the shore, across the narrow channel that fills and drains the pond, but at high tide you will have to detour around the west side of the pond. In either case, after crossing an open sandy area, you will reach Farm Slough, a shallow backwater of the Nicomekl River. At the optimal tidal levels of 3.4 to 4 m (11 to 13 ft), this sheltered slough may be full of shorebirds or ducks. A good viewing spot is at the north side of the slough's mouth, marked by a row of low pilings, remnants of an old oyster cannery. From this point, you may scan both Farm Slough and the Nicomekl estuary. *Common Yellowthroat* and *Yellow Warblers* nest in shrubby vegetation around the slough; a *Belted Kingfisher* might show up in any season. A cluster of tall pilings on the north side of the mouth of Farm Slough is festooned with nesting boxes for *Purple Martins*. This colony has grown impressively over the last decade and provides excellent viewing.

The main northward migration of shorebirds is compressed into approximately mid-April to mid-May; numbers may be fairly small, and their presence brief. The main southward migration in fall (July through September) produces the greatest variety of shorebirds, but some species are present all year. The *Killdeer* is resident in the area and may be found in any season. Small flocks of *Greater Yellowlegs* and *Long-billed Dowitchers* can usually be found all winter. A few *Semipalmated Plovers* may be found in late summer among the abundant *Western*, common *Least*, and very rare *Semipalmated Sandpipers*. Occasionally, some of the locally rare larger shorebirds have shown up at Blackie spit. The *Long-billed Curlew* and *Marbled Godwit* and (less commonly) *Willet* sometimes overwinter, and the *Bar-tailed* and *Hudsonian Godwit* may pass through on migration.

On the south side of Farm Slough, a narrow, rough path leads along the wooded dyke bordering the slough. This is a good area for resident passerines, such as sparrows, finches, robins, *Pine Siskins*, *American Goldfinches* and *Bushtits*, as well as transient species. The rough path joins the gravel walking path atop a wider, parallel dyke on the southern side of the slough's mouth. Pass the pumphouse, bear right (south) and walk along an unnamed road that parallels the railway tracks on the south side of Dunsmuir Farm Community Gardens. Scan the garden fields for a *Northern Shrike* (casual) in winter. The road is lined by dense shrub thickets and a few Lombardy poplars, in which one or two pairs of *Bullock's Orioles* may nest in summer.

# WHITE ROCK WATERFRONT — INTRODUCTION

The City of White Rock maintains a delightful waterfront promenade (2.2 km long) along East Beach and West Beach. The two beaches are divided by the wooden pier, which extends almost 500 m southwards into Semiahmoo Bay. The promenade and the pier comprise a local attraction that is heavily used year-round.

## DIRECTIONS

To reach the White Rock waterfront from Vancouver via Highway 99 (Oak Street) south, take the 8th Avenue exit (#3) onto Highway 99A (King George Highway), then turn right (west) onto 8th Avenue. After several blocks, 8th Avenue becomes Marine Drive. Pay parking lots are located at frequent intervals along the drive. Birders may want to note that parking is *free* until 10 a.m., and there is plenty of it. In afternoons during fine weather, one can expect to encounter hordes of visiting sightseers and limited parking spaces.

## BIRD SPECIES

In summer, resident **Canada Geese, Mallards, Double-crested Cormorants, Great Blue Herons** and one or two **Belted Kingfishers** may be seen. A few non-breeding **Common Loons** may be present, far out in the bay. **Northwestern Crows, Glaucous-winged** and **Ring-billed Gulls**, and perhaps a few non-breeding **Bonaparte's Gulls**, loaf on the beaches. Watch and listen for **Caspian Terns**. Resident raptors include the **Bald Eagle, Red-tailed Hawk** and the occasional **Cooper's Hawk**.

The long White Rock Pier provides many good bird–viewing opportunities. Al Grass

Transient species include the **Red-necked Grebe** (sometimes in very large numbers), **Western** and **Least Sandpiper** (April and May; July through September) and **Brant** (mostly March and April, but may be seen anytime in winter). A subspecies of **Brant**, the **Gray-bellied Brant**, has been occurring in the Pacific Northwest in increasing numbers and is worth noting. Currently under study, they may be raised to species status in the future.

A **Parasitic Jaeger** (casual in May and August to September) is sometimes seen harassing **Bonaparte's Gulls** and **Common Terns** over the bay. Watch for them around the commercial crab boats off shore.

The White Rock waterfront is one of the few places where it's possible to see all three scoter species at the same time.

Winter is the best time to look for birds in the waters of the bay, when large numbers of wintering waterfowl are present. Depending on the tide (mid-level to high tide is best), weather, wind and other variables known only to birds, loons, grebes and ducks may be plentiful. Scrutinize the rock breakwater at the end of the pier for **Black Turnstones**. Watch for a **Bald Eagle** overhead, or parked on "the

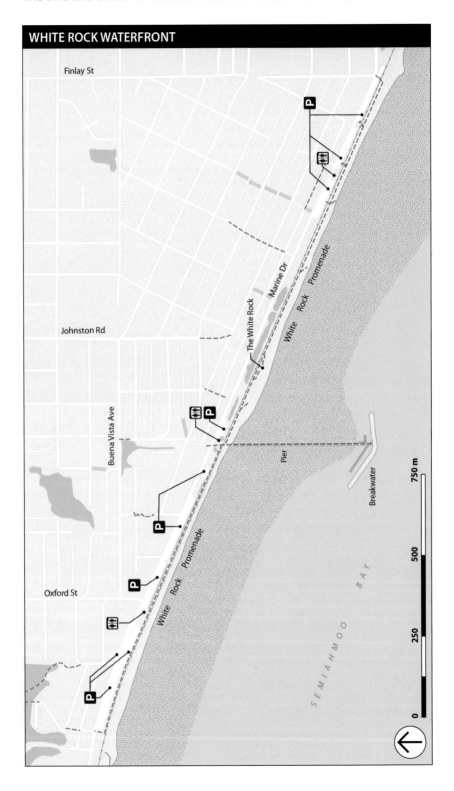

WHITE ROCK WATERFRONT

Finlay St

Marine Dr

The White Rock

White Rock Promenade

Johnston Rd

Buena Vista Ave

Pier

Breakwater

White Rock Promenade

Oxford St

White Rock Promenade

SEMIAHMOO BAY

750 m

500

250

0

Eagle Tree" (on "The Hump" above the big white rock), or on the tower at the west end of the rock breakwater. **Common Loon** is found easily. The **Red-throated Loon** is less common and **Pacific Loon** is uncommon to rare. **Horned Grebe** is abundant, **Western Grebe** is sometimes common, while **Red-necked Grebe** is fairly common. Look carefully for an **Eared Grebe**; some winter in the bay every year, usually far offshore, but occasionally a few will drift in close to the pier. Flocks of resident **Canada Geese** are seen often. Common puddle duck species include the **Mallard**, **Northern Pintail** and **American Wigeon** (rarely **Eurasian Wigeon**). Diving ducks that prefer the deeper water include scoters, **Red-breasted Mergansers**, **Greater Scaups**, **Common Goldeneyes**, **Buffleheads** and **Long-tailed Ducks**, all of which are fairly common. In some years, the **Ruddy Duck** also winters here.

A particular highlight is the large rafts of **Surf** and **White-winged Scoters** that are often feeding alongside the pier, where one can observe them gulp down whole clams and mussels—shells and all. A few **Black Scoters** can usually be detected among them. Large numbers of **Brants** are often present well off-shore for much of the winter season. Check the rocky shoreside area west of West Beach for the **Harlequin Duck** and **Barrow's Gold-eneye**. Alcids, such as the **Common Murre**, **Marbled Murrelet** and **Pigeon Guillemot**, are rare and usually far offshore. An assortment

Surf Scoters are seen regularly at the White Rock Pier and waterfront. Colin Clasen

of wintering gulls, mostly **Glaucous-winged**, **Mew** and **Ring-billed**, loiter about the pier and beaches, especially at the outflow of a freshwater drain at the west end of the promenade. Check carefully here for a **California Gull**; perhaps a **Western**, **Thayer's** or **Herring Gull** may also show up. Shorebirds are few, but **Killdeer** and **Greater Yellowlegs** are fairly regular along the beach in winter, and always watch for **Dunlins**, **Sanderlings** and **Black-bellied Plovers**, which are sometimes seen, often just flying by.

Rarities that have been observed along the pier and promenade over the last decade or so include the **Brown Pelican**, **Clark's Grebe**, **Black Tern**, **Franklin's Gull**, **Heermann's Gull**, **Black-necked Stilt**, **Willet** and **Ruddy Turnstone**. Who knows what might show up next!

*Note: Although local residents reach the shores east and west of the promenade by walking on the Burlington Northern Santa Fe Railway tracks, the practice is dangerous and not recommended. There are several blind corners, and the trains, becoming ever more frequent, are fast and quiet. Furthermore, track walkers risk being charged with trespass by railway police.*

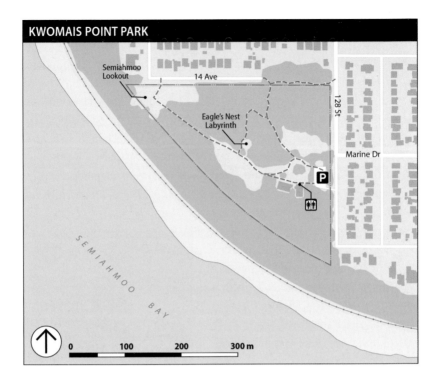

## KWOMAIS POINT PARK

This little gem of a park is fairly new; the area was used as a youth camp until it was purchased by the City of Surrey. Kwomais Point is on the southwest corner of the Semiahmoo Peninsula, near the intersection of 128th Street and Marine Drive, equidistant from Blackie Spit Park and the White Rock Pier. Access the park from Blackie Spit by driving south on 128th Street, or from the White Rock Pier by driving west about 3.5 km on Marine Drive.

The park sits on top of a bluff overlooking the Strait of Georgia and offers two features of interest to birders. There is a fine stand of mature second-growth forest with walking paths and a lookout with a clear overview of the water. In the woods, look for the usual forest birds, this being a good location for **Hutton's Vireos**. The **Bald Eagle** is common and nests in the park. The **Barred Owl** also nests and roosts here. From the lookout, one can scan for water birds, with gulls, cormorants, and ducks expected, and sometimes alcids may be present. It's a long way down to the water, so a scope is virtually essential.

*Blackie Spit and White Rock Waterfront subsections written and revised by Hue and Jo Ann MacKenzie, 2001, and updated by Carlo Giovanella, 2015.*
*Kwomais Point Park subsection written by Carlo Giovanella, 2015.*

# 19. IONA AND SEA ISLANDS

## INTRODUCTION

ONE OF THE WEST COAST'S PREMIER BIRDING LOCATIONS, IONA ISLAND is situated near Vancouver International Airport, less than a 30-minute drive from downtown. The area owes its incredible diversity to the sewage treatment plant, whose ponds allow birders to observe sandpipers and waterfowl up close, and whose discharge pipe, the South Jetty, provides an observation point over the Strait of Georgia.

The McMillan family first settled the island in 1885, and they named it after their Scottish home. The North Jetty, which attracts many species of shorebirds, was built between 1917 and 1935, and it has unique dune vegetation that was introduced from Oregon. Prior to 1958, when the causeway connecting Sea and Iona islands was completed, the only access to Iona Island was by boat. The sewage treatment plant and the South Jetty were completed in 1961, and an upgrade to the sewage plant's discharge pipe, completed in 1988, formed the present 4-km-long

The 4-km-long South Jetty at Iona Beach Regional Park. Ron Long

South Jetty. The Greater Vancouver Regional District (also known as Metro Vancouver) now oversees the public areas of the island, known as Iona Beach Regional Park. In the early 1990s, an area between the sewage ponds and the jetties became the new home for displaced *Yellow-headed Blackbird* in a marsh habitat restoration project. This was a joint effort by the Vancouver Natural History Society (Nature Vancouver), GVRD Parks and Environment Canada. The regional park includes the marsh and the "outer" pond, the beach area with its picnic tables and toilets, a large parking lot and a viewing tower at the base of the South Jetty.

In addition to the park, birders have access to the ponds at the sewage treatment plant. These are known as the "inner ponds," and you can get to them through the "birders' gate" (see below). A second gate in the west side of the fence now makes it possible to enter the marsh directly from the inner ponds and make a circular walk back to the gate via the road.

As with most urban parks, summer weekends bring out the crowds. If the jetties are busy, visit the sewage ponds, which are open to birders only. You can still scan the public ponds from the private side of the fence.

## DIRECTIONS

With the construction of the SkyTrain Canada Line and a new outlet mall under the Arthur Laing Bridge, there have been several recent changes in the traffic patterns at the south end of the bridge. Consult a good current city map before setting out, and in general, after crossing the Arthur Laing Bridge, follow signs first toward Vancouver International Airport, and then watch for the blue and white Metro Vancouver Regional Parks signs directing you to Iona Beach Regional Park.

To get to the Arthur Laing Bridge from downtown Vancouver, take Granville Street south (past 70th Street, where it curves left) onto the bridge. If coming to Iona from the south on Highway 99, or from the east on Highway 91, follow the signs for Vancouver International Airport and watch for the signs for Iona Beach Regional Park. Whichever route you take, after crossing the Fraser River you will be driving on Grant McConachie Way, heading west toward the airport. Continue past the exit to Richmond and follow the sign for Templeton Street North, keeping to the right-hand lane. Turn right onto Templeton Street North, continue past the next traffic lights, and follow the signs for Iona Beach Regional Park. Templeton Street becomes Ferguson Road and leads to Iona Beach. Partway along Ferguson Road, the only right (north) turn is at McDonald Road. This leads a short distance to McDonald Beach, where there are boat launch facilities and washrooms. At the end of Ferguson Road, across the causeway that links Sea Island and Iona Island, you will find Iona Beach Regional Park.

With the completion of the SkyTrain Canada Line, it is now easy to get to Sea

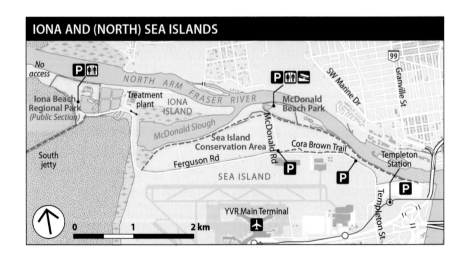

Island and Iona Island by SkyTrain and bicycle. From downtown Vancouver, take your bike on the Canada Line to Vancouver International Airport and get off at Templeton Station. There is no public transit to Iona Beach from Templeton Station. By bicycle from the station, take the short exit road to Templeton Street and turn right onto Ferguson Road, following the signs to Iona Beach Regional Park. It is approximately 5 km from Templeton Station to Iona Beach and there are bike racks located by the washrooms.

## BIRD SPECIES

Iona Island and vicinity has an ever-growing checklist of over 300 confirmed species, including 49 species of shorebirds, thanks to the variety of habitats available and the tolerance of the sewage treatment plant authorities toward eager birders searching for the rare and unusual. Happily, Iona Island is noted for these.

### Sea Island

At the beginning of McDonald Road, near the junction with Ferguson Road, is the Cora Brown Trail, part of the Sea Island Conservation Area (SICA). SICA consists of 140 ha of woodlands, old fields, hedgerows and wet habitats managed by the Canadian Wildlife Service and is designated to provide habitats for birds that do not contribute to aviation hazards at Vancouver International Airport. Limited parking is available at two pullouts at the start of McDonald Road. An information board with a map is present, and a trail goes both east and west from McDonald Road, running parallel to Ferguson Road.

A walk along the Cora Brown Trail or McDonald Road is good for the *Black-capped Chickadee*, *Bushtit*, *Spotted Towhee* and *Bewick's Wren* at any time of year, for the *Song*, *Fox* and other sparrows in winter, and for the *Willow Flycatcher*, *Black-headed Grosbeak* and *Rufous Hummingbird* in spring and summer. *Cinnamon Teal* and, with luck, *Green Heron*, may be encountered in summer along the drainage channels. Shrubby areas near the entrance to McDonald Beach Park and at the small woodlot by the intersection of Ferguson Road and the causeway are often frequented by *Bewick's Wrens*. *Rufous Hummingbirds* can often be seen along McDonald Road and along the portion of the north dyke near the small woodlot.

The fields on either side of Ferguson Road are hunted all year by the *Northern Harrier* and *Red-tailed Hawk*, and in winter by the *Rough-legged Hawk* and sometimes a *Short-eared Owl*. The airport fence and small trees and shrubs along the road are worth checking in winter for *American Kestrels*, *Northern Shrikes* and *Western Meadowlarks*, while *Savannah Sparrows* are common in the fields in summer. Marshy areas throughout Sea Island host numerous *Marsh Wrens* all year and *Common Yellowthroats* in spring and summer. The *Great Blue Heron* can be seen virtually anywhere at any time, but in winter, this species is especially common in fields, where it hunts voles instead of its usual fishy fare!

## Causeway

Ferguson Road eventually curves right (north) onto the causeway linking Sea and Iona islands. This is a good place to stop and look for water birds. The best time

is about 1 hour before high tide. Expect good numbers of waterfowl, *Great Blue Herons*, shorebirds and gulls. Across the road to the east is McDonald Slough. This is an excellent place year-round to see roosting gulls. The log booms and pilings in the slough often host loafing *Double-crested Cormorants*, *Great Blue Herons*, waterfowl and sometimes flocks of *Dunlins*. *Virginia Rails* regularly call from both the salt marsh along the western edge of the causeway and the southwestern corner of the slough, especially

Yellow-headed Blackbird. Michelle Lamberson

around sunrise and sunset. During low tides, large flocks of shorebirds (especially *Dunlins* in winter and *Western Sandpipers* during migration periods) feed on the tidal flats, and the *Caspian Tern* sometimes loafs here.

## Inner Ponds

Continue along the causeway and follow the road to the left into the park. *Do not drive into the sewage treatment plant parking lot.* Just past the yellow-gated entrance to the park, there is a parking area at the side of the road for birders. You will see the "birders' gate" in the fence on your right and a kiosk just inside the gate, which holds the sightings book and an Iona Island checklist.

*Note: In order to obtain the gate code to access the inner ponds, please go to this Nature Vancouver website (naturevancouver.ca/Birding_Birding_Sites) and read section 18.*

Feel free to sign the book with your day's observations or to check what has been seen in the area recently. If you intend to bird late in the day, take careful note of the park closing time posted near the yellow gate on the road. If you think you might be late, park beside the road outside the gate, which is locked at closing time.

The officials at the sewage treatment plant have been very helpful to, and tolerant of, birders for over 35 years. Please respect their property and remember that there are no public facilities here. You are welcome to bird the inner sewage ponds at any time during daylight hours. From the kiosk, you will see a path through the grass to your left, leading to the four ponds. The levels of the inner ponds are controlled according to the demands of the plant. During the height of the shorebird migration, at least one pond is kept at an ideal level. Another pond will likely have one year's growth of vegetation and may host breeding **Soras** and **Virginia Rails**. The sewage ponds are best known for their ability to attract shorebirds. They often number in the thousands and present an excellent possibility of finding rarities. On a rising tide, as the birds are pushed off the diminishing mud flats, they crowd into the ponds. Spring migration begins in early April, with numbers reaching a peak by mid-May. By the end of June a few northbound stragglers meet the vanguard of southbound returning adults.

The common spring shorebirds are **Western** and **Least Sandpiper**, **Long-billed** and **Short-billed Dowitcher**, **Semipalmated Plover**, **Killdeer**, **Dunlin**, **Greater** and **Lesser Yellowlegs** and **Wilson's Snipe**. In the late spring, **Spotted Sandpiper** is present. Less common but seen every spring are **Semipalmated**, **Pectoral** and **Baird's Sandpiper**; **American Golden-Plover**; and **Wilson's Phalarope**.

Spring migration is fast and purposeful, unlike fall with its more leisurely pace. The first southbound **Western Sandpiper** appears in the last days of June. This is the best time to look for adult **Red-necked Stint**, which is rare but has occurred many times. Numbers of returning **Western Sandpipers** build up dramatically through July. Other common species at this time are **Least**, **Baird's**, **Pectoral** and **Semipalmated Sandpiper**. As July gives way to August, the juvenile shorebirds start moving south. This time is always exciting, as numbers and species start to diversify dramatically. By mid-September the ponds will be packed with a great variety of

Common Goldeneyes have a dramatic courtship display that involves throwing their **heads far back.** Peter Candido

species. *Pectoral* and *Baird's Sandpiper*, *Greater* and *Lesser Yellowlegs* and *Wilson's* and *Red-necked Phalarope* are now more common. Less common species are *Ruff* (rare), *Solitary Sandpiper*, *Stilt Sandpiper* and *Buff-breasted Sandpiper* (rare). The vast numbers of shorebirds also attract other visitors to the ponds. Fall is an excellent time to see *Peregrine Falcons*, *Merlins*, *Cooper's Hawks* and *American Kestrels*. There is nothing more dramatic than watching a *Peregrine Falcon* chasing a huge flock of shorebirds; the sight is truly breathtaking.

By the beginning of October, the numbers of small shorebirds have diminished, but this is the time in which a rare visitor from Siberia might appear at Iona. In the fall, Iona is one of the best places outside Alaska to see juvenile *Sharp-tailed Sandpipers*. They increase in number along with the increase in *Pectoral Sandpipers*. The number varies each year, but at least one turns up annually.

As October ends, wintering flocks of *Dunlins* return in the thousands, with small numbers of wintering *Western Sandpipers* mixed among them. Other shorebirds that will stay for the winter in smaller numbers include *Greater Yellowlegs*, *Long-billed Dowitchers*, *Wilson's Snipes*, *Sanderlings*, *Black-bellied Plovers* and *Killdeers*.

Red–winged Blackbird—a very vocal and recogniz–able marsh bird. Colin Clasen

Iona's most famous visitor, a *Spoon-billed Sandpiper*, was seen by hundreds of lucky people in late July 1978. Other rarities that have contributed to Iona's top status as a location to find rare shorebirds include the *Black-necked Stilt*, *Snowy Plover*, *Upland Sandpiper*, *White-rumped Sandpiper*, *Red-necked Stint*, *Little Stint*, *Great Knot*, *Curlew Sandpiper* and *Red Phalarope*. With 49 confirmed species of shorebirds, Iona Island is hard to beat anywhere on the west coast of North America.

Large numbers of waterfowl also frequent the sewage lagoon ponds, especially the *Gadwall*, *Mallard*, *Northern Pintail*, *Northern Shoveler* and *Green-winged Teal* in winter, spring and fall, and the *Blue-winged* and *Cinnamon Teal* in spring. The northeastern pond is one of the most reliable places in the Vancouver area for visitors to find the *Mew* and *Thayer's Gull* in winter.

Although the sewage ponds have an enviable reputation among birding hot spots, that reputation goes beyond shorebirds. All six species of swallows can be found here, and in November 2012, BC's first *Cave Swallow* was found over the adjacent outer ponds (see below). Large flocks of *American Pipits* pass through, and *Vaux's* and *Black Swifts* are seen in approaching storm clouds. The trees and shrubs between the inner ponds and the outer pond and marsh sometimes harbour numerous passerines, notably the *Spotted Towhee* and *Song, Fox, Lincoln's, White-crowned* and *Golden-crowned Sparrow*, especially during migration and in winter. A few warblers may also be found here during migration. Some of the exciting non-shorebird finds over the years include the *Garganey; Forster's Tern; Say's Phoebe; Northern Mockingbird; Sage Thrasher;* and *Sagebrush, Clay-coloured, Brewer's* and *Harris's Sparrow.*

North outer marsh at Iona: the most reliable location for Yellow–headed Blackbirds. Bill Kinkaid

## Outer Pond and Marsh

After birding the inner ponds, you may wish to walk through the gate in the western fence into the marsh and from there to the large outer pond (or you can return to your car and drive around to the main parking lot). The new marsh was designed to attract the *Yellow-headed Blackbird,* an uncommon species in the Vancouver area, which was displaced from another marsh during the course of airport expansion. The blackbird population has relocated successfully to the present marsh and may

Tree Swallow, a cavity nesting bird, poses elegantly. Virginia Hayes

be seen there from April until mid-August. Also present in the marsh are the *Pied-billed Grebe*, *Virginia Rail*, *Marsh Wren* and *Red-winged Blackbird*.

The pond, with its several islands, is an excellent place to study ducks. Sometimes in the winter a *Tufted Duck* (rare) may be found in the flocks of *Greater* and *Lesser Scaups*. Look also for the occasional *Redhead* and the more common *Ring-necked Duck*. The *Ruddy Duck* is sometimes present in winter, as well as the *American Coot*, *Bufflehead* and one or two *Pied-billed Grebes*. In spring, *Cinnamon* and *Blue-winged Teal* might be found here. The best time to see the outer pond full of waterfowl is from November to April during a high tide. During winter, the *Mew Gull* often bathes communally in this pond.

## South Jetty

Vancouver's sewage, after treatment, is deposited more than 4 km offshore into the Strait of Georgia. Happily for birders, the means of transport is a sea-level jetty with an observation platform at the far end. A gravel road makes bicycling an attractive alternative to the 8 km round trip on foot. Motorized vehicles are prohibited on the jetty. There is a portable washroom at the end and there are

The migratory Willow Flycatcher has a unique "fitz–bew" call. Tak Shibata

two wind shelters partway along the jetty. The weather can change very quickly and visitors are advised to carry warm clothing, water and a snack.

Probably the most important consideration when visiting the South Jetty is the tide level, followed by the season. At low tide in the summer, there may be little to interest birders. However, a rising tide in the fall can be very productive. From July to the end of October, large numbers of *Western*, *Least* and *Semipalmated Sandpipers*, with smaller numbers of *Baird's* and *Pectoral Sandpipers*, *Black Turnstones* and *Surfbirds*, may be seen. The *Wandering Tattler* sometimes also turns up, usually from late August to early September. Fall also brings returning waterfowl and seabirds. Migrating *Bonaparte's Gulls* and *Common Terns* will draw the *Parasitic Jaeger*. The latter are most easily seen from the end of the jetty from late August through mid-October as they harass the terns and gulls. Other specialty species that the South Jetty may produce are the *Lapland Longspur* and *Snow Bunting*. These usually appear in October.

Winter is the most productive time at the South Jetty. The multitude of species commonly observed includes the *Common, Pacific* and *Red-throated Loon; Western, Red-necked* and *Horned Grebe; Double-crested* and *Pelagic Cormorant; Great Blue Heron; Canada* and *Snow Geese; Green-winged Teal; Greater* and *Lesser Scaup; Canvasback; Surf, White-winged* and *Black Scoter; Long-tailed Duck; Barrow's* and *Common Goldeneye; Red-breasted Merganser; Thayer's Gull; Mew Gull;* and *Dunlin.* Rarer but regularly seen species are the *Eared Grebe, Greater White-fronted Geese, Brant, Eurasian Wigeon, Redhead, Ring-necked Duck, Black Oystercatcher, Rock Sandpiper, Western Gull, Pigeon Guillemot, Common Murre, Marbled* and *Ancient Murrelet* and *Rhinoceros Auklet.*

Although birding from the jetty is good all winter, the chance of seeing local rarities increases dramatically during or just after a southerly or southeasterly storm system from May to early June, or from July to November. Records exist for the *Sooty Shearwater; Common* and *King Eider; Little, Black-headed* and *Sabine's Gull* and *Black-legged Kittiwake.*

Fox Sparrow. Jim Martin

## North Jetty

This sand-dune jetty, several kilometres long, is a worthwhile walk at any time but is more rewarding from July to November. In season, the dune grasses provide habitat for nesting *Savannah Sparrows, Killdeers* and *Spotted Sandpipers.* From September to November, flocks of *Lapland Longspurs,* sometimes accompanied by *Horned Larks* or *Snow Buntings,* occur here. The best birding is on a rising tide when the birds are pushed toward the shoreline of the jetty. Larger shorebirds, such as the *Black-bellied Plover,* are more likely to be observed here than on the inner ponds. Rarer species, such as the *Marbled Godwit, Whimbrel, Red Knot* and *American* and *Pacific Golden-Plover,* have all been seen in this area. At the very end of the sand dunes, another rock jetty extends for several more kilometres. A careful observer might be rewarded by views of shorebirds that prefer rocky areas.

*Caution: Walk this area only on a low tide, and pay close attention to the turning tide to avoid being cut off.*

The mud flats between the two jetties are a good place to find loafing *Bonaparte's, Glaucous-winged* and *California Gulls* and *Common* and *Caspian Terns.* Sometimes a *Franklin's Gull* can be found in the fall among the mixed flocks.

From offshore alcids to the finer points of shorebird plumages, from winter "dickey birding" to unravelling the mysteries of gulls—no matter what your birding interests, Iona Island holds the promise of good, and the possibility of exceptional, birding.

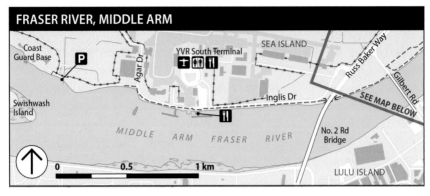

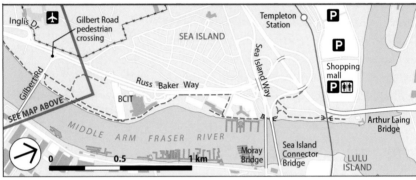

## Fraser River, Middle Arm

If time permits, birders visiting in winter may wish to check the Middle Arm of the Fraser River before leaving Sea Island. The best spot is the vicinity of a breakwater west of the seaplane base at the intersection of Agar and Inglis drives. To get there, take Russ Baker Way south toward the No. 2 Road Bridge. Turn right from Russ Baker Way onto Inglis Drive, follow it to its intersection with Agar Drive and then turn left immediately on a road leading to the Coast Guard Station.

*Western Grebes* often gather to the west of the breakwater, and *Common* and *Red-throated Loons*, *Horned* and *Pied-billed Grebes* and various diving ducks frequent the area. In some winters, a *Clark's Grebe* may also be present, occasionally with the *Western*, but usually somewhat aloof from them. *Double-crested Cormorants*, *Dunlins* and various gull species often loaf on the breakwater. The *American* and *Eurasian Wigeon* and *American Coot* frequently graze on the grass between the road and the river during high tide, while low-tide river flats attract the *Green-winged Teal*, *Killdeer* and various gull species.

*Written by John and Shirley Dorsey. Revised by Rick Toochin and Martin K. McNicholl, 2001. Updated by Peter Candido and reviewed by Mark Wynja, 2015.*

# 20. LULU ISLAND: TERRA NOVA NATURAL AREA / RICHMOND TRAILS

THE CITY OF RICHMOND ENCOMPASSES ALMOST 20 ISLANDS, THE LARGEST by far being Lulu Island. Much of Richmond's industry and almost all of its residential area is concentrated here between the North, Middle and South arms of the Fraser River. During the last ice age, this area was covered by glaciers; when they receded, they left a huge plain that has evolved into the delta of today. Three-quarters of Richmond's 110 square km lies only slightly above sea level. Sloughs crisscross the agricultural land, creating a haven for many species of waterfowl. The remaining cottonwood, birch, bog forest and crab apple stands, which once grew all across Lulu Island, provide a refuge for many species of land birds.

Of particular significance are the Terra Nova lands in the northwest corner, where in 1996 the voters of Richmond directed city council to preserve 26.7 ha of land as a park. Richmond council also set aside 13.7 ha of old-field habitat, which has subsequently been enhanced with the construction of ponds, plantings and a drainage system. Known as the Terra Nova Natural Area, funding for

View west from the West Dyke Trail, over the salt marsh toward the Strait of Georgia. Ron Long

its development came in the form of compensation for habitat lost due to the expansion of Vancouver International Airport.

Richmond's remaining farmland south of Steveston Highway, between No. 5 Road and Gilbert Road, offers good winter birding and complements a visit to Sea and Iona Island.

The West Dyke overlooking Sturgeon Banks and the Middle and South arms of the Fraser River all have extensive dyke sections worth exploring and have provided an extensive network of trails, a boon for the birder who enjoys walking or cycling. While walking along the dykes, watch for harbour seals disguising themselves as chunks of floating debris; in April and May sea lions may also be present.

Inland, the Shell Road Trail runs through fields of blueberries that thrive on the peat bog; small stands of birch, cedar, cottonwood and willow abound. Richmond Nature Park protects remnant peat bog and forest—an excellent example of how much of Lulu Island looked 100 years ago.

# TERRA NOVA NATURAL AREA —
## INTRODUCTION

Terra Nova Natural Area is bordered by the Middle Arm of the Fraser River to the north, the Quilchena Golf Course to the south, Sturgeon Banks to the west and residential housing to the east. On nice days the scenic vistas of the Fraser River, airport, marshes and distant Vancouver Island make this a very popular recreational area, so an early start is essential. Allow approximately 2 to 3 hours to cover the area thoroughly.

Habitat consists of a mosaic of hedgerows, successional field habitats, two ponds and small woodlots. The terminus of the old Westminster Highway intersects Terra Nova Natural Area. Both sides of Terra Nova are good birding areas offering slightly different vegetation mix and habitat type.

South of the old Westminster Highway, a wheelchair-accessible, gravel trail encircles the perimeter of Terra Nova, with a permanent water-filled ditch lined by a variety of shrubs, willows and a few conifers paralleling the path. Tall poplars and conifers border the southern boundary, the Quilchena Golf Course, and a viewing platform overlooks a pond and small birch-dominated woodlot located in the southwest corner. The southern block is dedicated to wildlife. It has a **Barn Owl** nesting box and the interior fields are mowed to produce winter pasture for grazing waterfowl.

North of Westminster Highway, the habitat includes community gardens (which have washrooms) and a small mixed-forest woodlot bordering the east side. In addition to the perimeter paths, several others intersect and border the interior fields and hedgerows. The northwest corner of the "northern block" has several large veteran deciduous trees located by the playground and a cattail-lined slough.

Immediately north of Terra Nova is the Middle Arm of the Fraser River, giving access to deeper-water waterfowl and a few marine species.

## DIRECTIONS

There are two main parking areas; one is located on the south side of Westminster Highway, which bisects the natural area and terminates at the west dyke, and one is at the northwest corner along the west end of River Road, which parallels the south side of the Fraser River Middle Arm.

To reach the Westminster parking area from Vancouver, take Highway 99 (Oak Street) south and take the No. 4 Road exit (#39B), continue south for 2 km, turn right onto Westminster Highway and drive west to the junction with No. 1 Road,

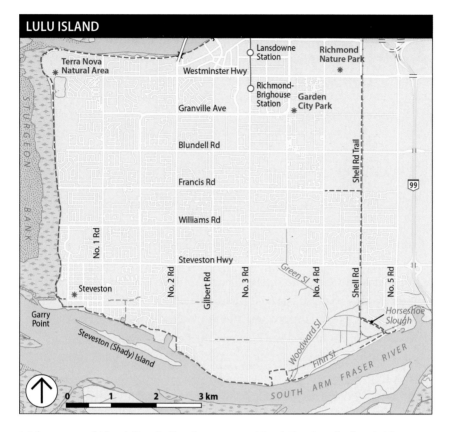

**LULU ISLAND**

4.8 km west of No. 4 Road. Continue across No. 1 Road and after 0.4 km, turn right at the stop sign onto Barnard Drive. Continue for 0.8 km and turn left onto Westminster Highway again (it is now a small residential street). In 0.2 km you will come to the Terra Nova parking area on the left.

For the River Road parking area: turn right at the junction of Westminster Highway and No. 1 Road, follow No. 1 Road north to River Road, then turn left (west) and drive to the end. There are several small parking areas here that provide excellent views across the Fraser River and Sturgeon Bank. Washrooms are also located here.

## BIRD SPECIES

This area is rapidly becoming a Vancouver hot spot due to its waterfront location and island effect due to rapid urbanization. Beginning in December 1998, monthly bird surveys by Nature Vancouver have produced over 100 species, and several rarities, including the *Snowy Egret*, *Black Phoebe* and *Western Scrub-Jay*, have shown up in the last decade. Migration and winter are the best seasons to visit (August to June).

The Terra Nova Natural Area is now most notable as a site from November to February, when one can walk within a few metres of hundreds of grazing *Snow Geese* that are now accustomed to people. Several thousand of these noisy birds winter on Lulu and Sea islands, feeding in the tidal marshes of Sturgeon Bank and during high tide (when feeding areas are covered) on short-grass school fields in west Richmond and at Terra Nova. It is always worth scanning through them, as others geese species have shown up. Fields within Terra Nova are actively managed by following a mowing regime that produces pasture for grazing waterfowl.

Flooded fields in winter attract mainly *Mallards* and *American Wigeons*, with the occasional *Eurasian Wigeon*, and small numbers of *Northern Pintails* and *Green-winged Teal*. Ponds on fields during April and May occasionally attract small numbers of shorebirds, mainly yellowlegs, dowitchers and *Least Sandpipers*, with drying mud edges having *Killdeer*, *Spotted Sandpiper* and *American Pipit*.

Field habitat supports Townsend's vole populations, which in turn are fed on by *Great Blue Herons*, *Red-tailed Hawks*, *Northern Harriers* and occasionally *Northern Shrikes* in winter. The *Bald Eagle* is found year-round, as well as *Cooper's Hawk*, which nests in the area. Scarce but regular raptor species in migration and winter are the *Sharp-shinned Hawk*, *Merlin* and *Peregrine Falcon*.

The pond located in the southwest corner of Terra Nova (south of Westminster Highway) has deeper water, which attracts a variety of wintering waterfowl like the *Gadwall*, *Northern Shoveler*, *Bufflehead*, *Lesser Scaup*, *Ring-necked Duck* and *Hooded Merganser*. *Green-winged Teal* frequent the perimeter ditches with a few *Cinnamon* and *Blue-winged Teal* in late April to June. The slough located at the northwest corner of Terra Nova almost always has *Pied-billed Grebes*, *Ring-necked Ducks* and *Hooded Mergansers* from October to April, and *American Bitterns* have been seen here in winter on a couple of occasions.

Emergent vegetation at both wetlands has *Marsh Wrens* all year, as well as the *Common Yellowthroat* and sometimes the *Virginia Rail* and *Sora* from April to September.

A couple of *Barn Owl* boxes have been erected and this species is a regular resident; however, a nighttime visit is required. The *Great Horned* and *Barred Owl* have been seen in the woodlot immediately south of the community gardens and *Northern Saw-whet Owl* in hedgerows nearby. The *Long-eared Owl* has roosted in the thick vegetation bordering the west dyke during winter and probably occurs with more frequency than the few records indicate. This species is extremely difficult to locate; however, significant whitewash is a good clue of roosting owls. Squeaking during night visits in winter may produce more records, as the old-field habitat is very good.

Fields and ponds attract aerial insectivores. *Violet-green* and *Tree Swallows* arrive in early March, followed by *Northern Rough-winged*, *Barn* and *Cliff Swal-*

lows in April. During spring and fall, migrating *Vaux's Swifts* sometimes join them.

Common breeding birds include the *Rufous Hummingbird*, *Bewick's Wren*, *Bushtit*, *Spotted Towhee* and *Black-headed Grosbeak*.

Cherries, hawthorn and other fruit-bearing shrubs along the hedgerows attract many *American Robins*, a few *Varied Thrushes* in migration, *Cedar Waxwings* and *Purple* and *House Finches* during fall and winter. The abundant fruit can also bring in the *Hermit Thrush*, *Western Tanager* (fall) and, rarely, *Townsend's Solitaire* and *Bohemian Waxwing* in season. Migrants, including flycatchers, vireos, warblers and sparrows, use this shrub habitat, with small numbers in spring and larger numbers during fall migration.

Check the shrubs and trees across the road from the Westminster Road parking lot toward the north, as you may find an *Evening Grosbeak* in spring. The large birch trees bordering the west dyke, and to a lesser degree alder trees, regularly attract the *Common Redpoll* in winter, especially every other year. Therefore, carefully examine any *Siskin* or *Goldfinch* flock for a *Common Redpoll*; when they are quietly feeding, these birds can be surprisingly easy to pass by.

## STURGEON BANKS AND THE MIDDLE ARM OF THE FRASER RIVER — DIRECTIONS

Parking at the west end of River Road gives access to the deeper waters of the Fraser River and a different set of birds. One can check the river from the top of the dyke, and there are several viewing platforms, including one at 1.7 km near the corner of Lynas Lane, which has a short pier. Good views of the river are possible here, but you can walk onto the dyke at almost any point and scan the river. A scope is handy for checking the river and Sturgeon Banks.

The parking areas at the west end of River Road mark the beginning of the Sturgeon Bank marshes. The west dyke forms the western boundary of Terra Nova and overlooks Sturgeon Banks, with Terra Nova trails connecting to the dyke near the southwest and northwest

The Middle Arm of the Fraser River, at the north end of Lulu Island. Ron Long

corners and the end of Westminster Road. The West Dyke Trail can be followed all the way south to Steveston's Garry Point Park if you feel like a good walk of 5.5 km one way, or have your bicycle. Cycling is a very attractive option in this flat city surrounded by dykes.

The Merlin is a small falcon that feeds mainly on small birds. Mike Tabak

## BIRD SPECIES

Species farther out at the river mouth and venturing upriver are the *Double-crested Cormorant*, *Common* and *Red-breasted Merganser*, *Surf Scoter*, *Bufflehead*, *Common Goldeneye*, *Red-throated* and *Common Loon*, *Pied-billed* and *Horned Grebe* and less regularly, *Western* and *Red-necked Grebe*.

In fall and spring, the calls of *Snow Geese* fill the air as they gather for migration, while *Trumpeter Swans* spend the winter here. The *American Bittern*, *Sora* and *Virginia Rail* are secretive inhabitants in this area. Uncommon visitors to the area, such as the *Great Egret* and *Long-eared Owl*, have been seen in the marsh and ditches from this trail. *Great Blue Heron* are common along the length of the dyke along the Fraser River, and *Canada Geese* can be seen at most times. Scan flocks in autumn and winter for *Greater White-fronted Geese*.

## STEVESTON

The historic community of Steveston, in the southwest corner of Richmond, provides the visitor with many attractions in addition to its wildlife. Several eco-tour companies offering boat trips have their base here, and there are historic buildings to visit as well as a variety of shops and restaurants. This fishing and tourist village is an excellent place for lunch after a morning's birding on Lulu Island. The West Dyke Trail ends here at Garry Point Park, but the dyke walk continues eastwards as the South Dyke Trail and Dyke Road. To reach Steveston by car, drive south from Westminster Highway on No. 1 Road for 4.8 km, crossing Steveston Highway and turning right (west) onto Chatham Street. Continue for a few blocks to reach Garry Point Park and the south end of the West Dyke Trail.

## GILBERT BEACH —
## DIRECTIONS

Gilbert Beach can be reached by driving south on Gilbert Road until you come to Dyke Road, which follows the north edge of the South Fraser, from No. 5 Road to No. 2 Road. Turn right and drive west; there are several areas to park along the river and at Gilbert Beach. Gilbert Road runs in a north–south direction between No. 2 and No. 3 Roads.

At the southwest corner of Lulu Island is Garry Point Park, where you get this view across the South Arm of the Fraser River toward the Gulf Islands. Colin Clasen

## BIRD SPECIES

Gilbert Beach, at the south end of Gilbert Road, is a good area to check for ducks and small numbers of migrating shorebirds, especially during low tide. Flocks of **Canada Geese** in migration sometimes have **Greater White-fronted Geese**. Several dabblers in small numbers are found on the brackish marsh from October to April, including the **Mallard**, **Northern Pintail**,

Western Sandpiper. John Lowman

**Green-winged Teal**, **American** and the occasional **Eurasian Wigeon**. **Double-crested Cormorant**, **Red-throated** and **Common Loon**, **Western** and **Horned Grebe**, **Bufflehead** and **Common Goldeneye** frequent the river here during winter. All three merganser species can be seen at Gilbert Beach and the Steveston Harbour Channel. **Bald Eagles** nest annually in veteran cottonwoods on Shady Island. Look for **Thayer's**, **California**, **Glaucous-winged**, **Mew**, **Ring-billed** and **Bonaparte's Gulls** in the appropriate season on the log booms and foreshore of Gilbert Beach. This is a good site for seeing a **Belted Kingfisher** in winter.

During spring and fall, migrating yellowlegs and dowitchers, and occasionally other species, shelter in the pond areas of Britannia Heritage shipyards and the adjoining Imperial Landing Park during high tides. **Belted Kingfisher** also uses these areas in migration.

# NO. 3 ROAD TO NO. 5 ROAD SOUTH OF STEVESTON HIGHWAY — DIRECTIONS

You can park at several areas south of Steveston Highway between No. 3 and No. 5 Roads: at the dog-walking area at the foot of No. 3 Road; at the foot of Garden City Road just outside the Crown Packaging plant (limited parking); along the dyke on River Road between No. 4 and No. 5 Roads; or at the Woodward Landing Girl Guide Camp (Horseshoe Slough) parking lot. From the parking areas you can walk east or west along River Road and loop back to your vehicle via the railway tracks paralleling the dyke. An early start is ideal, as many joggers, cyclists and dog walkers use this area, especially during weekends.

## BIRD SPECIES

### Riparian Habitat

The woodlot immediately east of the foot of Garden City Road is a great place to start birding. By going east along the railway tracks, one can access the woodlot. *Barn Owl* boxes erected in the woodlot occasionally hold a pair; almost every year, the *Bald Eagle*, *Red-tailed* and *Cooper's Hawk* nest in the woodlot, and recently a *Common Raven* pair has raised a family at the Crown Packaging plant. Other breeding species to watch for in the area include the *Rufous Hummingbird*, *Downy Woodpecker*, *Willow Flycatcher*, *Bewick's Wren*, *Bushtit*, *Swainson's Thrush*, *Cedar Waxwing*, *Yellow Warbler*, *Black-headed Grosbeak* and *Bullock's Oriole* (scarce). In winter, this woodlot hosts the occasional *Orange-crowned Warbler* and during fall migration, the *White-throated Sparrow*. A slough bordering the woodlot always has *Green-winged Teal*, *Mallards* and often *American Wigeons* during winter, and occasionally others like the *Wood Duck* (rare) or *Hooded Merganser*.

Along the tracks east of the woodlot are fields and hedgerows that support open country birds. Check for *Lincoln's*, and (rarely) *White-throated* and *American Tree Sparrows* among the large numbers of migrating and wintering *Golden-crowned*, *White-crowned*, *Song*, *Savannah* and *Fox Sparrows*. Numbers of *Lincoln's Sparrows* can be found along ditches, weedy fields, and hedgerows from August to May. A *Northern Shrike* is occasionally seen along this stretch between October and March. A kilometre east of Garden City Road, the tracks cross the foot of No. 4 Road. You can continue east to Horseshoe Slough or retrace your steps by heading west along Dyke Road and Finn Slough. *Barn*, *Tree* and *Violet-green Swallows* are a common sight, foraging throughout the summer over the fields.

The river along this stretch is usually pretty quiet, with a few wintering *Double-crested Cormorants* and sometimes *Common Goldeneyes*, *Buffleheads*, *Lesser Scaups*

The Northern Shoveler has the largest beak of any duck in North America. Colin Clasen

and *Common Mergansers*. Kirkland Island on the south side of the Fraser River has a few pairs of nesting *Bald Eagles*.

The riparian habitat along Finn Slough, located along the dyke at the foot of No. 4 Road, holds another nesting pair of *Bald Eagles*, as well as *Anna's Hummingbirds* (attracted by feeders), *Willow Flycatchers*, *Yellow Warblers*, *Common Yellowthroats*, *Swainson's Thrushes*, *Cedar Waxwings*, *Bullock's Orioles* (uncommon) and *Black-headed Grosbeaks*. During winter, a *Peregrine Falcon* frequently uses the dead cottonwood snags as a perch. A *Swamp Sparrow* has been recorded a few times in the cattail marsh bordering the slough in winter.

Horseshoe Slough is located at the Woodward Landing Girl Guide Camp, roughly 100 m west of No. 5 Road along Dyke Road. From the parking lot one can complete a 3.5 km level loop trail bordering the Horseshoe Slough. In winter (November through March) a few *Varied Thrushes* are present (local in Richmond), and *Cooper's Hawks*, *Downy Woodpeckers*, *Northern Flickers*, *Bewick's Wrens*, *Brown Creepers* and *Bushtits* are seen all year. In most years a *Cooper's Hawk* nests here, along with the *Warbling Vireo*, *Swainson's Thrush*, *Black-headed Grosbeak* and sometimes *Bullock's Oriole*.

## Agricultural Fields and Hedgerows

Good winter birding can be had in the agricultural, old-field, hedgerow and woodlot habitats between Gilbert Road and No. 5 Road. During late fall and winter, some excellent birds such as the *Blue Jay*, *Northern Mockingbird* and *Yellow Warbler* have shown up, as well as many lesser rarities. Flooded fields in winter can have hundreds of *Mallards*, *Wigeons* and *Northern Pintails*, and in late November to January, a few *Trumpeters* and (rarely) *Tundra Swans*. A few *Ring-necked Pheasants* persist, mainly as dispersals from hunt/game club releases on Kirkland and Westham Islands. *Cooper's* and *Red-tailed Hawks* and *Northern Harriers* (October through April) are relatively common, with the odd *Merlin*, *Peregrine Falcon* or *Northern Shrike* seen.

During this same winter period, gull flocks sometimes congregate in the fields, especially if the fields are flooded. Working through the *Glaucous-winged* and *Mew Gulls*, one can find a few *Thayer's*, *Ring-billed*, *Herring* (uncommon) and *California Gulls* (rare).

On a dry, calm night, a slow drive will usually yield a *Barn Owl* or two, as a few pairs breed in farm buildings in the area. Stopping to squeak will increase your chance of seeing one. Very rarely, *Great Horned* and *Long-eared Owls* (especially along the dykes) are seen during winter.

Short grass fields hold the *Savannah Sparrow* and *Western Meadowlark* but are difficult to find unless you walk the fields. Fields between No. 5 Road and Gilbert Road host large blackbird flocks during winter (late October through January). However, the *Red-winged* and *Brewer's Blackbirds* and *European Starlings* wander widely depending on foraging opportunities. If they settle close to the road, they should be thoroughly scanned for *Brown-headed Cowbirds*, *Rusty* and *Yellow-headed Blackbirds*. Safe parking is limited, so a scope is extremely useful.

The area along No. 4 Road (south of Steveston Highway) between the Richmond Golf Course and Finn Road can also be productive. Many songbirds use the riparian vegetation and gardens along this stretch. The *Eurasian Collared-Dove* now resides all year, with up to 40 wintering. The red alder and birch trees lining the slough are good in winter for the *Pine Siskin*, *American Goldfinch*, sometimes *Yellow-rumped Warbler* and the occasional *Common Redpoll*.

## SHELL ROAD TRAIL — DIRECTIONS

One can park at the east end of Francis Street (on the east side of No. 4 Road) and walk east to the Shell Trail, or from Steveston Highway drive south on Shell Road and park at the end.

Shell Road Trail runs north–south alongside a railway line for 6.5 km between Westminster Highway and Francis Street and provides good songbird birding. While the whole trail is worth exploring, the southern end and the section between Westminster Highway and Francis Road provide the best birding. Intermediate points on the trail can be reached where it intersects Westminster Highway, Granville Avenue, Blundell Road, Williams Road or Steveston Highway; each crosses the trail 5.6 km east of No. 1 Road.

# BIRD SPECIES

The hedgerows along the trail provide a year-round home for the *Spotted Towhee*, *Bewick's* and *Pacific Wren*, *American Robin*, *Bushtit*, *Black-capped Chickadee*, *House* and sometimes the *Purple Finch*, *Pine Siskin* and *American Goldfinch*. The fall migration brings the *Yellow-rumped Warbler*, *Western Tanager*, *Red Crossbill* and birds that winter here, such as the *Downy Woodpecker*, *Northern Flicker*, *Varied Thrush*, *Dark-eyed Junco*, *Golden-crowned* and *Ruby-crowned Kinglet*, and *White-crowned* and *Golden-crowned Sparrow*. Spring brings the migrant breeding birds, such as the *Rufous Hummingbird*; *Wilson's*, *Townsend's*, *Orange-crowned* and *MacGillivray's Warbler*; *Black-headed Grosbeak*; and *Swainson's Thrush*. The *Hermit Thrush* is a common migrant. Between Francis and Blundell roads, listen for the song of a *Willow Flycatcher*; each spring these birds return to breed and can be heard on almost any summer day.

The Bushtit constructs a very unique, long sock–like nest. Jim Martin

## GARDEN CITY PARK

The parking for this small urban park is located on the north side of Granville Street, between No. 4 Road and Garden City. Habitat consists of two small ponds and mixed deciduous tree patches. This park is worth a visit during migration in April to May and August to September, as it acts as a "trap" or "oasis," a patch of habitat surrounded by residential housing and busy roads. Small numbers of migrant flycatchers, vireos, kinglets, warblers, *Western Tanagers* and sparrows are found, especially in days of inclement weather or low-pressure systems. During winter, the ponds attract several waterfowl species (in small numbers). Be sure to come early in the day, as this park is heavily used.

## RICHMOND NATURE PARK

This municipal park protects remnant bog forest, which once covered much of Richmond. Access is on the north side of Westminster Highway, about 400 m west

The male Purple Finch has a pale red wash down its back. Jim Martin

of Highway 99. This park is the only regular location in Richmond for *Hutton's Vireo*. A few can be heard singing in the more mature hemlock stands from late March to June. A small pond and wetland areas add to the diversity, and feeders attract birds, allowing great looks at many common species. These feeders are the only reliable location for a *Hairy Woodpecker* (winter) in Richmond.

## NORTH RICHMOND/RIVER ROAD

There is a fairly recently built small grain storage terminal called Ray-Mont Logistics, where River Road meets the north end of No. 7 Road. Huge flocks of feral *Pigeons* and large flocks of *Eurasian Collared-Doves* gather here. The *Cooper's Hawk*, *Red-tailed Hawk*, *Merlin* and *Peregrine Falcon* have been sighted hunting the doves and pigeons.

*Written and revised by Eric Greenwood, 2001. Revised by Steffany Walker, with advice from Eric Greenwood and Margaret Butschler. Reviewed by John Chandler. Updated by Tom Plath, 2015.*

# 21. BURNS BOG AREA

## INTRODUCTION

IN SATELLITE PHOTOGRAPHS OF THE LOWER MAINLAND, BURNS BOG stands out as the largest green space in MetroVancouver. It is both the largest urban green space and the largest raised peat bog in western North America.

Over 2,000 ha are protected as the Burns Bog Ecological Conservancy Area and not accessible to the public. However, those wishing to explore bog habitat can visit the Delta Nature Reserve (details below), a 24 ha park on the eastern perimeter of the bog. This forested park lies just west of the North Delta escarpment. Typical bog and heathland plants occur in wetter areas of the reserve, and the birdlife reflects the mix of deciduous and coniferous forests, shrubs and open habitats. Level, gravel trails and boardwalks traverse the reserve and a greenway trail links it with Watershed Park to the south. The park is popular with dog walkers and cyclists and can be busy on weekends.

Meandering forested boardwalk through the Delta Nature Reserve. Colin Clasen

For many generations, Coast Salish used the natural resources of the bog, including sphagnum mosses, wild berries, waterfowl, black bear and deer. The Katzie believed *Sandhill Cranes* were the guardians of the bog. Much of the bog was purchased by the Marquis of Lorne for a dollar an acre when the land was surveyed in 1882. The land transferred to Dominic Burns in 1905 and he later sold it for peat farming, which continued through to the 1980s. Following strong requests from the public, spearheaded by the Burns Bog Conservation Society, over 2,000 ha of Burns Bog were acquired by the federal, provincial, regional and Delta municipal governments in 2004 and protected as the Burns Bog Ecological Conservancy Area. The remaining peat lands outside this protected zone are in private ownership and mostly zoned agricultural or industrial. The drier perimeter of the bog is known as the "lagg" and is an important habitat in its own right.

*Note: In this area, streets run north–south and avenues run east–west; both are numbered. Consult your map for clarity. Some directions need to be double-checked, as highways are under construction and changing frequently in Delta.*

# DIRECTIONS: DELTA NATURE RESERVE

To reach the Delta Nature Reserve from north of the Fraser River, follow Highway 91 south and take the Nordel Way exit shortly after crossing the Alex Fraser Bridge. Stay in the lane with signs toward Highway 17 and Highway 1. Follow the lane as it curves around the overpass until you reach the first set of lights (be careful not to turn onto the truck scale lane). Turn right at the lights on Nordel Way. At the second set of lights (Nordel Court), turn right and follow this road into the parking lot of Planet Ice Delta (formerly known as Grand Pacific Forum) at 10388 Nordel Court. Park in the far left of the parking lot. Follow the bricked pathway to the left around the side of Planet Ice to the Delta Nature Reserve, following signs that welcome you. Once you pass the entrance sign, follow the level trail running parallel to the creek (Davies Creek) until you reach the entrance to the first boardwalk loop. You have the option of entering here or passing on to a smaller loop at the second boardwalk entrance. A trail connecting the inner and outer boardwalk loops is under construction. Note that after heavy rainfall, the creek running parallel to the reserve can sometimes flood the walking path. Rubber boots will be necessary at almost any time of year.

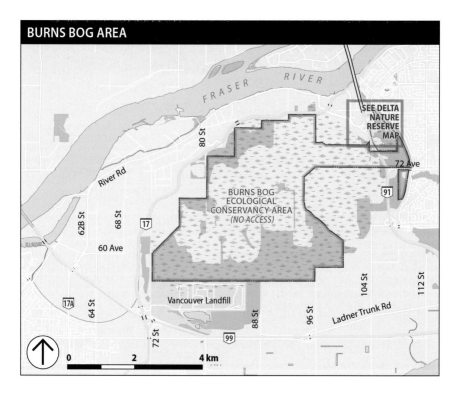

**BURNS BOG AREA**

FRASER RIVER

SEE DELTA NATURE RESERVE MAP

80 St

72 Ave

River Rd

BURNS BOG ECOLOGICAL CONSERVANCY AREA (NO ACCESS)

91

62B St

68 St

17

60 Ave

104 St

112 St

17A

64 St

Vancouver Landfill

88 St

96 St

Ladner Trunk Rd

72 St

99

0    2    4 km

# BIRD SPECIES AND ECOLOGY

The Burns Bog Ecological Conservancy Area and some of the surrounding areas are home to small mammals, insects and plants that are unusual for a location this far south, being more typical of bogs in the northern part of the country. Several are listed as endangered in Canada. Larger mammals, other than Columbian black-tailed deer and coyote, are absent; several black bears inhabited the bog up to the last decade. Small mammals include Pacific water shrew and a number of vole species. The endangered southern red-backed vole was rediscovered in the bog in 1999. Over 4,000 species of invertebrates are estimated to occur in Burns Bog, including many butterflies and dragonflies. Forty-six species of moths and butterflies have been identified, including the mariposa copper and pine elfin. Burns Bog is one of the best places in the Lower Mainland to find dragonflies, with 25 species documented so far, including the crimson-ringed whiteface, yellow-legged meadowhawk, chalk-fronted corporal, zigzag darner and subarctic darner. Most of these species can be hard to find elsewhere in the Vancouver area.

Within the Ecological Conservancy Area, former peat excavation has created deep ponds and water-filled ditches, many of which are concealed by vegetation.

These wetlands are home to nesting water birds such as the *Pied-billed Grebe, Mallard, Gadwall, Green-winged Teal, Northern Shoveler, American Wigeon* and *American Coot. Blue-winged* and *Cinnamon Teal* are uncommon nesters. These ponds are also an important breeding location for the *American Bittern, Sora,* and *Virginia Rail.* Various species of shorebirds pass through on migration, including *Least, Pectoral* and *Baird's Sandpiper,* while others, such as the *Spotted Sandpiper, Killdeer* and *Wilson's Snipe,* stay to breed. *Bald Eagles* are often seen in large numbers on the western side of the bog, near the Vancouver Landfill.

Burns Bog is one of a few locations in the Vancouver Checklist Area where

The Northern Flicker regularly forages for insects on the ground. Peter Candido

*Sandhill Crane* nests. (Others include the Pitt-Addington Marsh Wildlife Management Area in Pitt Meadows and the George C. Reifel Migratory Bird Sanctuary in Delta.) More cranes pass through during migration. Migrating crane flocks can be observed in Delta agricultural fields, particularly those immediately to the west of Burns Bog in the Crescent Slough area (immediately north of Highway 99 and east of River Road). Search the fields in spring and fall in the vicinity of 60th Avenue and 68th Street. Please note that this is an active farming area, so park with care along the roadside and respect farmers' activities while looking for birds. Similar back roads around Burns Bog can be used to access views of the lagg (edge) habitat of the bog.

A number of good bird habitats are found in the vicinity of the Delta Nature Reserve and the greenway footpath and cycle trail along the foot of the North Delta escarpment. An early morning visit will be most rewarding.

Boardwalk trails, about 2 to 3 km long, go through boggy areas of salal, Labrador tea and shore pine, and around very wet areas with skunk cabbage and sphagnum mosses. Common species throughout the Reserve include the *Black-capped* and *Chestnut-backed Chickadee, Spotted Towhee, American Robin, House Finch, Bushtit* and *Song, Golden-* and *White-crowned Sparrow.* The dense, young coniferous forest has nesting *Townsend Warblers, Brown Creepers, Pacific-slope Flycatchers, Downy* and *Pileated Woodpeckers* and *Northern Flickers,* while wetter, open areas attract breeding *Common Yellowthroats.*

Where the forest opens up into heathland, before looping back to the main trail, there is a chance of the *Northern Shrike* in winter or *American Kestrel.* Check open areas for overhead raptors, which are common throughout the Burns Bog area, especially in winter. The *Red-tailed Hawk* and *Northern Harrier* are year-round residents, and *Rough-legged Hawk* spends the winter. Watch for a *Peregrine*

The Great Horned Owl averages twice the weight of the Barred Owl. Jim Martin

*Falcon*, *Merlin*, or *Cooper's* or *Sharp-shinned Hawk*. It is not uncommon to find a roosting *Barred* or *Great Horned Owl*, and in open areas, the *Short-eared Owl* hunts at dusk and dawn.

Farther south along the greenway, Cougar Creek descends from the escarpment. The *American Dipper* has been seen feeding in the small pond at the foot of Blake Drive, as well as in the first kilometre of Cougar Creek. The ravine at the foot of Blake Drive can be quite rewarding for songbirds, and sometimes a *Barred* or *Great Horned Owl* can be found there. The bog vegetation in this area is primarily deciduous and harbours many songbird species in summer, such as *Hutton's*, *Cassin's*, *Red-eyed* and *Warbling Vireos*; *Black-throated Gray*, *Yellow* and *Orange-crowned Warblers*; *Black-headed Grosbeak* and *Bullock's Oriole*. The wetlands around Cougar Creek (the small stream next to the trail) may produce the occasional *Green Heron*, *Virginia Rail* or *Sora* in summer. It was one of the last remaining strongholds of *Ruffed Grouse* in the Vancouver Checklist Area, but this species has not been recorded in recent years. Wintering species include the *Fox Sparrow* and *Golden-crowned Sparrow*.

## GULL-WATCHING AREAS

Agricultural areas around Burns Bog are among the best places to observe roosting gulls in winter. The Vancouver Landfill at 5400 72nd Street in Delta attracts the largest winter congregation of gulls in British Columbia, with tens of thousands feeding there during dumping periods (most weekdays from daybreak until

The Glaucous–winged Gull is by far the most common large gull in our region. Colin Clasen

4 p.m.). Although *the landfill itself is strictly out of bounds to birders*, most of the gulls spend a significant amount of time lounging around the fields surrounding Burns Bog, particularly in wet weather—a common occurrence during Vancouver winters! In addition, the landfill supports the largest number of wintering eagles in the Vancouver Checklist Area. Over 1,200 **Bald Eagles** have been counted at one time. Roosting eagles can often be seen in trees around the bog, particularly beside Highway 99 and Highway 17. Use side roads to view, as there are no pull-offs on the major highways. Other raptors, such as the **Red-tailed Hawk** and **Northern Harrier**, also visit the area. Keep a lookout for the tame *Harris's Hawk*, which a falconer employs to discourage gulls from feeding at the landfill.

The landfill currently hosts a free Open House each June, which includes driving tours around the site.

The best fields for observing winter gull flocks are found to the south of the bog along Burns Drive, which parallels Highway 99, and can be reached by exiting Highway 99 onto Highway 10 (Ladner Trunk Road) at the Matthews exchange (Exit #20). Go north on 96th Street and immediately west onto Burns Drive. Alternatively, travel along Hornby Drive on the south side of Highway 99, also accessed from Exit #20. Other good locations, to the north of Burns Bog, include the log booms in the Fraser River along River Road, the fields along River Road (especially those around 68th Street), agricultural areas adjacent to 72nd Street and 64th Street and the fields at 68th Street and 60th Avenue. Please note that many of these streets are active agricultural or industrial areas, often with high levels of traffic and minimal parking areas. Be considerate of people working in the area and be sure to pull well off the road when parking. Do not block access roads or driveways. Consider leaving your car and walking or cycling these back roads as a better method of birding safely.

Burns Drive provides viewpoints over several very large, cultivated fields that attract large flocks of roosting gulls in winter. Gulls to be expected here, in decreasing order from abundant to very rare, are the **Glaucous-winged, Thayer's, Ring-billed, Mew, Herring, California, Western** and **Glaucous Gull**. **Glaucous Gull** is the rarest of this group. One or two **Slaty-backed Gulls** have been seen in the past, and should be looked for along Burns Drive or Hornby Drive, and off 72nd Street, the **Iceland Gull** and the **Common Black-headed Gull** have also been reported as very rare vagrants among gull flocks.

For more gull-watching locations, see the 72nd Street information in the "Boundary Bay: 64th Street to 112th Street" section.

*Extensively revised by Anne Murray, Nature Guides BC, 2015. Based on Kyle Elliott's original version, with input from Tom Bearss and Maureen Vo from the Burns Bog Conservation Society, 2015.*

# 22. BURNABY LAKE REGIONAL PARK

## INTRODUCTION

BURNABY LAKE REGIONAL PARK, SITUATED IN THE MIDDLE OF THE CITY OF Burnaby's Central Valley, is bounded on the south by Highway 1 (the Trans-Canada Highway) and on the north by a main railway line. The north side of the park and its eastern and western ends all offer excellent birding. On the southside trails, although birding can be very good, the vehicle noise from the adjacent Trans-Canada Highway can be quite intrusive.

While the lake and its surrounding forests and wetlands provide year-round birding, visits can be particularly worthwhile during spring and fall migrations. There is always the chance here for an occasional rarity to show up. Summer presents the birder with opportunities to observe many of the typical breeding birds of the forested and freshwater habitats of the Lower Mainland. In winter, the park offers good locations to observe a large variety of the birds that winter in the Lower Mainland, including many species of water birds and forest species.

A scene from the viewing tower overlooking the popular Piper Spit boardwalk, extending from the north side of Burnaby Lake. Colin Clasen

What is now parkland was extensively logged around the turn of the last century. On many forest trails you can still see much evidence of this activity. Large western red cedar stumps, with the springboard holes still visible, dot the forested areas. Just west of the Nature House at the foot of Piper Avenue, the remnants of a sawmill can be identified by the large mound of sawdust and wood waste now being colonized by birch and western hemlock trees.

The major habitats of the park are the shallow lake itself, the lowland second-growth mixed forest through which most of the trails travel, and the extensive marshy wetlands forming the margins of the lake. The marshes reach their greatest extent at the eastern end where the lake empties into the Brunette River, which then flows east to the Fraser River. Still Creek feeds Burnaby Lake from the west. Flowing into the lake on the southern side, near the Rowing Pavilion, is Deer Lake Brook, which is the outlet stream of Deer Lake.

# BURNABY LAKE REGIONAL PARK

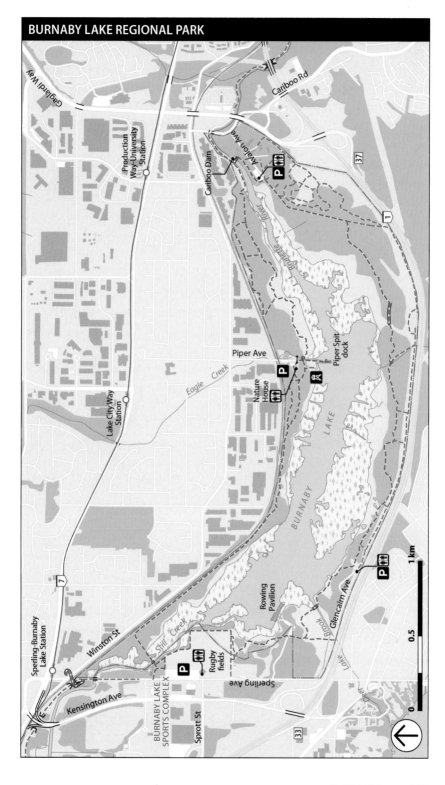

## DIRECTIONS

There are many access points to the park, but the three recommended for birders are the Nature House on Piper Avenue, the Avalon Avenue (Cariboo Dam) entrance at the eastern end of the lake and the Burnaby Lake Pavilion (Rowing Pavilion) at the western end of the lake. All have good parking, but the Nature House parking lot often fills up on sunny weekends. Unfortunately, the parking areas have a high rate of car thefts. **Do not leave valuables in your car while birding**. Washrooms are available at the Nature House and the Avalon Avenue entrance. It is also possible to make a complete circuit of the lake on foot—approximately 9 km via the trail network, which will include all the locations mentioned above. All directions given here are based on driving east from Vancouver on Highway 1.

To get to the Nature House on Piper Avenue, take the Sprott Street exit (#32). Turn left onto Sprott Street, continue 0.6 km to the first set of traffic lights and turn left onto Kensington Avenue heading north. Travel north 1 km, following the signs for Lougheed Highway East over the Kensington overpass. Keep to the right on the overpass and as you come down the off-ramp, turn right immediately at its foot onto Winston Street. Follow Winston Street east for 2.7 km, watching out for the blue and white metal Metro Vancouver Regional Parks advance sign and the old wooden green and yellow GVRD Parks sign on the right at Piper Avenue. Turn right on Piper Avenue and continue past Warner Loat Park on your left, over the railway tracks, and at the south end of Piper, look for a parking spot.

*Note: From the Nature House, trails lead east and west along the lakeshore. The trail heading east is recommended for birders and is described in the text below. However, the trail heading west is also good, particularly if you continue about 1.5 km to the turn north to Still Creek. The section of trail from here to the creek bridge can be very productive. Also worth visiting is the observation tower about 100 m west of Piper Spit and clearly visible when standing on the boardwalk at Piper Spit.*

To get to the Avalon Avenue (Cariboo Dam) area, take the Gaglardi Way exit (#37) on Highway 1. Turn right at the first set of traffic lights onto Cariboo Road, and almost immediately turn left at the next set of traffic lights onto Cariboo Road North. As you travel under the Gaglardi Way overpass, watch for Avalon Avenue almost immediately on your left. Turn left and continue west on Avalon, past the sign that indicates Burnaby Lake Regional Park (Cariboo Dam), to the parking area on the right at the end of this short road.

To get to the Burnaby Lake Pavilion, take the Sprott Street exit (#32). Turn left onto Sprott Street and continue straight until the second set of traffic lights at Kensington Avenue North. Cross Kensington, drive past the tennis courts on your right to the T-intersection and turn right onto Sperling Avenue. Drive past the rugby fields on the left, and turn left following the sign to the Canada Games Rowing Course, Burnaby Lake Pavilion. If you are here in winter, check the goose flocks on the rugby fields. *Cackling Geese* are regular here, numbering up to 100 birds. After a short distance you will arrive at a parking area. (The left turn off Sperling is Roberts Street, but at the time of writing it was not signposted.)

The observation deck of the pavilion provides an elevated view over the lake. From late summer through winter and spring, it is a good place to observe waterfowl and shorebirds. The latter are frequently visible feeding along the far shore of the lake. In recent years, the *Purple Martin* has been investigating the nest boxes provided for them at the west end of the lake.

**Burnaby Lake has the highest concentration of Wood Ducks in the Metro Vancouver area.**
Virginia Hayes

The trail that leaves the pavilion parking lot at its southwest corner is recommended. It heads south and then turns east to skirt the lake after crossing Deer Lake Brook. After the bridge, the trail goes through a productive riparian area for the next 200 to 300 m and gives good views of the lake.

## BIRD SPECIES

Start at the Nature House at the foot of Piper Avenue. A short walk south of the Nature House brings you to Piper Spit, which is bordered on its eastern side by a large mud flat created by Eagle Creek. This is one of the best places in the park to observe shorebirds. In spring and fall migrations, *Long-billed* and *Short-billed Dowitchers* and *Western*, *Least* and *Pectoral Sandpipers* may be found on the mud flats. In winter, *Greater Yellowlegs* are regularly found here, and there is usually a winter resident flock of *Long-billed Dowitchers*, which allows very close views along the boardwalk. Walk out on the spit for good views of the lake. This is a prime location for the *Wood Duck*, and Burnaby Lake has the largest population in the Vancouver area. The *Mallard*, *Common Merganser*, *Bufflehead*, *Lesser Scaup*, and *Green-winged Teal* are among the common ducks of winter. Also seen are the *Northern Pintail*, *Northern Shoveler*, *Gadwall*, *American Wigeon* and *Common Goldeneye*. Occasionally, a *Blue-winged* or *Cinnamon Teal* can be seen in spring and summer. *Bald Eagles* nest on the south shore of the lake; it requires a scope to observe, looking south across the lake from the spit. The spit provides excellent

The commonly seen Green–winged Teal (left) and much rarer Eurasian Teal (right) at Piper Spit. Colin Clasen

views up and down the lake and over the surrounding marshes where, in spring and summer, *Red-winged Blackbird*, *Brown-headed Cowbird*, *Common Yellowthroat* and *Marsh Wren* are common. Many *Great Blue Heron* stalk the lakeshore and marshes here year-round. *Double-crested Cormorant* is common in winter. The *Northern Harrier* and, less commonly, the *Short-eared Owl* hunt over these marshes. In recent years, a *Green Heron* has been breeding on the lake, and in winter, look for the *Northern Shrike*.

Looking from Piper Spit across Eagle Creek to the east, a large number of swallow nest boxes have been erected, and along the creek itself you'll find many *Wood Duck* boxes. In spring, there are large numbers of swallows here, mainly *Tree* and *Violet-green*, and the lake itself is a good location for *Northern Rough-winged*, *Cliff* (less common) and *Barn Swallows* too.

Take the trail that heads east across Eagle Creek and is signposted to the Cariboo Dam. This trail passes through an attractive sample of the mixed forest that is very typical of the area and contains the birds you would expect to see in this habitat. Spruce Loop and Conifer Loop trails, which both return you to the main trail, are worth walking too. In the forest, look for *Black-capped* and *Chestnut-backed Chickadees*. In the cooler months, they are often found in mixed flocks with *Golden-crowned* and *Ruby-crowned Kinglets*, *Red-breasted Nuthatches* and the occasional *Brown Creeper*.

Also look for the *Downy Woodpecker* and the less common *Hairy Woodpecker*. The *Red-breasted Sapsucker* is resident here in small numbers, but this species may increase in winter when snows are heavy in the North Shore Mountains. In the understorey, *Pacific* and *Bewick's Wren, Song Sparrow, Dark-eyed Junco* and *Spotted Towhee* are common. At all times, the raucous *Steller's Jay* is a noisy presence in the forest, as are the *Northwestern Crow* and *Common Raven*. In fall, winter and early spring, these forested areas often have flocks of *Pine Siskin, Evening Grosbeak* and *Red Crossbills* feeding in the upper canopy of the forest. In the spring, the forests attract good numbers of *Yellow-rumped, Black-throated Gray* and some *Townsend's Warblers. Wilson's Warbler* is also fairly common and breeds here. The *Western Tanager* is regular here in spring and summer, and the *Olive-sided Flycatcher* is often heard ordering beer here in spring. At a number of points, the trail comes close to the edge of the marshes, where beavers are actively putting their stamp on the local hydrology. The *Willow Flycatcher* sings from the riparian areas in spring, and from March on, the *Virginia Rail* is quite vocal here.

You can continue to walk along this trail, cross the Brunette River via the Cariboo Dam and walk around the entire lake. After crossing the Cariboo Dam, the trail soon arrives at the parking area for the Avalon Avenue entrance. The forest surrounding this parking area is probably the most consistent location in the park to see *Pileated Woodpecker*. The large cottonwoods between the parking area and the Brunette River are usually good in the late spring for *Red-eyed Vireo*, and

The Red–tailed Hawk, clearly showing the rusty red coloured tail of an adult. Tak Shibata

in migration, *Cassin's* and *Warbling Vireo. Wood Duck* nests here in the many nest boxes erected by members of the Burnaby Lake Advisory Committee.

Continuing on the main trail, a large area of hardhack with many equestrian trails through it is an excellent place to observe displaying *Rufous Hummingbird* in March and April. From the parking area, the section of the main trail that heads south for about 300 m is an excellent place for many warblers in spring, including the *Yellow-rumped* and *Orange-crowned Warbler,* in addition to the species mentioned above.

*Written and revised by George Clulow, 2015.*

# 23. DEER LAKE PARK

## INTRODUCTION

DEER LAKE PARK, LIKE ITS CLOSE NEIGHBOUR BURNABY LAKE REGIONAL Park, is located in Burnaby's Central Valley. South of the Trans-Canada Highway, it sits in a much quieter, more secluded location than its partner park north of the highway. Surrounded by quieter suburbs, it also offers stunning views of the North Shore Mountains from its southern slopes. Its extensive fields and forests, along with the lake and its riparian areas, offer a wide range of habitats for a variety of birds. The area that is now Deer Lake Park was logged around the turn of the last century; its remaining forested areas are now dominated by mixed, second-growth forest.

Deer Lake as seen from the beach at the east end of the lake. Colin Clasen

The lowland western part of the park, between Royal Oak Avenue and the lake itself, was once the farmland for the Oakalla Prison Farm. In 1991 the prison was closed and replaced by the Oaklands development of townhouses and apartments that now overlook the park from the south. Over the years, these old farm fields have transformed into valuable, old-field habitat, adding substantially to the park's diversity of birds.

## DIRECTIONS

By car from downtown Vancouver, take Highway 1 east, exiting onto Willingdon Avenue South (#29B). Travel 2.7 km south on Willingdon Avenue to Grange Street. Turn left at the traffic lights onto Grange Street (which becomes Dover Street as you drive east), and proceed east 1.1 km to Royal Oak Avenue. Turn left on Royal Oak Avenue and continue down the hill 1.1 km. The park and lake will be visible on your right as you head downhill. At the base of the hill, before the traffic lights at Deer Lake Parkway, turn right into a small, unmarked parking lot.

*Note: This entrance is easily missed if travelling at speed. This rather circular route*

# DEER LAKE PARK

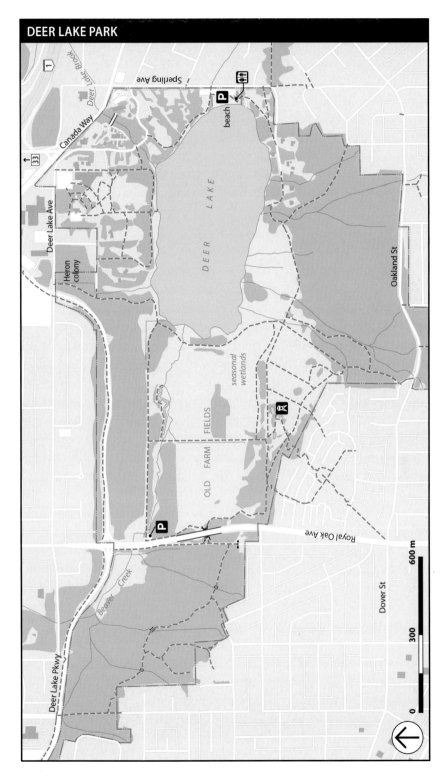

*is necessary, because the parking lot can only be reached from the northbound lanes of Royal Oak Avenue.*

A second access route is to leave Highway 1 at the Canada Way exit (#33). Stay in the left lane when exiting, go through the first set of lights and then turn left at the lights at Canada Way. You are now heading east. At the next set of lights, at Canada Way and Sperling Avenue, turn right. Continue straight on Sperling Avenue past Deer Lake Avenue on your right. The lake is about 400 m ahead on your right. The large parking area here has washrooms at its south end. The walk described below is taken from the Royal Oak entrance, but exploration of the lake and meadows may instead be started from the Sperling Avenue end.

## BIRD SPECIES

The trail into Deer Lake Park from the small parking lot at Royal Oak Avenue parallels Beaver Creek. In spring, look for migrants in the forest, hedges and meadows. April and May ought to produce *Orange-crowned, Yellow-rumped, Black-throated Grays*; and *Townsend's, MacGillivray's, Yellow* and *Wilson's Warblers. Warbling Vireo* and *Western Wood-Pewee* are common migrants, a few staying to breed. *Cassin's Vireo* is less common. *Hutton's Vireo* is a resident breeder in the park and is often quite vocal as early in the season as late February. Breeding *Black-headed Grosbeaks* are common in late spring and summer throughout much of the park. Listen for its robin-like song or creaking call note, and watch for the spectacular display flights of the males when they fly out from the forest edges. *Western Tanager* breeds in the park's forested areas too, and in recent years *Eastern* and *Western Kingbirds* have been showing up in May in the meadows, but at time of writing, they haven't yet stayed to breed.

At the first junction in the trail, turn right, head south, cross Beaver Creek and continue out through the meadows, where a few *Ring-necked Pheasant* are still hanging in. This is a good location to see breeding *Common Yellowthroats* and *Savannah Sparrows*. In spring and fall migrations, *Golden-crowned* and *White-crowned Sparrows* move through in large numbers. The *Bushtit* is regular year-round and is one of the earliest nesting species in the park, along with *Hutton's Vireo*. The *American Goldfinch* is also seen year-round but most frequently in the summer, when the bouncing display flights of the males attract attention. The *House Finch* is common here too. In fall, winter and spring, *Lincoln's Sparrows* (most common in migration) and *Fox Sparrows* are found in the hedges around the fields. The latter are common in winter in the extensive blackberry thickets that provide cover and food. *American Robins, Song Sparrows* and *Spotted Towhees* are common year-round. *The Dark-eyed Junco* is absent during the summer. The *Purple Martin*, which breeds on nearby Burrard Inlet, is an irregular visitor to the

Pied–billed Grebe with a chick on its back. Tak Shibata

lake in summer. Particularly when clouds are low, flocks of **Vaux's** and **Black Swifts** may be seen over the park in summer. Less regular are very small numbers of the **Common Nighthawk**.

A walk around the old fields may produce several raptors. The **Red-tailed Hawk** and **Northern Harrier** both nest in the park. You'll see the signs protecting the harrier nesting areas in the meadows. Occasionally, **Rough-legged Hawk** is found in winter. **Merlin** and **American Kestrel** are uncommon in fall, winter and spring. **Peregrine Falcon** is a rare visitor, whereas **Bald Eagle** is regular year-round and may hunt wintering waterfowl here, particularly **American Coot**. There are several **Cooper's Hawk** nesting pairs in the park, and they are regular year-round. The **Sharp-shinned Hawk** is rare at any time of year and is absent in summer.

Owls frequent the park but are not easily found. The **Great Horned Owl** and **Barred Owl** both breed here. The **Barn Owl**, which bred here for many years in the old prison farm outbuildings, is now the subject of a City of Burnaby project to reintroduce it as a breeding species in the park. You'll see the specially designed nest boxes (installed in 2015) in the old-field meadows. The **Northern Saw-whet Owl** is a rare winter visitor.

Follow the path that skirts the fields heading south and then turn left to head east. You will now be walking toward the forest that comprises the southeast slope of the park, with meadows on your right and left. In spring and summer, you can expect a wide variety of species in or at the edge of the forest, including **Brown-headed Cowbirds**, **Willow Flycatchers**, **Swainson's Thrushes** and, less commonly, **Olive-sided Flycatchers** in spring. The **Pacific-slope Flycatcher** breeds in the forest, and in spring migration, the **Hammond's Flycatcher** is also seen regularly. **Northern**

*Flicker*, which breeds in the park, is often seen in large numbers in the fall. In March and April, large numbers of **Ruby-crowned Kinglets** migrate through; much smaller numbers overwinter.

At the trail junction near the southwest corner of the lake, you can turn left and head north, taking the boardwalk along the west shore of the lake instead of heading east toward the forested areas. The boardwalk is a good location for **Virginia Rail** in all seasons. Vigorous mimicking of their calls is usually required to get a look at the birds. A **Sora** may also be present but is not common. Year-round resident **Anna's Hummingbird** is most easily found along the boardwalk trail. Look at the tips of willows and Pacific crab apple shrubs for the highly territorial males. The lakeshore vegetation here will offer many chances to see the **Common Yellowthroat** (abundant), **Yellow-rumped**, **Yellow**, **Black-throated Gray** and **Orange-crowned Warbler** in spring. The **Marsh Wren** sings from the willow thickets near the bridge over Beaver Creek. In late summer and fall, the **Cedar Waxwing** feasts on the Pacific crab apple trees in this area, as does the **Purple Finch** in fall and winter. From the boardwalk, you can complete the circuit back to the Royal Oak parking lot, or backtrack to the trail junction noted above and continue on the longer loop through the forest. The boardwalk loop is approximately 2 km.

Barn Swallow numbers have drastically declined in the last decade. Jim Martin

If you have more time to explore, the trails that run along the upper, south edge of the south slope below the Oaklands development can be very productive.

Not to be missed is the relatively new, established **Great Blue Heron** colony in the northeast area of the park, bounded by Rowan Avenue, Price Street and Deer Lake Drive. The best place to view the colony is from Deer Lake Drive, just east of Deer Lake Parkway. Over 140 nests were counted here in 2014. To access this area from a walk around the lake, take the trail that heads north from the west end of Price Street and turn right where it emerges onto Deer Lake Drive.

There are many trails that can be taken into the forested area from the fields. To complete a circuit of the lake, the suggested route is to follow the trail through the fields that heads east to the wooden arch, marking the entrance to the forest. At this point, the choice is to continue around the lake on the lower trail or turn right and head uphill, across the small wooden bridge, and through the forest. This is the most reliable area for the **Pileated** and **Downy Woodpecker**, and less frequently, the *Hairy Woodpecker*. *A Red-breasted Sapsucker* can also be seen here and elsewhere in the park, but it is the least common woodpecker found here. *Swainson's Thrush* commonly breeds through a large portion of the park's forests. *Varied Thrush* forages here in good numbers in the winter, and occasional *Hermit Thrush* may also be seen in both winter and in spring migration. Year-round forest residents include the *Pacific* and *Bewick's Wren*, *Hutton's Vireo*, *Black-capped* and *Chestnut-backed Chickadee*, *Brown Creeper* and *Red-breasted Nuthatch*. Flocks of *Golden-crowned Kinglets* are common in winter, as are the *Pine Siskin* in the treetops.

By following the path uphill through the forest, you will eventually emerge from the park at its extreme southeast corner and enter a residential area on Strawson Avenue. Continuing east onto Haszard Street through the residential area will bring you to a long set of stairs that lead down to the lake again, this time at its eastern end. The beach area and children's playground area next to the Sperling Avenue parking lot are excellent for gulls and ducks in winter. In winter look here for the *Ring-billed*, *Glaucous-winged* and the occasional *Thayer's Gull*. Continue around the lake on the trail that generally follows the north side of the lake, but does so at some distance in places. It finally connects to the trail that skirts the old-field meadows on their north side, heads west and returns to the parking area at the foot of Royal Oak Avenue. This longer loop will make a circuit of about 6 km.

*Belted Kingfishers* may be seen around the lake in all seasons. In winter, the *Hooded Merganser* is common, along with the *Mallard*, *Gadwall*, *American Wigeon*, *Bufflehead* and *Ring-necked Duck*. Rarely, a *Greater White-fronted Goose* or a *Snow Goose* joins the resident flocks of *Canada Geese*, and occasionally a *Trumpeter Swan* will drop in for a visit. In spring, the lake is a good location to watch swallows in migration, some of which remain all summer. *Tree*, *Violet-green* and *Barn Swallows* are the most common. *Northern Rough-winged* and *Cliff Swallows* are more unusual. The lake also attracts a number of other interesting but transient species, including the *Caspian Tern* in late summer, *Common Merganser* in spring and the occasional *Common Loon* or *Horned Grebe* in migration. *Ospreys*, although not breeding at the lake, are seen regularly in spring and summer. In August, numbers of six or more are common as young birds perch in the trees around the lake, where they are fed by their parents.

Burnaby Lake and Deer Lake parks are geographically very close, so combining visits to both makes for a good day's birding. They contain a modest but interesting variety of habitats, including forests, riparian areas, marshes, mossy bogs, rough fields and grassland, and freshwater streams and lakes. The parks are of interest to birders in all seasons.

*Written and revised by George Clulow, 2015.*

# 24. BURNABY MOUNTAIN CONSERVATION AREA

## INTRODUCTION

THIS 576 HA PARK IS THE LARGEST COMPONENT OF THE BURNABY PARKS system and is a significant natural area in the Lower Mainland. In common with the other Burnaby parks described in this guide, Burnaby Mountain was logged around the turn of the last century and is now covered in second-growth forest of mainly deciduous trees, such as red alder, big leaf maple and black cottonwood. Small patches of coniferous forest do occur, and some larger original forest trees may be found in ravines on the northern and southern slopes. Notable for its birding, the spectacular views to be enjoyed here are why many people visit. Vistas of the North Shore Mountains, the City of Vancouver, Burrard Inlet and Indian Arm, the Strait of Georgia and the mountains of Vancouver Island are among the most outstanding viewscapes in the Lower Mainland.

Simon Fraser University and the UniverCity community occupy the top of the mountain, with access roads from the south and west. The park is shaped roughly like a doughnut surrounding the university. On the western side of the mountain, overlooking the steep northern side of the park and Burrard Inlet, is the Centennial Pavilion area that once comprised the core of the old Burnaby Mountain Park, now absorbed into the larger Burnaby Mountain Conservation Area.

Although the park can be birded in all months, Burnaby Mountain is most notable as a spring migrant trap where, under the right weather conditions in late April and May, spectacular passerine fallouts may happen.

The east end of Burrard Inlet, as seen from the top of Burnaby Mountain. Bill Kinkaid

Burnaby Mountain Park sign, with the very popular Horizons Restaurant in the background. Ron Long

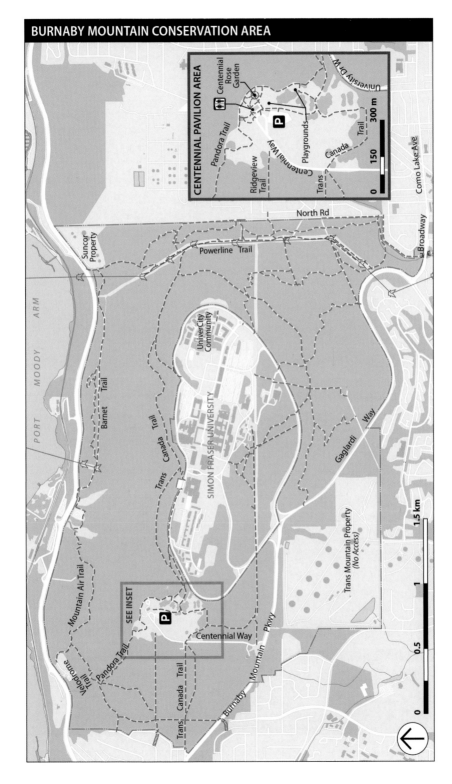

*Note: The north side of the mountain is fenced off for good reason. The area north of Pandora Trail is extremely dangerous. People have died there. It is deceptively treacherous and steep. Respect the warning signs.*

## DIRECTIONS

From downtown Vancouver, take Highway 1 east and exit onto Gaglardi Way (#32). Set your odometer to zero at this point. As you drive north on Gaglardi Way, the road begins to ascend Burnaby Mountain. In 6 km, you will reach a main intersection with traffic lights. University Drive East is to the right and Burnaby Mountain Parkway on the left. Turn left onto Burnaby Mountain Parkway, drive for another 1 km and turn right onto Centennial Way. Follow this winding road up the hill for an additional 1 km and park in the large parking area below the Horizons Restaurant. Public washrooms are at ground level at the western end of the restaurant building.

From this point, you can walk the many trails that wander through the park. The most productive areas in spring are frequently those surrounding the formal and informal Centennial garden areas, and the Trans Canada Trail, which traverses the mountain roughly southwest to northeast. The Pandora Trail is good to follow both upslope and downslope. The forested areas to the east (upslope), toward

The Yellow-rumped Warbler (Myrtle Variety) has a white throat. John Lowman

and beyond the upper and lower children's playgrounds, can be very productive in spring. All trails are worth exploring, including those that head down toward Burrard Inlet, such as the Velodrome Trail. Expect hilly terrain wherever you walk in the park.

## BIRD SPECIES

Burnaby Mountain Conservation Area is an excellent area to observe large numbers of warblers, flycatchers, sparrows and thrushes in spring, particularly *Yellow-rumped*, *Wilson's*, *Townsend's*, *Orange-crowned* and *Black-throated Gray Warblers*. Less frequently, *MacGillivray's* and *Nashville Warblers* have been recorded. In migration, both the *Pacific-slope Flycatcher* (which breeds in the park) and *Hammond's Flycatcher* are common. *Swainson's Thrush* is also common and breeds here. *Hermit Thrush* may be seen in migration. The *Black-headed Grosbeak* breeds in the park and is common, particularly on the western and southern slopes of the park, as is the *Western Tanager*. Substantial flocks of *American Robin* are sometimes seen on the grassy slopes below the parking area. Migrating *Townsend's Solitaire* and *Olive-sided Flycatcher* frequent the field edges and also the tall treetops in the meadows and cliff edge.

The grassy areas below the parking lot also attract migrating sparrows. Among the flocks of *Golden-crowned* and *White-crowned Sparrows*, look for the rarer *White-throated Sparrow*. The salmonberry thickets surrounding the grassy areas attract many *Rufous Hummingbirds* in spring, and in some years a migrating *Calliope Hummingbird* or two.

The brushy areas along forest edges and power line rights-of-way are good places to find a *Hutton's Vireo*, particularly in February and March, when they are more vocal. Other typical birds of the park include the *Pine Siskin*, *Ruby-crowned* and *Golden-crowned Kinglet*, *Black-capped* and *Chestnut-backed Chickadee*, *Red-breasted Nuthatch*, *Dark-eyed Junco*, *Spotted Towhee*, *Song Sparrow*, *Pacific Wren* and *Bushtit*.

The extensive forests of the park provide habitat for *Pileated*, *Hairy* and *Downy Woodpeckers*, which are frequently seen and heard. *Red-breasted Sapsuckers* are also a regular species here and are often found in the forest west (downslope) of the parking area, where they use the metal power pole caps to rap out their syncopated drumming. September often sees considerable numbers of the *Northern Flicker*.

Small movements of raptors made up of the *Turkey Vulture*, *Cooper's Hawk* and *Red-tailed Hawk* are sometimes seen in spring. *Black* and *Vaux's Swifts* use the skies above the mountain to forage in spring and summer.

The *Sooty Grouse* is a highlight species here. The small population on the

Cedar Waxwings sometimes get intoxicated from eating fermented berries in winter.

Ilya Povalyaev

mountain is an extreme southerly outlier from the more mountainous areas across Burrard Inlet and farther east. In April and May, listen for the deep hooting of the male. If lucky, you will be treated to close views of him in full display. Otherwise, search the conifers around the upper playground where the birds are often found.

This is a huge park and it would take days to explore its many trails. Walking the trails within 1 to 2 km of the parking area will provide good opportunities to observe its birdlife.

*Written and revised by George Clulow, 2015.*

# 25. BURNABY FRASER FORESHORE PARK

## INTRODUCTION

BURNABY FRASER FORESHORE PARK IS A LONG, NARROW PARK THAT stretches along Burnaby's portion of the Fraser River flood plain. It is populated with tall northern black cottonwood trees, with an understorey of red-osier dogwood, Pacific ninebark, salmonberry, thimbleberry and hedges of Himalayan blackberry. It is, in fact, a very good example of a locally threatened flood plain habitat.

## DIRECTIONS

From downtown Vancouver, take Oak Street or Cambie Street south to SW Marine Drive and turn left (east). Follow SW Marine Drive (which becomes SE Marine Drive at the intersection of Ontario Street) east into South Burnaby. Just past the intersection of Kerr Street, bear right onto Marine Way. Access to the park is via Byrne Road. Turn right (south) at Byrne Road (a main intersection) and go straight to the end, where you will find washrooms, an information board with map and a parking lot.

Part of the deciduous forest and trail through Burnaby Fraser Foreshore Park. Al Grass

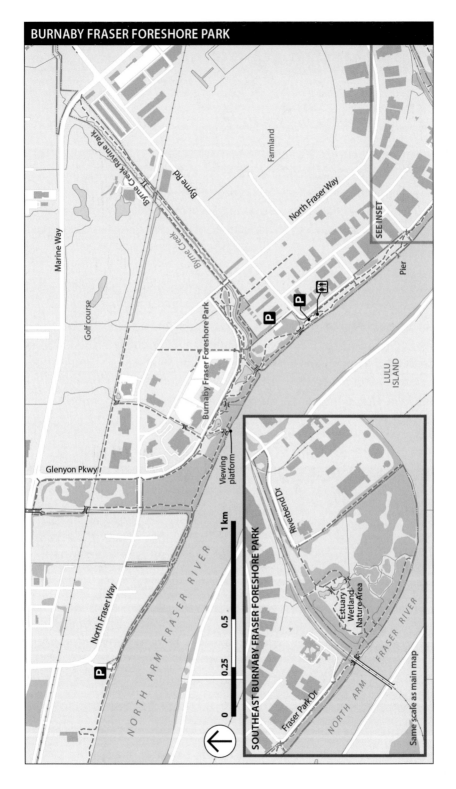

BURNABY FRASER FORESHORE PARK

Great Blue Heron with fish at Burnaby Fraser Foreshore Park. Colin Clasen

## BIRD SPECIES

Standing at the edge of the parking lot, you will get a good view of the mighty and often muddy Fraser River as it churns its way down to the sea. Check the river for **Common Merganser** and **Great Blue Heron** (on pilings). There is almost always a **Bald Eagle** perched somewhere nearby or circling overhead. In spring, when the eulachons (small, herring-like fish) are running, various gulls, such as the **California**, **Mew**, **Ring-billed** and sometimes the **Herring Gull**, are attracted to the fishy feast. **Western Grebes** may also be spotted here.

Take the trail to the west of the parking lot toward the big cottonwoods. Entering the tall, cathedral-like cottonwood grove is an inspiring experience in itself. Spring is the best season here; the air is fresh and fragrant from bursting cotton-

A brilliantly coloured Yellow Warbler. John Gordon

wood buds, and the birds are active and singing. This is Burnaby's best place to locate a *Bullock's Oriole* (early morning is the best time). *Downy* and *Hairy Woodpeckers* and *Northern Flickers* may be heard hammering and pecking. In spring migration, both the *Hermit* and *Swainson's Thrush* can be found here, with the latter nesting in the park. The *Swainson's Thrush* is especially attracted to salmonberry thickets for food, shelter and nesting sites. On some days in April, the bushes are alive with *Ruby-crowned Kinglets* migrating through, and a few overwinter here. Scan the birch trees, especially in winter, when the *American Goldfinch*, *Pine Siskin* and sometimes *Common Redpoll* gobble up the nutritious "seeds."

Byrne Creek enters the river just to the west of the parking lot (watch for the floodgate). The murky water is a good place to find a *Hooded Merganser* and possibly a *Green Heron*. Extensive riparian vegetation provides habitat for migrating *Yellow-rumped*, *Yellow*, *Wilson's* and other *Warblers*. In winter, the *White-crowned*, *Fox* and *Song Sparrow* call it home. The *White-throated Sparrow* has occasionally been sighted here. The creek water looks like root beer these days, but cutthroat trout could once be caught in the creek. Conservation efforts are aimed at helping this ailing stream.

Fish-eating mammals to be watched for include harbour seals, sea lions and river otters. Sit patiently for a while near Byrne Creek and you might get a good look at a beaver or muskrat.

Burnaby Fraser Foreshore Park makes a nice half day of birding and will be even better when nearby enhancement work is completed. There is a pier and a picnic area. In addition, you can walk upriver to the adjacent Estuary Wetland Nature Area, an excellent spring bird site for warblers, vireos, etc. Nearby farmlands offer some good birding opportunities, including raptors.

*Written and revised by Al and Jude Grass, 2015.*

# 26. BARNET MARINE PARK

## INTRODUCTION

BURNABY'S BARNET MARINE PARK, WHICH HUGS BURRARD INLET, IS A visually spectacular site where land and sea meet, providing excellent bird habitat. To the north, the inlet is framed by the North Shore Mountains, with easily recognizable peaks, such as Mount Seymour, in the distance. Burnaby Mountain is to the south.

The sandy beach at Barnet Marine Park, with a viewing platform at the west end. Ron Long

A mixture of large coniferous and deciduous trees lends a special charm to this park. Mature bigleaf maple, tall red alder, black cottonwood and western hemlock are the dominant tree species. Wildlife-friendly understorey shrubs include thimbleberry, salmonberry, red elderberry and blackberry hedges. Dead or dying trees (wildlife trees) provide feeding and nesting opportunities for a variety of species, including *Downy*, *Hairy* and *Pileated Woodpeckers*.

Marine habitats consist of rocky shore, some pebble and mud beach and deeper open water. The lack of well-developed mud flat habitat is a limiting factor in shorebird activity at Barnet Marine Park.

## DIRECTIONS

To get to the park from downtown Vancouver, drive east on Hastings Street until it becomes the Barnet Highway, and when you see the Burnaby City Parks sign, turn left and follow the road to the parking lot on the right before the train tracks. Facilities here include picnic tables and washrooms.

From the washroom complex, follow the shoreline trail to the west. There is a public pier, and a structure, part of an old burner, which is all that is left of an old mill. This makes a great viewing platform in lieu of a purpose-built tower. The trail follows Burrard Inlet for several kilometres, and shorter trails snake through the forest.

# BARNET MARINE PARK

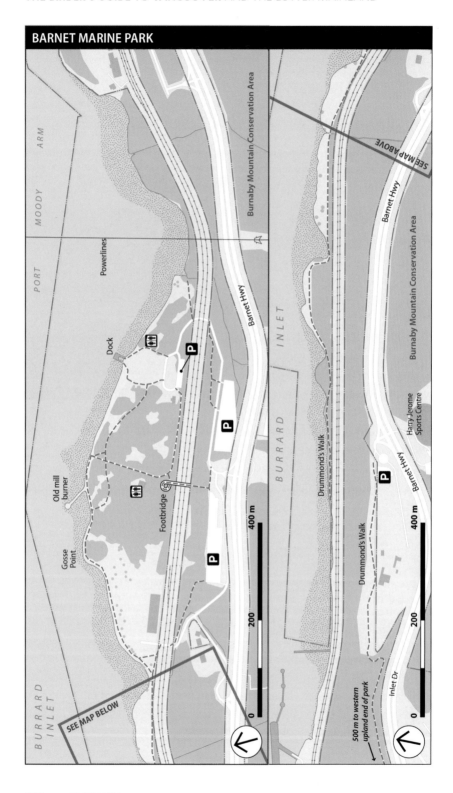

# BIRD SPECIES

In spring migration, the park may host a "fallout" of warblers and vireos, which can be quite spectacular if you are there at the right time. Watch for *Black-throated Gray, Townsend's, Orange-crowned, Wilson's, Yellow-rumped* and *MacGillivray's Warbler*, as well as *Cassin's, Hutton's* and *Red-eyed Vireo. Townsend's Solitaire* has also been observed here in migration. Resident birds of the shrubby areas include *Chestnut-backed* and *Black-capped Chickadee, Bushtit, Spotted Towhee* and *Song Sparrow. Ruby-crowned Kinglet* flocks pass through in good numbers each spring.

Resident raptors include *Cooper's* and *Red-tailed Hawks, Bald Eagles* and *Osprey,* often perched or soaring somewhere near the park or across the mouth of Port Moody Arm (directly opposite the park). The *Turkey Vulture* is fairly common here in summer and is usually seen soaring on thermal air currents above the hills and ridges.

On the marine side, the *Marbled Murrelet* has been recorded here at various times of the year, including summer, and

Male Common Merganser with its distinctive green hood and bright red beak. John Lowman

it probably nests in the subalpine area of nearby mountains. The only other alcid seen regularly here is the *Pigeon Guillemot*. In open water, it is sometimes possible to see three cormorant species—*Pelagic, Double-crested* and *Brandt's. Pelagic Cormorant* is the most common and can be seen year-round. Gulls and terns usually gather offshore or rest on nearby rocks and pilings. All the common Vancouver-area gulls have been seen here. *Caspian Tern* is observed in summer, plunge-diving for fish. *Common Tern* is usually seen in fall migration, and you may be fortunate enough to spot a *Parasitic Jaeger* in hot pursuit of the terns. Closer inshore, *Common* and *Red-throated Loons* and *Horned Grebes* are all regularly seen.

On the shore itself, the *Killdeer* are residents. *Spotted Sandpipers* may be present in the summer, and *Solitary Sandpipers* may turn up in fall migration. Winter is the best time to observe sea-going waterfowl. Watch for the *Harlequin Duck* fishing for small shore crabs along the rocky shore. *Barrow's Goldeneye* and *Surf Scoter* are seen here, with the latter diving for (and often bringing to the surface) blue mussels. The *Common Merganser, Bufflehead, Greater Scaup* and *Common Goldeneye* are other regulars at Barnet Marine Park.

Also watch for river otters, harbour seals and sea lions. In 1999 a pilot whale was spotted here.

*Written by Al Grass, 2001. Revised by Al Grass and Jude Grass, 2015.*

# 27. MINNEKHADA REGIONAL PARK / ADDINGTON MARSH / DEBOVILLE SLOUGH

## INTRODUCTION

MINNEKHADA REGIONAL PARK, ADDINGTON MARSH (PART OF THE Pitt-Addington Marsh Wildlife Management Area) and DeBoville Slough are tucked beneath the shadow of Burke Mountain in northeast Coquitlam, less than an hour's drive from downtown Vancouver. They are contiguous with each other, bordered by the Pitt River to the east and blueberry farms between DeBoville Slough and Minnekhada Park.

Minnekhada (meaning "Rattling Waters") became a regional park in 1984. In 1934 Lieutenant Governor Eric Hamber built a lodge here as a base for hunting.

**Minnekhada Marsh.** Colin Clasen

This lodge is open to visitors most Sundays from 1 to 4 p.m. A large wetland was created in the centre of the park to attract waterfowl, and this remains a productive waterfowl spot today. The adjacent Minnekhada Farm was added to the park in 1995, but at the time of writing, it is not accessible to the public.

Addington Marsh, on the east side of Minnekhada Park, was also once a private hunting preserve of approximately 283 ha. It was purchased in 1977 by the Nature Trust of BC in order to create a wildlife reserve.

DeBoville Slough is south of Minnekhada Park and Addington Marsh and runs east from the mouth of Hyde Creek for 2 km to the Pitt River. From there, the dyke continues northeast along the Pitt River to reach Addington Marsh and Minnekhada Park.

These three areas offer exceptionally varied terrain. Minnekhada Park features coniferous and mixed forests and rocky outcrops, including some steep terrain leading to lookouts. In contrast, Addington Marsh and DeBoville Slough offer easy walking and views along sloughs and the Pitt River. Together, these three areas provide excellent birding opportunities in a relatively small area.

Black-tailed deer and coyotes can be seen anywhere in the area. Black bears are often seen in spring through summer, as they are attracted by adjacent blueberry fields. Give them a wide berth!

# MINNEKHADA REGIONAL PARK — DIRECTIONS

There is no public transit to Minnekhada Park. Parking is available either at Minnekhada Lodge or at Quarry Road. If you want to park at the lodge, check beforehand whether there is a private function, which will make the parking lot off limits. There is no parking along the entrance road, so signs will redirect you to the Quarry Road entrance.

To reach Minnekhada Park from Vancouver, take the Lougheed Highway (Highway 7) east. At the intersection with the Barnet Highway in Coquitlam, turn right (east), staying on Lougheed, and continue for 3.5 km. Turn left (north) onto Coast Meridian Road. Continue for 2.5 km to Apel Drive, turn right and after 0.7 km, turn right onto Victoria Drive.

For the Quarry Road entrance, continue for 1 km and turn left, staying on Victoria Drive. At the junction with Gilley's Trail, Victoria Drive becomes Quarry Road. Continue on Quarry Road for about 600 m and turn right into the Quarry Road parking lot to reach the park trailhead, where maps are available at the kiosk.

For the Minnekhada Lodge entrance, follow the same route, but turn right onto Gilley's Trail and drive 0.5 km to a T-intersection. Turn left onto Oliver Road

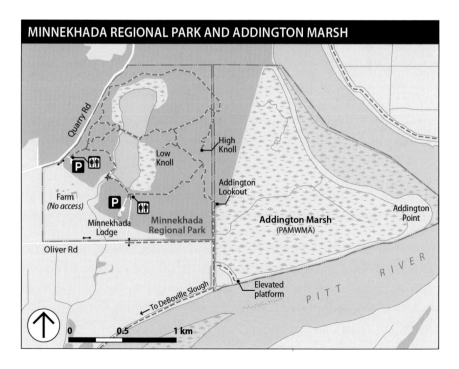

MINNEKHADA REGIONAL PARK AND ADDINGTON MARSH

and continue down this single-lane road for 1.2 km, turning left onto the narrow entrance road to the lodge. Follow that road for about 0.5 km to the parking area behind the lodge. Pit toilets are available at both parking lots, and there are picnic tables near the lodge. A wheelchair-accessible washroom is located inside the lodge when it is open.

Minnekhada Regional Park has superb scenery, pleasant woodland and marsh walks with good maps at the trail junctions, and interesting birding in varied habitat year-round. The bird list for Minnekhada Park stands at 157 species on eBird at the time of writing.

## BIRD SPECIES

The marsh in the centre of the park is a focal point. The fastest way to reach it is by parking at the lodge, where it is only about a 300-m walk to the viewing platform at the south end of the marsh. From the Quarry Road parking lot, follow the maps along the trails. Follow the trail from the parking lot and turn left at the first fork. At the second fork take the right trail, and at the third fork take the left trail. A few metres after the last fork, a rocky outcrop allows you to scan the marsh. Continue down the trail to the dyke (which divides the Upper Marsh from the Lower Marsh) and scan the Upper Marsh from there. At least 19 species of waterfowl have been counted from this point.

Winter is the best time for waterfowl watching: *Ring-necked Ducks* can be seen in large numbers, as well as the *Lesser Scaup, American Wigeon, Green-winged Teal, Common Goldeneye, Common* and *Hooded Merganser* and *Bufflehead. The American Dipper* can also be found around the lake. In spring, look for the *Wood Duck*, and if you're lucky you may see a *Cinnamon* or *Blue-winged Teal. Great Blue Heron* can be found all year and a *Sandhill Crane* is also a good possibility any time of the year. Watch for the occasional beaver and river otter. The Lower Marsh is thickly vegetated with hardhack and holds large numbers of *Marsh Wrens* all year and *Common Yellowthroats* in summer. The *Sora, Virginia Rail, Pied-billed Grebe* and *American Coot* may also be found.

In the forest areas, look for the *Hairy, Downy* and *Pileated Woodpecker; Red-breasted Sapsucker; Steller's Jay; Black-capped* and *Chestnut-backed Chickadee; Red-breasted Nuthatch; Brown Creeper; Golden-crowned Kinglet; Pacific Wren; Spotted Towhee;* and *Varied Thrush.* In some years, you can find the *Evening Grosbeak, Red Crossbill* and *Pine Siskin* year-round. The *Great Horned Owl* inhabits the park and one of the best places to see this species is on the south side, along the Panabode Trail near the marsh, just east of the picnic area. The *Common Raven* is resident and may be seen or heard anywhere in the area. In spring, *Sooty Grouse* can be heard hooting from the surrounding hills.

Check out the Low Knoll (reached from the Dyke Trail). There are splendid views across the Lower Marsh, the Pitt River and beyond. Scan above the marsh for the *Red-tailed Hawk* and other raptors soaring above at any time of year, and look for the *Black* and *Vaux's Swift* and *Common Nighthawk* in the summer months. Summer brings the *Cassin's Vireo, Swainson's Thrush, Western Tanager* and *Hammond's* and *Pacific-slope Flycatcher*. The *Hermit Thrush* nests on the slopes of nearby Burke Mountain and can be found passing through the park on migration. Local warblers include *Orange-crowned, Yellow-rumped, Black-throated Gray, Townsend's* and *Wilson's*.

Deciduous woods, dominated by red alder, form a small part of the park, accessible from the Quarry Road parking lot. The dense understorey of salmonberry provides protected nesting for the *Bewick's Wren, Spotted Towhee* and *Song Sparrow*. Watch for the *Rufous Hummingbird, Western Wood-Pewee, Red-eyed* and *Warbling Vireo, Orange-crowned* and *Black-throated Gray Warbler* and *Black-headed Grosbeak* in summer.

From the Panabode Trail, a side trail leads to the Addington Marsh Lookout—a rocky outcrop with partial views over the marsh (see the marsh section that follows). A short path leads down from the lookout to the north end of the gated service road. Addington Marsh is now on the left; to the right, the woods hold nesting *Red-breasted Sapsucker* and *Hairy Woodpecker*. A few hundred metres farther on, you come to the east end of Oliver Road, which runs west (right). It can offer some very good birding, with hedgerows and thickets along the road hosting a variety of sparrow species, including *Fox, Lincoln's, Golden-crowned* and *White-crowned Sparrows* in fall and winter. In spring and summer, watch for *Willow Flycatchers, Yellow* and *MacGillivray's Warblers* and *Common Yellowthroats*.

Continue west on Oliver Road and take the first right toward Minnekhada Lodge. To get back to the Quarry Road parking lot (a 20-minute walk), go left past the picnic tables, skirting the marsh. When the trail emerges into the open, scan the High Knoll; a *Turkey Vulture* is sometimes observed soaring along the edge.

## ADDINGTON MARSH
## — DIRECTIONS

To get to Addington Marsh, follow the directions for Minnekhada Regional Park (previous section). The marsh can be reached on foot via the park trail

Addington Marsh. Colin Clasen

system, or from the north dyke of DeBoville Slough by walking 1.9 km northeast of its confluence with the Pitt River. Addington Marsh is the western section of the larger Pitt-Addington Marsh Wildlife Management Area, which lies mostly on the east side of the Pitt River in Pitt Meadows (see section 28).

## BIRD SPECIES

Addington Marsh is best viewed from either the Addington Marsh Lookout or the elevated wooden platform on the edge of the Pitt River. If you are coming from Minnekhada Park, turn south along the dyke from Oliver Road. After about 200 m you will see a left turn toward the Pitt River. If you are coming from DeBoville Slough, turn left when you reach the Pitt River and walk 1.9 km northeast, with the Pitt River on your right. The platform is 250 m along a curved trail leading to the edge of the Pitt River from the main dyke. In winter, scan the marsh for *Rough-legged Hawks*, *Bald Eagles* and *Northern Harriers*, and the *Marsh Wren* is hard to miss. A *Northern Pygmy-Owl* can also be found here on occasion. Check the Pitt River for *Pied-billed Grebe*, *Common Merganser* and *Double-crested Cormorant*. In the non-summer months, this area is also good for *Trumpeter Swans*. The area around the blue house often has *Cooper's Hawks* and *American Kestrels* hunting

Start of DeBoville Slough, looking east. Colin Clasen

over the blueberry fields and *Bushtits* in the bushes. In summer, there are also *Cliff Swallows*.

## DEBOVILLE SLOUGH — DIRECTIONS

There are parking lots on either side of the start of the slough, at the intersection of Victoria Drive and Cedar Drive, at the northeast corner of the City of Port Coquitlam. For clarification, the public washrooms and southern parking lot are in the City of Port Coquitlam, but the northern parking lot and DeBoville Slough are in the City of Coquitlam. You can walk along either the north or south dyke. However, a large housing development currently underway along the south dyke makes this walk less than a "wilderness experience," so we recommend the north dyke, which also has the advantage of connecting to Addington Marsh and Minnekhada Park. Although the adjacent blueberry fields are somewhat sterile, the sloughs along this trail still provide excellent birding.

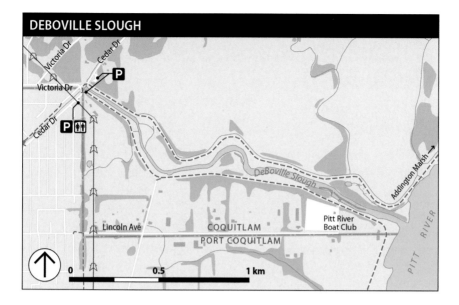

DeBoville Slough proper is 2 km long before it reaches the Pitt River. Another 1.9 km northeast of the confluence of DeBoville Slough and the Pitt River is Addington Marsh, with the blue house at its southern boundary.

## BIRD SPECIES

At the time of writing, 167 species are listed for DeBoville Slough in eBird, which for many people includes species seen at Addington Marsh. A typical visit from DeBoville Slough up to Addington Marsh in winter can yield 40 or more species, and 50 or more species are often seen during spring visits. Specialty species for this area include the *Green Heron*, which nests along DeBoville Slough and adjacent Pitt River to the northeast, as well as *Gray Catbirds*, *Bullock's Orioles* and *Eastern Kingbirds*. All of these species are most commonly seen along the last (east) half of the north side of DeBoville Slough and along the first 500 m of the Pitt River dyke. *Sandhill Crane* is also seen or heard frequently.

Other species to watch for along DeBoville Slough are the *Northern Pygmy-Owl* in winter, as well as the *Mute Swan* at the Pitt River Boat Club (these birds are considered legitimate naturalized breeders). The *Evening Grosbeak* can also be found in some years.

*Written by Christine Hanrahan, 1993. Revised by Larry Cowan, 2001. Updated by John Reynolds, 2015. New DeBoville Slough section written by John Reynolds and reviewed by David Mounteney, Hilary Maguire and David Schutz, 2015.*

# 28. PITT-ADDINGTON MARSH WILDLIFE MANAGEMENT AREA AND VICINITY

## INTRODUCTION

THE PITT-ADDINGTON MARSH WILDLIFE MANAGEMENT AREA IS 40 KM east of Vancouver. It is in a narrow valley, 12 km long, with the larger eastern section being bordered by the Pitt River and the Coast Mountains. The eastern section is comprised of four adjacent individual marshes defined by internal berms: Katzie

**Katzie Marsh and north viewing tower.** Colin Clasen

Marsh, Pitt Marsh, Homilk'um Marsh and Crane Ponds Marsh. Also officially part of the Pitt-Addington Marsh Wildlife Management Area, but on the west side of the Pitt River, is Addington Marsh, which is covered in Section 27.

Pitt Lake at the northern end is 26 km long and drains an area as far north as Mount Garibaldi in Garibaldi Park. Pitt Lake is the second-largest freshwater tidal lake in the world.

The Pitt River was named by James McMillan in 1827, possibly honouring William Pitt (the Elder), Earl of Chatham and twice Prime Minister of England. In the early 1870s, the first white settlers in the area dyked portions of the Alouette and Pitt rivers, and the disastrous flooding of 1894 was followed by a more complete dyking program.

The valley north of Sturgeon Slough was marshland until the early 1950s, when the Dutch, under the guidance of Dr. Blom, began a program of dyking and ditching to claim the 2,900 ha we now know as Pitt Polder. This had been attempted previously in 1911 and again in the 1920s, when a Mennonite settlement there was flooded and abandoned.

From the Lougheed Highway (Highway 7) north past Sturgeon Slough, much of the land is used for the production of blueberries, raspberries, cranberries and commercial horticultural enterprises. Some dairy farming still persists. Once past the hydro power line, however, the ground becomes wetter and the marsh

# PITT-ADDINGTON MARSH WILDLIFE MANAGEMENT AREA AND VICINITY

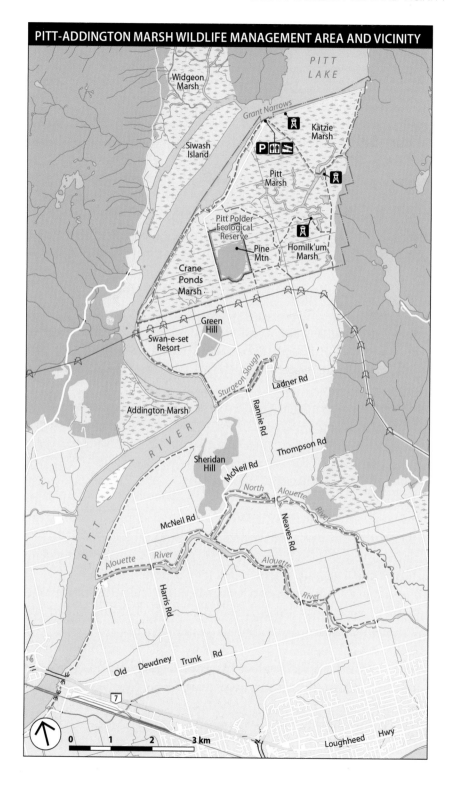

PITT LAKE

Widgeon Marsh

Grant Narrows

Katzie Marsh

Siwash Island

Pitt Marsh

Pitt Polder Ecological Reserve

Pine Mtn

Homilk'um Marsh

Crane Ponds Marsh

Green Hill

Swan-e-set Resort

Ladner Rd

Sturgeon Slough

Addington Marsh

Rannie Rd

Thompson Rd

Sheridan Hill

McNeil Rd

North Alouette River

McNeil Rd

Neaves Rd

PITT RIVER

Alouette River

Alouette River

Harris Rd

Old Dewdney Trunk Rd

7

N

0    1    2    3 km

Loughheed Hwy

predominates, with hardhack, cattail and sedge. There are a few thickets of willow and alder providing good cover for birds, but in the late 1990s a lot of this cover was lost as land was converted to the production of cranberries and blueberries.

There are three hills on the flood plain. Menzies Mountain, now called Sheridan Hill on most maps, is the highest, at 100 m. It lies along the edge of the Pitt River between the North Alouette River and Sturgeon Slough. Green Hill is 2 km to the north and Pine Mountain 1 km farther north again, east of Rannie Road. All three hills are well treed. Sheridan and Green have Douglas-fir, western red cedar, vine maple, alder, willow and birch. Pine Mountain was burned over twice by the Dutch in the early 1950s and has a narrow band of lodgepole and white pine as well as other species. Sheridan Hill is private land that is dotted with homes and contains the Pitt River Quarry. Green Hill is in the centre of the Swaneset Bay Resort and Country Club and Pine Mountain in the Pitt Polder Ecological Reserve.

## DIRECTIONS

There is no public transit to the Pitt-Addington Marsh Wildlife Management Area. To reach it by car, take Highway 1 (Trans-Canada Highway) east to Exit #44 (Highway 7/7B) and follow the signs for Highway 7B East, Maple Ridge. **Caution:** *pay very close attention to signage.* This exit leads onto the Mary Hill Bypass. (The Fraser River will now be on your right.) The bypass ends in about 7 km at the junction with Highway 7. Follow the sign for Highway 7 East Pitt Meadows/Maple Ridge/ Mission. Once on the Pitt River Bridge, move into the left-hand lane. On crossing the bridge, turn left at the first traffic lights onto Dewdney Trunk Road. This is the southern edge of the area described.

A second route is to take the Lougheed Highway (Highway 7) through Burnaby and Port Coquitlam to the Pitt River Bridge. A third alternative is to take East Hastings Street in Vancouver through Burnaby to the Barnet Highway, which runs east along the edge of Burrard Inlet to Port Moody. Here you once again join the Lougheed Highway and continue to the Pitt River Bridge.

There are no gas stations or stores in the valley. There are portable toilets adjacent to the Grant Narrows parking area at the north end of Rannie Road. The Swaneset Bay Resort and Country Club on Rannie Road has a coffee shop, and birders are welcome. Another coffee shop is at the Golden Eagle Golf Club at the east end of Ladner Road, just south of Sturgeon Slough. For gas and provisions, return to the Lougheed Highway and the communities of Pitt Meadows and Maple Ridge.

# BIRD SPECIES

Travel east on Dewdney Trunk Road to a T-intersection with Harris Road and turn left (north). Continue on Harris Road and cross the Alouette River in 2.4 km. (Look for waterfowl here in the winter months.) After another 0.7 km, turn right onto McNeil Road. The area you are heading for starts to open up to your left, ringed on its eastern side by the mountains of Golden Ears Provincial Park (Alouette, Blanshard, Judge Howay and Robbie Reid). The low, rounded peaks to the west of Pitt Lake are unnamed on most maps. Behind and to the left are Widgeon Peak, Coquitlam Mountain and, farther back, Peneplain and Obelisk mountains.

McNeil Road skirts the base of Sheridan Hill, while the dyke on your right encloses the North Alouette River. The mixed woodland at the base of the hill is home to a rich assortment of birds in most seasons. In summer *Rufous Hummingbird, Pacific-slope* and *Willow Flycatcher, Red-eyed* and *Warbling Vireo, Cedar Waxwing, Swainson's Thrush* and *Orange-crowned, Wilson's* and *Yellow Warbler* may be sighted.

This area supports the Lower Mainland's largest concentration of *Osprey,* which nests on the many wooden pilings lining the Pitt River immediately to the west. In 3.8 km, McNeil Road

This area is one of the most reliable locations for American Redstart in the Metro Vancouver area.

Mark Habdas

meets Neaves/Rannie Road, the main north–south artery in the area. The name changes at McNeil Road, with Neaves Road leading off to the south on your right and Rannie Road to the north on your left. Furthermore, McNeil Road changes names to Thompson Road on the east side of Neaves/Rannie Road. The fields along Neaves/Rannie Road are good for raptors during the winter months and in migration, including *Red-tailed* and *Rough-legged Hawk, Bald* and (rarely) *Golden Eagle, Cooper's* and *Sharp-shinned Hawk, Northern Harrier, Peregrine Falcon* and *Northern Shrike.* The hedgerows should be checked for *White-crowned, Golden-crowned, Song* and *Fox Sparrows,* flocks of *Bushtits* and *Western Meadowlarks.* In summer months this is a good area to look for *American Kestrels.*

A short side trip can be taken here by crossing over Neaves/Rannie Road and travelling along Thompson Road (posted "No Through Road"), which ends at a

The Gray Catbird is commonly found in this area. Colin Clasen

gated gravel road in 1.4 km. Check the weedy roadside and trees for sparrows and *Wilson's Snipe* in the winter months. The slough attracts **Belted Kingfishers** in all seasons. The end of the road can have a good variety of passerines in migration. Listen for warblers, vireos and thrushes in spring and summer months. The **Brewer's Blackbird** is common near dwellings.

Retrace your route to Neaves/Rannie Road, turn right, and head north toward the mountains. After 1.8 km the road crosses Sturgeon Slough. Park on the right immediately after the slough and walk the gravel road on the north side for 0.8 km, heading west to the junction with the Pitt River dyke. The brush at the western end of Sturgeon Slough occasionally has a **Green Heron** in it, and the pilings will often be occupied by an **Osprey** or **Double-crested Cormorant**. Also here are **Gray Catbird** and **Bullock's Oriole**, along with an occasional **Lincoln's Sparrow**. A **Willow Flycatcher** can sometimes be seen in the alders, while in winter the slough holds **Common Goldeneyes**, **Buffleheads** and a **Belted Kingfisher** or two.

After passing Sturgeon Slough, you approach Green Hill and soon, on your left, the imposing entrance to the Swaneset Bay Resort and Country Club. Birders have permission to bird Green Hill, and as mentioned earlier, you can take advantage of the resort's amenities, including the coffee shop and toilets in the main clubhouse at the end of the 1.5 km entrance drive.

*Note: The resort management has asked that birders sign a register at the front desk and also report their sightings. Their intention is to produce a checklist, and your sightings will help in its accuracy. We are greatly appreciative of the resort's cooperation in allowing us access to a valuable piece of treed habitat, since there is not a lot of it left in Pitt Meadows.*

Continuing north along Rannie Road; after 1 km a twin hydro line crosses the valley. About 300 m north of the power line, gravel roads lead off to both the left (west) and right (east). Both sides are gated and usually locked. **Do not drive these roads if the gates are open, as you may get locked in.** You can park by the roadside and walk in. In 2.1 km, the western road leads to the Pitt River dyke. The walk is a pleasant one, but there is unlikely to be anything along this trail that cannot be found elsewhere in the Pitt-Addington Marsh Wildlife Management Area. The eastern road parallels a dyke; in 1.7 km a gate leads onto dyke trails going off to the north and northwest. Check out the various sloughs beyond the gate. In summer both the *Eastern* and *Western Kingbird* can be found. In Homilk'um Marsh to the northeast you may see the *Sandhill Crane*, *Pied-billed Grebe*, *Cinnamon* and *Blue-winged Teal* and *Black* and *Vaux's Swift*. These last two species nest on the steep cliffs of the UBC Research Forest that forms the eastern edge of the valley. Check the power pylons for raptors.

Farther north, Rannie Road runs through a band of dark coniferous trees on both sides of the road. To the east (right) is the Pitt Polder Ecological Reserve on the slopes of Pine Mountain (a small hill). On a walk along this portion of Rannie Road, you might see or hear the *Black-headed Grosbeak*; *Willow* and *Pacific-slope Flycatcher*; *Orange-crowned*, *Wilson's* and *Yellow Warbler*; *Cedar Waxwing*; *Black-capped* and *Chestnut-backed Chickadee*; *Red-breasted Nuthatch*; and *Brown Creeper*. The *Chipping Sparrow* has nested here.

In another 1.5 km, Rannie Road meets the Pitt River dyke and curves to the right. About 200 m after this curve, on the left, is a small slough that birders call Catbird Slough, and for good reason. From here to the stand of tall cottonwood trees 1.2 km farther along, the dyke and roadside habitat to the west should be carefully checked in summer for *Gray Catbirds*. Not common anywhere else in the Vancouver area, this is the most reliable spot in the Lower Mainland to find this bird. It sings in the early morning and sometimes later, on overcast days. This is also a good spot for the *Eastern Kingbird* and *Bullock's Oriole*. This stand of cottonwoods also holds the *Western Tanager*, *Downy Woodpecker*, *Tree* and *Violet-green Swallow*, *Red-breasted Nuthatch* and *Black-headed Grosbeak* in summer months. Check the open fields on the eastern side for *Sandhill Crane* and *Osprey*. In winter months, the *Northern Harrier* and *Short-eared Owl* are also attracted to this area.

After another 2 km, Rannie Road ends at Pitt Lake and Grant Narrows, where there is a boat launch, paved parking for cars (free day parking), canoe rental and portable toilets. This is a busy area on weekends, so be careful to lock your car securely and hide valuables. A system of trails and dykes leads off from here, making this the most productive birding spot in the entire Pitt Meadows area. Late spring and summer bring in a number of species that are rarely found elsewhere in the Lower Mainland. There is a dyke walk around the triangular Katzie Marsh (about a 6 km loop), and two observation towers give views out over the marsh, which is productive in any season.

The most productive of the three sides of the marsh is a path signed "Nature Dyke Trail," which begins between the caretaker's house and the canoe rental stand. This section of the trail is overgrown with small trees, shrubs, salmonberry and blackberry vines and is a very productive area for passerines. It is a 1.8 km walk to the south viewing tower. All of the woodland species previously mentioned can be found along this section of the trail. Look for the *Black-throated Gray*, *Townsend's*, *Yellow* and *Orange-crowned Warbler*; *Red-breasted Sapsucker*; *Hairy Woodpecker*; *Bullock's Oriole*; and *Marsh* and *Bewick's Wren*. An *American Redstart* is a good possibility. Few spring migrations pass that a rarity isn't found along this trail. There have been *Least Flycatchers*, *Nashville Warblers*, *Black-throated Sparrows* and many more over the years. Near the south tower, the shrubbery gives way to grass and an open dyke trail. Listen and look for the *Wilson's Snipe* winnowing over the marsh. The many nest boxes are used by *Wood Ducks* and *Hooded Mergansers*.

In the winter months, the other two arms of the triangle, Pitt Lake dyke and Swan dyke, yield a wide assortment of waterfowl: *American* and *Eurasian Wigeon*, *Northern Pintail*, *Gadwall*, *Green-winged Teal*, scaup, goldeneyes, *Western* and *Horned Grebe* and *Common* and *Hooded Merganser*. There is usually a contingent of swans here—look for *Trumpeter*, *Tundra* and *Mute*. During hard winters farther north, *Snow Bunting* and *Common Redpoll* have been reported. During spring migration, look for *Townsend's Solitaire* and *Mountain Bluebird*. The entire loop of the Katzie Marsh perimeter will take 2 to 2.5 hours—longer if the birding is good—and will usually produce something out of the ordinary.

In addition to the Nature Dyke Trail, the dyke on the east side of the Pitt River between Catbird Slough and Grant Narrows has been reliable the past few years for an *American Redstart* in the spring. They are very few in number and challenging to see in the tall cottonwood trees, but following their song will often reward you with a sighting.

Both the Pitt River and Pitt Lake are frequented by a small gull assortment, mostly in the winter months. Look for *Glaucous-winged*, *Mew*, *Ring-billed* and *Thayer's Gulls*. In warmer months, you may find a wandering *Bonaparte's Gull*, *Caspian Tern* or *Common Tern*, mainly in migration.

There are over 50 km of readily accessible dykes in the Pitt-Addington Marsh

A male Common Yellowthroat with its very distinctive colouration. Peter Candido

Wildlife Management Area. They can all be walked or cycled, and we urge you to get a map and explore them. A map from the Pitt Meadows/Maple Ridge municipal website shows all biking, hiking and dyke trails in the Pitt Meadows/Maple Ridge area (mrpmparksandleisure.ca/DocumentCenter/View/9). There is also a north viewing tower on the main dyke, near the northwest corner of the Katzie Marsh.

Outside of (but immediately adjacent to) this area, the farmlands south of Highway 7 provide potential habitat for bluebirds in migration. There are cultivated fields, still with real hedgerows around them, and on the river side of the dykes, huge stands of cottonwood and alder with brushy thickets at their base.

Another walk, which is 5 km one-way, goes from the Harris Road Bridge over the Alouette River, west down the Alouette to the Pitt River, then northeast to Sheridan Hill. Plan to walk back along Harris Road, birding as you go. On a bicycle, this route takes about 1 hour. The area north of Dewdney Trunk between Neaves Road and Hale Road, north to the Alouette River, is mostly pasture and open fields and is your best chance for *Gyrfalcon* in winter. Finally, you can rent a canoe at Grant Narrows, where Pitt Lake empties into the river, and explore Widgeon Marsh on the other side of the river. This is a wilderness park with water access only. By all reports, the birding can be good there.

*Written by Brian Self. Revised by Larry Cowan, 2015.*

# 29. COLONY FARM REGIONAL PARK

## INTRODUCTION

COLONY FARM REGIONAL PARK CONSISTS OF 262 HA STRADDLING THE lower end of the Coquitlam River, near its confluence with the Fraser River. It is composed of two sections: the Wilson Farm on the east side of the Coquitlam River (in Port Coquitlam) and the Home Farm on the west side of the Coquitlam River (in Coquitlam). Colony Farm got its start in 1904, when it produced food for a new mental health facility called Riverview Hospital. It was a working farm until 1983. Through the concerted efforts of local naturalists and concerned citizens, it was designated a Regional Park in 1995.

Although the entire park is important to wildlife, only some fields (mainly on the Port Coquitlam side) are designated in the Park Management Plan for wildlife habitat (111 ha). The rest of the fields are designated for either agricultural use (75 ha) or integrated management, which is intended to be a blend of wildlife use and compatible agriculture (46 ha).

The park contains a wide range of habitats that support both resident and migratory birds. Its old-field habitat is of particular interest, as it represents one of the largest protected areas of its kind west of the Pitt River.

The arched footbridge across the Coquitlam River joins the east and west sides of Colony Farm Regional Park. Colin Clasen

Indeed, this habitat is disappearing rapidly east of the Pitt River too, due to conversion to blueberry and cranberry farms. Other habitat types in, or bordering on, the park are riparian, deciduous woods, mixed deciduous and coniferous woods and several small marshes. The adjacent Fraser River and the Coquitlam Wildlife Management Area are also home to many bird species. Colony Farm provides a link in a wildlife corridor that stretches from the mountains in the north to Surrey Bend Regional Park on the south shore of the Fraser River.

Birders can see 50 to 60 species during a spring visit or 20 to 30 species in winter. Specialties include a small breeding population of *Lazuli Bunting*, which is rare elsewhere in the Vancouver area, as well as the *Mountain Bluebird*, which

# COLONY FARM REGIONAL PARK

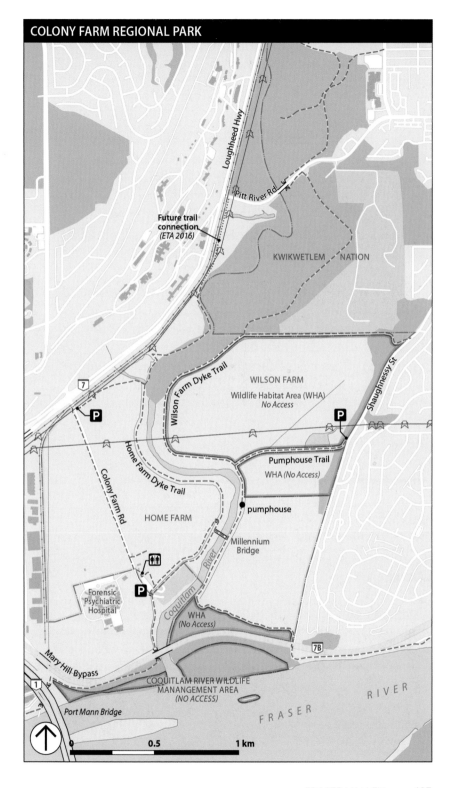

Loughheed Hwy

Pitt River Rd

**Future trail connection** *(ETA 2016)*

KWIKWETLEM NATION

WILSON FARM
Wildlife Habitat Area (WHA)
*No Access*

Wilson Farm Dyke Trail

Shaughnessy St

7

P

P

Pumphouse Trail
WHA *(No Access)*

Home Farm Dyke Trail

Colony Farm Rd

HOME FARM

pumphouse

Millennium
Bridge

P

Coquitlam River

Forensic
Psychiatric
Hospital

WHA
*(No Access)*

Mary Hill Bypass

7B

1

COQUITLAM RIVER WILDLIFE
MANANGEMENT AREA
*(NO ACCESS)*

Port Mann Bridge

FRASER      RIVER

0        0.5        1 km

usually stops in during spring migration. The **Virginia Rail** and **Sora** can be found at the pond on the Pumphouse Trail at any time of the year. A checklist with seasonal bar charts was produced by the Burke Mountain Naturalists in 2015 and is available on their website at (bmn.bc.ca/assets/bmn/doc/CFPbirds.2015.pdf).

## DIRECTIONS

The west section of the park (Home Farm) is best reached from the south end of Colony Farm Road, which runs south from the Lougheed Highway (Highway 7). Go almost to the end of the road to the parking lot on your left, at the community gardens.

The east section (Wilson Farm) is best reached from Shaughnessy Street, approximately 1.2 km north of the Mary Hill Bypass (Highway 7B). There are two small paved parking areas, one on each side of the road.

If you are using Highway 1 (Trans-Canada Highway) to get here, either from the west or east, take Exit #44 and follow the signs for either Highway 7 East/ Lougheed Highway to get to the Home Farm side or Highway 7B East/Mary Hill Bypass to get to the Wilson Farm side, as noted above.

A footbridge crossing the Coquitlam River allows access to both sides of the park, regardless of your starting point, allowing you to cover the entire park from either entrance. The flat trails are also ideal for cycling or wheelchairs.

## BIRD SPECIES

### Home Farm (West Section)

On the drive along Colony Farm Road, watch for the **Mountain Bluebird** in March/April and for **Lazuli Bunting** in spring and summer. In winter, watch the fields for **Northern Shrikes** and **American Kestrels**. A kiosk at the parking lot by the community gardens has a map of the area. There are also washrooms and a drinking fountain.

From the parking lot, you can take a short walk south along the gated extension of the road that you drove in on, to reach the confluence of the Coquitlam and Fraser Rivers. Check the large stand of cottonwood trees here for nesting **Bullock's Orioles** in spring and summer. This is also a good area for **Black-headed Grosbeak**, and watch for **Osprey** too. During the non-breeding season, **Common Loons** and other water birds can be found near the mouth of the Coquitlam River.

Retrace your steps and walk north along Colony Farm Road past the Forensic Institute. There are more fields to explore on the left. In spring and summer, this area has the most reliable population of **Lazuli Bunting** in the Vancouver area.

Walk west along the gated gravel road (marked 200 Colony Farm Road) on the north side of the Forensic Institute. As the road peters out near some park works buildings, scan the fields ahead (west) and listen for the birds. If you haven't found them, you may need to bushwhack through the field toward the line of cottonwoods along the west perimeter of the park. At the time of writing, there are plans for a trail along the west side of the park, so this connection may make this area more accessible.

Back at the parking lot, you can follow the trail that leads along the southeast side of the community gardens to a small bridge over the slough on your right. When you walk up the stairs to the dyke, you'll be on the Home Farm Dyke Trail and will see a much larger rust-coloured bridge on your right. This is the only bridge that crosses the Coquitlam River, connecting the east and west sections together. Cross that bridge and you are now on the Wilson Farm (East Section). Turn left on the Wilson Farm Dyke Trail, continue to the T-intersection, turn right on the Pumphouse Trail and continue to the pond.

## Wilson Farm (East Section)

The other way to reach the pond is from the small parking area on the side of Shaughnessy Street. This is the east end of the Pumphouse Trail. You will pass a kiosk with a map of the

Top: **Virginia Rail.** Michelle Lamberson

Bottom: **Sora.** Liron Gertsman

park and then go down through a small deciduous forest to the pond. This pond was established in the fall of 1998 and is the focal point of the park for most birders. Most of the common duck species in the Vancouver area have been seen here, with the most common species including *Gadwall*, *American Wigeon* and *Mallard*. Outside of the breeding season, you can often find a few *Ring-necked Ducks*. The *Pied-billed Grebe* nests here and is present year-round. *Sora* and *Virginia Rail* also nest here, and if you are lucky, you might see one at any time of year from the bench beside the pond. The *American Bittern* has been seen and heard, though it is less common now. *Tree*, *Violet-green*, *Northern Rough-winged*, *Barn* and *Cliff Swallows* may be seen in spring and summer in the vicinity of the marsh, as well as lots of *Common Yellowthroats*.

As you continue past the pond (which will be on your right), watch for the many species of sparrows that are typically found here. *Song* and *White-crowned Sparrows* are present all year in varying numbers, while other sparrows are seasonal: *Fox* and *Golden-crowned* are present in winter, *Lincoln's* in spring and fall, and *Savannah* is a common summer visitor. Occasionally, during migration, *American Tree Sparrows* and *White-throated Sparrows* have also been found here. As the elderberries ripen, they often attract large flocks of *Band-tailed Pigeons* and good numbers of *Black-headed Grosbeaks*. Both *Vaux's* and *Black Swifts* are sometimes seen high over the fields in summer, especially on cloudy days. The *Ring-necked Pheasant* is often seen and heard in the fields on either side of the trail, and watch for *Red-tailed Hawks* hunting for Townsend's voles. The *Great Blue Heron* also stalks voles in the fields, while coyotes are often seen stalking both the voles and the pheasants.

As you continue west on the Pumphouse Trail toward a T-intersection with the Wilson Farm Dyke Trail, check the sloughs for *Wood Ducks* and *Hooded Mergansers* at any time of year, as well as *Cinnamon Teal* in spring. The *Belted Kingfisher* can be found here, and if you are lucky, you might see a *Green Heron* in summer. River otters are sometimes seen here and elsewhere too. At the T-junction, you will see the Coquitlam River, where you should watch for *Buffleheads*, *Common Goldeneyes* and *Common Mergansers* in winter.

Now you have a choice. At the T-junction, you can take the left (south) turn on the Wilson Farm Dyke Trail to reach the bridge that spans the Coquitlam River, as described above. You can go over this bridge and then turn right on the Home Farm Dyke Trail for about 50 m to another small bridge over the ditch on your left. If you take that route and turn left after the small bridge, you will arrive at the parking lot by the community gardens at the end of Colony Farm Road.

Alternatively, at the T-intersection you can turn right (north) and continue along the Wilson Farm Dyke Trail, with the Coquitlam River on your left and fields on your right. Check these fields for migrating *Mountain Bluebirds* and *Western Meadowlarks* in April. In summer, this can be a good place to watch for the *Mourning Dove* as well as the *Eastern Kingbird* and some of the many *Rufous Hummingbirds* zinging through the air. *Anna's Hummingbird* can also be found here. The trail will curve to the right as it approaches the park's largest area of forest on the left. In spring, as you approach the forest, watch for *Yellow-rumped*, *Orange-crowned*, *Wilson's*, *Yellow* and *Black-throated Gray Warblers*. This is also a good place for the *Downy* and *Hairy Woodpecker*, as well as the *Warbling Vireo*. A *Red-eyed Vireo* can sometimes be found here too. Additional forest species include the *Bewick's* and *Pacific Wren*, *Golden-crowned Kinglet* and *Brown Creeper*.

In spring and summer, the *Western Wood-Pewee* and *Willow Flycatcher* are common here too.

Several pairs of Eastern Kingbirds breed annually at Colony Farm. Colin Clasen

The trail leads to a junction, where the branch to the right goes past a large housing development that is under way. You can take a short walk along this branch to the end of the trail at a small forest beside Shaughnessy Street. Otherwise, bear left past the chain-link gate on either side of the trail. Technically, you will now be out of the park, but at the time of writing, there are still nice forests along the start of this trail, though there has been recent clearing of the forest to the right, opposite the backwaters of the Coquitlam River. This wetland is a good place to see *Wood Ducks*, *Green-winged Teal* and beavers. This is also a good place to watch for *Merlins*, *Varied Thrushes* and *Pileated Woodpeckers*. If you continue to the end of this trail, you will end up at Pitt River Road.

Retrace your steps and find the birds you missed on the way out. In fall and winter, look for a *Northern Shrike* perched on top of the elderberries in the fields, and if you are lucky, you might see one of the resident *Barn Owls* putting in a rare daylight appearance. The *Short-eared Owl* used to be seen quartering over the fields, though it is rare.

*Written by Larry Cowan, 2001. Updated by John Reynolds, 2015. Reviewed by Larry Cowan, Hilary Maguire, Monica Nugent and Elaine Golds, 2015.*

# 30. BRYDON LAGOON

## INTRODUCTION

BRYDON LAGOON BEGAN AS A SEWAGE SETTLING POND IN 1963 IN THE City of Langley and was used until 1975. After Langley joined the Greater Vancouver Regional District sewage system, the Langley Field Naturalists began to take an interest in the lagoon as an area with high wildlife value. They petitioned the City of Langley to designate the area as a Nature Park, which occurred in 1985. The Langley Field Naturalists, using a grant from the Public Conservation Assistance Fund, began their work of enhancing the habitat and building a nature trail around the lagoon. Brydon Lagoon and the surrounding floodplain is an excellent birding location at all times of the year.

The aerated Brydon Lagoon hosts a good variety of waterfowl. Colin Clasen

## DIRECTIONS

Driving east on Highway 1 from Vancouver, take the 200th Street exit (#58), head south on 200th Street for about 7 km and turn right (west) onto 53rd Avenue. There is a small parking area a couple of blocks on the left, as well as street parking.

## BIRD SPECIES

Immediately adjacent to the parking area is a natural marshy area officially known as Brydon Pond. A scope is useful at this location given that it is not accessible except from the main trail. The best viewing location is from the two elevated green metal platforms between the marsh and the parking lot. In the winter, large flocks of **Long-billed Dowitchers** and **Green-winged Teal** are common. **Virginia Rails** can occasionally be heard from this location as well. Migration brings a variety of shorebirds, waterfowl and gulls. The water level here can fluctuate quickly, with far fewer birds found when the water level is high.

While walking west on the main trail toward Brydon Lagoon, a number of

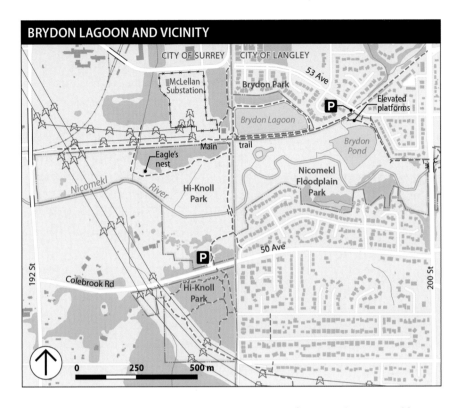

**BRYDON LAGOON AND VICINITY**

species may be seen in the floodplain to the south (left) along the Nicomekl River. A *Red-tailed Hawk* is common, and other raptors, including the *Bald Eagle*, *Cooper's* and *Sharp-shinned Hawk* and *Northern Harrier* may be seen. Spring and fall may bring the *Lincoln's* and *White-crowned Sparrow* along the trail. *Marsh Wrens* and *Common Yellowthroats* are easily heard in the summer months. Four species of swallow are common over the floodplain and lagoon—*Barn*, *Violet-green*, *Tree* and *Northern Rough-winged*.

From fall through spring, Brydon Lagoon is very productive for waterfowl. A number of species are commonly found here, including the *Mallard*, *Northern Shoveler*, *Canvasback*, *Scaup*, *Common Goldeneye*, *Ring-necked Duck*, *Bufflehead*, *Common* and *Hooded Merganser*, *Gadwall*, *American Wigeon* and occasionally *Ruddy Duck*. The *Cormorant* is found here in good numbers in the winter. The *Pied-billed Grebe* is regularly found throughout the year. Occasionally, a *Green Heron* may be found. The *Golden-crowned Sparrow* is easily found near the mallard feeding area at the entrance to the lagoon. The *Belted Kingfisher* is often seen fishing on the west edge of the lagoon. A variety of songbirds can be found in the trees surrounding the lagoon.

At the western edge of Brydon Lagoon, a trail runs north–south along a wooded area. This trail is the north–south municipal boundary between the City of

Langley and the City of Surrey. It is great during migration for warblers, *Black-headed Grosbeaks* and *Western Tanagers*. The *Brown Creeper* is found all year, and kinglets are easily found (*Golden-crowned Kinglet* in the winter and *Ruby-crowned Kinglet* in spring and fall). Both *Black-capped* and *Chestnut-backed Chickadees* are often found here. Occasionally, a *Barred Owl* or *Pileated Woodpecker* may be found in these woods.

If continuing west along the main trail, south of the McLellan Substation (you will now be in the City of Surrey), watch for the *Spotted Towhee*, *Savannah Sparrow*

Male Hooded Merganser, with its white head–patch similar to that of Bufflehead. Peter Candido

and *Rufous Hummingbird* in the summer. Flycatchers, including *Western Wood-Pewee*, *Pacific-slope* and *Willow Flycatchers*, are generally easily seen in the summer.

Once you cross McLellan Creek, the main trail branches off north and south. The trail north leads into another wooded area and follows the creek. In mid-November, salmon can be seen swimming up the creek. Listen for the *Pacific-slope Flycatcher* in the summer. The *Pacific Wren* and *Ruby-crowned Kinglet* may be heard singing in the spring, and the *Golden-crowned Kinglet* and *Brown Creeper* are commonly seen in the winter.

By following the trail south along McLellan Creek, you enter Hi-Knoll Park. After about 100 m, where the trail bends eastward (left), you get closer to the Nicomekl River. This location will occasionally provide some interesting species, such as the *Wood Duck*. *Savannah* and *Song Sparrows*, *Marsh Wrens* and *Common Yellowthroats* are easily heard in the summer. A *Belted Kingfisher* is often seen and heard from this location as well. An active *Bald Eagle* nest is seen at the corner where the trail turns east.

Walking east, the wooded area along the north side of this trail often has *Brown Creeper*, kinglets and *Varied Thrush* in the winter, *Pacific Wren* in the spring and *Bewick's Wren* year-round.

At the east end of this trail, there is an option to turn south and cross the Nicomekl River. If you continue south along this trail, you can cross Colebrook Road to the entrance to the southern part of Hi-Knoll Park. This part of the park has some excellent trails to explore and provides a variety of woodland bird species.

*Written by Randy Walker, 2014. Reviewed by Annabel Griffiths, 2015. Introduction ©2013 BC Nature, used with permission.*

# 31. CAMPBELL VALLEY REGIONAL PARK

## INTRODUCTION

CAMPBELL VALLEY REGIONAL PARK IS 50 KM SOUTHEAST OF VANCOUVER in the Hazelmere District of south Langley. The 545 ha park is in a narrow valley approximately 2.5 km long, with the Little Campbell River meandering through its length. In the mid-1800s, the Hudson's Bay Company farmed and trapped in Campbell Valley. Pioneers moved into the area in the late 1800s, using the land for cattle and for hay production. In 1886 Alexander Annand homesteaded in what is now the south part of Campbell Valley Regional Park. After two changes of ownership, the property was acquired from Len Rowlatt in 1973 and opened as a Greater Vancouver Regional District park in 1979. The Annand/Rowlatt Farmstead is preserved as a heritage site and visitors are welcome, but they are asked to respect the privacy of the caretakers living in the farmhouse. There is a Nature House at the 8th Avenue park entrance area, which is open on weekends from May through the end of August, 1 to 4 p.m. The wildlife garden and pond at the Nature House can be good for migrant and nesting birds, especially hummingbirds feeding on flowers.

One of many convenient boardwalks and viewing decks at Campbell Valley Regional Park. Bill Kinkaid

The area around Campbell Valley consists of farmland and a number of old gravel pits. The valley floor is 300 to 700 m wide, and the steep sides are 30 m high. The east and west slopes of the valley are covered with deciduous and coniferous trees. Maple, western hemlock, Douglas-fir, western red cedar and red alder are the dominant species. On the floor of the valley, where it is damp and marshy, willow, black cottonwood, Pacific crab apple and hardhack take over. Interspersed with the trees are shrubs, such as saskatoon berry, ocean spray, false azalea, salal and hazelnut. In spring and summer, the valley is full of the flowers of salmonberry, wild rose, thimbleberry and blackberry. Wildflowers abound, and the moist, boggy areas are full of mosses and ferns.

The Little Campbell River meanders sluggishly through the flood plain, where reeds, cattails, skunk cabbage, monkey flowers, water lilies and many other water-loving plants grow. The lower part of the river supports fish such as trout and salmon. The Semiahmoo hatchery aids in the stocking of the river.

Equestrians are very active in the park, which includes the Campbell Downs Equestrian Centre and extensive riding trails. While horses are not permitted on walking trails, hikers are allowed on horse trails. When walking on horse trails, please be alert, yield to horses and be courteous to approaching horses and riders, especially on curves and in dense woods. Horses can be spooked easily.

There are 174 bird species listed for Campbell Valley Regional Park, including such extreme rarities as the *Great Gray Owl* and *Yellow-breasted Chat*. There have also been sightings of some relatively uncommon species, such as the *Lazuli Bunting*, *American Redstart*, *Northern Goshawk* and *Calliope Hummingbird*. Nine species of owls have been seen at one time or another, including the *Western Screech*, *Long-eared*, *Northern Saw-whet*, *Great Horned*, *Barred*, *Northern Pygmy* and *Barn*. All but the *Western Screech-Owl*, *Long-eared Owl* and *Northern Pygmy-Owl* are known to nest in the park. The *Barn Owl* is often seen at night, flying across 8th, 4th or 16th Avenues.

Take time to explore this beautiful park in all seasons; you never know what you might find!

## DIRECTIONS

To reach Campbell Valley Regional Park from Vancouver, take Highway 99 and exit east on 16th Avenue. Continue for 8 km to reach the North Valley entrance located at the bottom of the hill on the right, just past 200th Street. Driving on Highway 1 from the North Vancouver area or eastern Fraser Valley localities, take Exit #53, then take Highway 15 (176th Street) south to 16th Avenue and turn left (east). Continue about 6 km to the North Valley entrance just past 200th Street.

For the South Valley entrance, travel south on 200th Street and turn left (east) on 8th Avenue. Alternatively, from Highway 99 South, take the 8th Avenue East exit (#2A) and drive 7.5 km along 8th Avenue to the South Valley entrance. Watch for the Metro Vancouver Parks signs on both 16th and 8th Avenues. Wear suitable footgear in fall, winter and spring. Some trails, especially horse trails, can become quite muddy in wet weather. Unfortunately, vehicle break-ins are very common in the 16th and 8th Avenue parking lots, so do not leave any valuables in your vehicle.

By bicycle from the west, take 8th Avenue from Surrey, which is scenic and less busy than 16th Avenue. We would not recommend 16th Avenue as a safe bike route. You can ride from Surrey along 8th Avenue east, but just be aware that it is

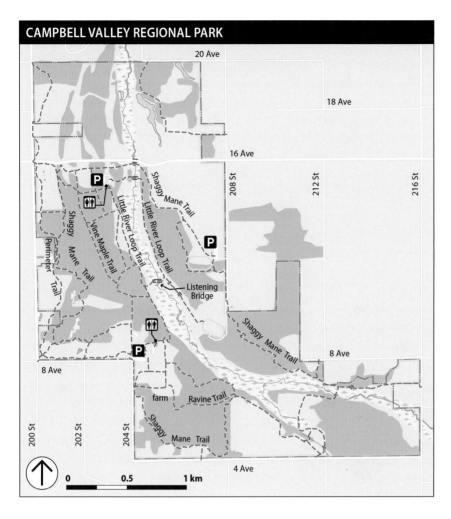

**CAMPBELL VALLEY REGIONAL PARK**

20 Ave

18 Ave

16 Ave

Shaggy Mane Trail

Little River Loop Trail

Little River Loop Trail

Shaggy Mane Trail

Vine Maple Trail

Perimeter Trail

Listening Bridge

Shaggy Mane Trail

8 Ave

8 Ave

farm    Ravine Trail

Shaggy Mane Trail

208 St    212 St    216 St

200 St    202 St    204 St

4 Ave

0        0.5        1 km

a busy road (with wide shoulders) until you get to 176th Street. There it becomes a rural two-lane road with a steep hill just before 200th Street. Alternatively, to approach by bike from northern Langley, travel south on 200th Street and at 40th Avenue there is a bike path that begins on the east side of 200th which will take you all the way to Campbell Valley Park. The bike entrance is about 500 m north of 16th Avenue. The Perimeter Trail is the bike trail and pay attention to the signs because not all trails allow bikes. You can lock up your bike at racks at the 16th Avenue and 8th Avenue parking lots. The closest amenities to Campbell Valley Park are at 24th Avenue and 200th Street (pub, grocery store and gas station).

There are no stores on the periphery of this park. There are, however, gas stations, grocery stores, pubs and restaurants just a 5-minute drive or 10-minute bike ride north of the park along 200th Street at 24th and 40th Avenues. At the North Valley entrance (16th Avenue), you'll find a parking lot, picnic tables and toilets (one of which is wheelchair accessible). Walking trails start from here, including an excellent trail (Little River Loop) designed for wheelchairs. At the South Valley entrance (8th Avenue), there are parking spots, toilets, drinking water, a large picnic area and the Nature House.

The main birding trails through the park are listed below. However, there are a number of other entrances: on 200th Street, 4th Avenue, 208th Street, 216th Street and 20th Avenue. A trail map is posted on kiosks at the 16th and 8th Avenue entrances.

## BIRD SPECIES

### Little River Loop Trail

This walk is approximately 2 km long. Start at the North Valley entrance (16th Avenue) and take the trail to the east from the south end of the parking lot. It is also marked as a wheelchair trail. After walking approximately 160 m through the forest, you will come to the first boardwalk and bridge across the Little Campbell River and wetlands. Along this river you could see a *Great Blue Heron*, *Green Heron*, *American Wigeon*, *Hooded Merganser*, *Killdeer*, *Spotted Sandpiper* and a

The delicate–voiced Brown Creeper usually spirals its way up tree trunks.

Jim Martin

variety of waterfowl, including the *Ring-necked Duck*, *Green-winged Teal* and *Common Goldeneye*. Past the bridge, and parallel to the river, *Black-capped* and *Chestnut-backed Chickadees* are common in the trees. In spring, *Wilson's Snipe* may be heard winnowing, and the *Marsh Wren; Common Yellowthroat*; and *Violet-green, Tree* and *Barn Swallow* can all be seen. The *Pileated Woodpecker* frequents the area at the east end of the boardwalk.

As you follow the trail, it continues south, with steep slopes on the left and marsh to the right. Many birds can be found on this section of the trail, among them the *Bewick's Wren*, *Spotted Towhee* and *Downy* and *Hairy Woodpecker*. *Red-tailed Hawks* and *Barred* or *Great Horned Owls* occasionally roost in the trees on the slope, sometimes very close to the path. The *Sharp-shinned* and *Cooper's Hawk* are regularly seen in this area. In spring, watch for vireos, *American Robins* and *Red-breasted Nuthatches*. From the marshy area to the west, it is not unusual to hear a *Virginia Rail* or *Sora*. Both the *Black-capped* and *Chestnut-backed Chickadee* in this area will come to an outstretched hand offering sunflower seeds.

Because the slope faces west, it attracts large numbers of passerines. In winter it is a sun trap and much warmer than other areas of the park, so birds tend to congregate here. *Varied Thrush, Fox Sparrow* and *Ruby-crowned* and *Golden-crowned Kinglet* are common, especially in migration.

The south end of the trail divides, with one part continuing southeast, but make a hard right turn here to continue on the Little River Loop Trail. A boardwalk called the Listening Bridge crosses back to the west side of the park. Take your time here. The *Common Yellowthroat, Wilson's Warbler, Willow Flycatcher, Song Sparrow* and *Rufous Hummingbird* are common in spring and summer. Look also for *Anna's Hummingbird*. There are benches halfway across the boardwalk on which to sit and enjoy a packed lunch or snack. Look up and you may see a *Turkey Vulture* circling above in spring and fall, or the more common *Red-tailed Hawk* or *Bald Eagle* at any time.

After crossing the bridge, follow the trail marked Little River Loop to the right (north). At first the trail is heavily treed with western red cedar, Douglas-fir, alder and bigleaf maple. The *Brown Creeper* and, in winter, *Fox Sparrow* may be seen. The trail next passes through a meadow where the *Golden-crowned* and *White-crowned Sparrow* can be found in winter. In spring, the *Orange-crowned Warbler* and *Black-headed Grosbeak* are attracted to this area. Continue north to a shrubby area. The honeysuckle here attracts the *Rufous* and *Anna's Hummingbird, American Goldfinch* and *Cedar Waxwing*. As it nears the parking lot, the trail passes through an abandoned hazelnut grove. This is home to *Chestnut-backed Chickadee* and *Hutton's Vireo*. In spring, the *Purple Finch* sings from the tops of the high firs in this area. The trail ends back at the 16th Avenue parking lot.

## Vine Maple Trail

Start at the south end of the North Valley (16th Avenue) parking lot and take the south-heading trail, which is to the right of the kiosk and toilets. Walk south approximately 170 m and then turn right onto the Vine Maple Trail, which passes through dense fir trees, where the *Cooper's Hawk* sometimes nests. Stay on the main trail going west, and some 250 m farther on, turn left (south). The next 600 m section of trail passes through mixed forest and shrubs, an ideal place to find the *Pacific-slope Flycatcher, Pacific Wren, Dark-eyed Junco, Swainson's Thrush, Western Wood-Pewee* and, in migration, *Hermit Thrush*. This is an excellent spot to hear, and perhaps see, a *Yellow-rumped, Black-throated Gray* and *Townsend's Warbler* and *Hutton's Vireo* during their breeding season (May through June). Throughout this trail, look for a *Barred Owl*. The owls quite often roost in the trees and shrubs, and a summer's evening is a good time to look. Sometimes the young can be heard giving a hissing call. Enjoy, but please do not approach too close to the owls. They

The bright yellow Wilson's Warbler has an obvious black skullcap. Liron Gertsman

are best seen through binoculars. On this trail, a *Great Gray Owl* has been spotted in winter, but it is very rare.

Continue south to stands of very large bigleaf maples. Woodpeckers inhabit the tall trees and a variety of warblers may be found in the shrubby, more open areas. At this junction in the trail, you can turn left and meet the Little River Loop Trail (see above) and continue north back to the 16th Avenue parking lot. As mentioned, the Little River Loop Trail offers a wide variety of forest and meadow bird species as you go north to 16th Avenue.

## McLean Pond

To find the entrance to the park for this trail, travel east on 16th Avenue from 200th Street; turn north (left) onto 208th Street and then left at 20th Avenue. The entrance to the park, and also identifying it as a route to McLean Pond, is marked with signage and also numbered (20480 20 Avenue, which is handy for your GPS). You must park outside the No Parking signs along 20th Avenue, which means you will park about 50 m away on the shoulder of the road. The loop route described here is about 2 km of easy walking.

At 20th Avenue you enter a heavily wooded area and can see or hear forest species such as the *Brown Creeper*, *Pacific-slope Flycatcher* and *Pacific Wren*. In the winter, look for *Varied Thrush* and sometimes a *Barred Owl* or *Great Horned Owl*. Follow this trail for about 500 m to where it splits, and take the right-hand trail out to McLean Pond. The trail is well worn and easily found. There is a bench overlooking the pond just as the trail leaves the forest. At McLean Pond, depending on the season, look for **Mallards**, **American Wigeons**, **Common Goldeneyes**, **Wood Ducks**, **Ring-necked Ducks**, **Canada Geese**, **Great Blue Herons**, **Gadwalls**, **Green-winged Teal** and, rarely, **Pied-billed Grebes** or **Double-crested Cormorants**. Sometimes you can also see a **Northern Shoveler** or **Hooded Merganser**. There is usually a **Belted Kingfisher** in the area. Both species of **Chickadee** are found around the pond, as well as the **Song Sparrow** and occasionally **Bewick's Wren**. Sometimes an **Osprey** will turn up near the pond.

Bear right from the trail entrance and from the woods, and take the path that winds around the pond; keep your eyes and ears open. The Little Campbell River valley will be on your right, and it is surrounded by large trees. Often, a **Northern Flicker** or **Pileated Woodpecker** flies over. You just might see a **Red-tailed Hawk** nesting or hunting in the area, or you might spot one of the 24th Avenue nesting **Bald Eagles** fly by. As you walk around the dyke above the pond and follow the path into a meadow, you may hear and see a diversity of birds. In the spring, **Wilson's Snipes** may be seen in wet spots in the meadow. The **Savannah Sparrow** is very common in this grassy area in spring and summer. Later in the summer, you may find an **American Goldfinch** feeding on seeds. In the spring and summer, the trees on the right side of the meadow toward 16th Avenue occasionally contain a **Bullock's Oriole**. Follow the path nearly to 16th Avenue, and loop to your left and toward the north–south road that is beside the tree farm. (This road is not shown on the map.)

On the tree farm itself, there usually is an abundance of **American Robin**, **Dark-eyed Junco** and sparrows, especially **Song** and **White-crowned**, and when you get to the gate, under the shrubs, often **Golden-crowned Sparrow** is present in the winter season. In winter and spring, there are usually a lot of **Killdeers** around, and nesting is highly likely when they do their broken-wing display. Follow the road beside the tree farm, and it eventually becomes a trail that connects back to the trail that you came in on (off 20th Avenue). On the trail that connects the tree farm to the forest, but closer to the tree farm, the **Northern Goshawk** has been seen.

Alternatively, another way to reach McLean Pond is from the south side of 16th Avenue. If you are already in the park and near the 16th Avenue parking lot, head north and turn right onto the Shaggy Mane Trail, but pay attention, as this is also a horse trail. After 100 m or so, you will come to an old bridge over the Little Campbell River. From the bridge, you may see a **Mallard**, **Ring-necked Duck**, **Common Goldeneye** or **Wood Duck** in the winter. In spring, you may hear an **American Bittern**, **Virginia Rail** and **Common Yellowthroat**. Have a look to see if the trail under the bridge is in a good shape. In winter and spring, it often gets flooded and boots may not be sufficient. If it looks good, turn left from the Shaggy Mane trail onto a small trail near the bridge, and after a few metres, turn left again and then go to the right under the bridge and up to the old road. From there you head east (to the right) along the old road until you find the steps up the hillside into the meadow area described above.

## Ravine Trail

This route is approximately 5 km round trip and we recommend a loop, except for a short diversion up onto the Shaggy Mane Trail to check the open fields for birds. Note that the trails may be rough or wet in some places. From the 8th Avenue parking lot, walk through to the south edge of the field that the Annand/Rowlatt Farmstead is in. Turn left and follow the gravel trail into the forest, and you will be on the Ravine Trail. As you walk along the gravel trail, but before you enter the forest, look in the hedgerows in spring for *Yellow-rumped*, *Townsend's* and *Black-throated Gray Warblers*. Also keep an eye open for the *Sharp-shinned* and *Cooper's Hawk*, *Merlin* and *Peregrine Falcon* over the field or on the forest edges. Take

the Ravine Trail into the woods. *Hammond's Flycatchers* and *Western Tanagers* are common migrants throughout these woods. A *Barred Owl* can sometimes be seen in early morning or late evening. As you walk through these woods, look for *Downy* and *Hairy Woodpeckers* and *Pacific Wrens*.

After about 1 km, you will come to a sharp dip and a boardwalk, and then up a steep bank, you will see a viewing platform to your left. On this trail and visible from the viewing platform, the *Great Gray Owl* has been spotted on the forest's edge in winter, but they are very rare. Back

This boardwalk is at the north end of Campbell Valley Regional Park. Al Grass

on the main trail, walk up a hill and down steeply to where the trail splits. This is where you can take a side trail by crossing the small bridge and walking up to the top of the ravine onto a horse trail called Shaggy Mane Trail. Turn left onto Shaggy Mane Trail and follow it as it winds across open ground; fields are to the right, and the river and wetlands are below to the left. This open area is excellent for a variety of birds—raptors soaring above and warblers in the trees, especially *Yellow-rumped*, *Black-throated Gray* and *Townsend's*. Look also for the *American Goldfinch* and *Savannah Sparrow*. Once you have checked this area out, go back to the small bridge, cross it and return to the Ravine Trail.

Once back on the Ravine Trail, travel west. Birds to look for include the *Swainson's* and *Hermit Thrush*, *Steller's Jay* and, in spring, *Townsend's Solitaire* and

*Hutton's Vireo*. Look for the *Pine Siskin* and sometimes, in winter, the *Common Redpoll*. As you emerge from the forest, look for *Bushtits*, as well as fly-bys high in the sky, such as *Evening Grosbeaks*, *Bald Eagles*, *Peregrine Falcons* and *Turkey Vultures*. The gravel trail passes by the Annand/Rowlatt Farmstead and a large red barn where *Barn Owls* nest. Swallows often feed over the grassy open area, so look for them as you follow the gravel trail across this open area back to the 8th Avenue parking lot, bathrooms and nearby Nature House. Check the gardens around the Nature House for migrants and hummingbirds.

## Southeast Section of Shaggy Mane Trail

This is a **grassland and wetland walk** that can be reached via the entrance to the park on 4th Avenue between 208th Street and 212th Street. This is also a horse trail, so be alert for horses and riders. There is a small parking area near the entrance (be careful not to block the emergency access gate), or you can park on the other side of 4th Avenue along the shoulder of the road. The length of this walk is roughly 2 km (early return) to 3 km (loop around outside edge of park), depending on what you choose to do. Described here is a route starting from 4th Avenue, about 50 m west of 212th Street, and heading to 216th Street, which comes out at approximately 7th Avenue. You can turn around there and retrace your steps or walk along 216th Street to 4th Avenue and back to the trailhead. If you elect to walk on 216th Street, turn south and walk on the shoulder of the road along the edge of the park, past the entrance to the Critter Care facility, and then west along 4th Avenue to your parking spot. By doing this, you can bird the edge of the park, and you never know what might turn up!

Pacific Wren—a tiny forest floor dweller with a very long, loud song. Colin Clasen

As you start the trail from 4th Avenue, look around on both sides; *Downy Woodpecker* sometimes nests in the dead trees on the right-hand side of the trail. On the left-hand side, you may see a *White-crowned Sparrow*, *Cedar Waxwing* or *American Goldfinch*. The *European Starling* is also around. Over the open areas, the *Barn Swallow* is often gliding, and sometimes you will see a *Violet-green* or *Tree Swallow* too. The *Savannah Sparrow* is found in the grassy areas on lower shrubs or in the grasses.

The trail quickly splits, but keep to the left and just past the water, splash in the shrubs to the right; there have been very secretive *Steller's Jays* nesting in the last few years. Just a bit farther, the trails meet up again and you are back on the main stem of the Shaggy Mane Trail. As you move along this trail, look for the *Orange-crowned Warbler*, *Spotted Towhee*, *Swainson's Thrush* and *American Robin* in the shrubbery. In the winter, there are usually a lot of *Golden-crowned Kinglets* and some *Ruby-crowned Kinglets* as well. Diverse warblers and vireos may be heard or seen in the trees on the right-hand side. The *Barred Owl* is usually nesting in the forest area and sometimes the *Great Horned Owl*.

When you go around the corner to the right and into the valley, you will pass a former pond, which has slowly filled in over the years. The whole area has gotten marshier, and a bit farther along the trail, birds like the *Virginia Rail*, *Sora* and *American Bittern* have been seen and heard. A *Great Blue Heron* may be seen. The *Mallard*, *Common Yellowthroat*, *Marsh Wren*, *Song Sparrow* and *Spotted Towhee* are among the birds nesting in this area. Across from the pond in the big trees, the *Cooper's Hawk* has been nesting, and you may see this species in this area if it is quiet. You may see a *Cedar Waxwing* catching insects at the pond and, in the evening during spring migration, lots of *Red-winged Blackbirds* dropping down in the vegetation. Continue on the Shaggy Mane Trail as it veers to the right toward some large cedars, and you can usually find a *Rufous Hummingbird*. You may also hear *Canada Geese*. Woodpeckers in this wooded area are *Northern Flicker*, *Hairy*, *Downy* and *Pileated*. *Black-capped* and *Chestnut-backed Chickadees* and *Red-breasted Nuthatches* may be seen, as well as *Pacific* and *Bewick's Wrens*. Once you get to the bridge, keep your eye out for species such as the *Red-tailed Hawk* and *Bald Eagle*. A *Green Heron* has also been seen here in the past.

Continuing on the Shaggy Mane Trail to the right and toward 216th Street, there is sometimes a *Mourning Dove*. As you slowly get out of the wooded area, there may be different birds again depending on the season. The *Ring-necked Pheasant* may be seen or heard, and overhead it is possible to see a *Glaucous-winged Gull*. In fall and winter, look for a *Trumpeter Swan* overhead. You may see the first flight of a *Great Horned Owl* just before dusk in spring.

*Written by Mary Peet-Leslie. Updated by Christine Bishop, Wim Vesseur, Jude Grass, Al Grass and Tineke Goebertus, 2015.*

# 32. GOLDEN EARS PROVINCIAL PARK

## INTRODUCTION

GOLDEN EARS PROVINCIAL PARK LIES IN THE COAST MOUNTAINS ABOUT 48 km east of Vancouver on the north side of the Fraser River. From its southern boundary near Maple Ridge, the park extends 55 km northwards through mountain wilderness to the southern boundary of Garibaldi Provincial Park.

The lower forests were logged in the 1920s, and the resulting second growth consists of western hemlock, western red cedar and Douglas-fir. Significant areas of old-growth forest still exist at higher elevations and in remote valleys. There are some spectacular mountains in the park, including Golden Ears itself, at 1,706 m. Open subalpine parkland is present between 1,000 m and 1,500 m elevation.

The park contains a number of quite distinct aquatic habitats. Alouette Lake, a 2.5-km-long, fjord-like lake, is deep and cold, with little shore vegetation. It supports fish populations and is thus attractive to birds such as mergansers. The recreational focus of the park is centred here, with a boat launch and picnic and beach facilities for visitors. Mike Lake is a small, shallow lake surrounded by bog vegetation with well-developed emergent shore vegetation and floating species. This is the richest bird area in the park, which is no doubt a reflection of the varied plant communities creating good habitat.

In addition to the natural habitats, there are several areas that have been modified for recreational use, including two campgrounds and a large day-use area with a vast expanse of lawns.

Entrance to Golden Ears Provincial Park. Al Grass

Golden Ears East Canyon Trail. Nancy Prober

## DIRECTIONS

Access to the park is through the Municipality of Maple Ridge, 41 km east of Van-couver. To reach the park from downtown Vancouver, take Highway 1 east to Exit #44 and follow the signs for Highway 7B East/Maple Ridge. This will take you onto the Mary Hill Bypass, which leads to the Lougheed Highway (Highway 7), across the Pitt River Bridge and through Pitt Meadows to Maple Ridge. Watch for signs in town directing you to the park. If following 232nd Street, go north to Fern Crescent (the road that leads to the park). Once you are in downtown Maple Ridge (Haney), the route is well signed. The route is also signed from the east. Total travel time from Vancouver is about 1 hour. There is no public transit access to Golden Ears Park.

A 10-km paved highway extends from the park entrance to the day-use areas, campgrounds and Gold Creek Corridor. A park brochure containing a map is avail-able on the park's website (env.gov.bc.ca/bcparks/explore/parkpgs/golden_ears).

The Ruby–crowned Kinglet raises and flashes its red crown when agitated. Liron Gertsman

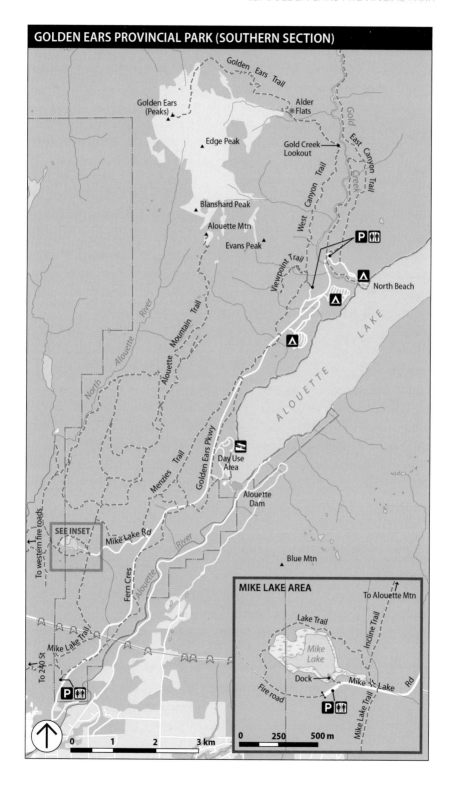

GOLDEN EARS PROVINCIAL PARK (SOUTHERN SECTION)

Golden Ears Trail

Golden Ears (Peaks)

Alder Flats

Edge Peak

Gold Creek Lookout

East Canyon Trail

Gold Creek

Blanshard Peak

West Canyon Trail

Alouette Mtn

Evans Peak

Viewpoint Trail

North Beach

Alouette River

North Alouette River

Alouette Mountain Trail

LAKE

ALOUETTE

Menzies Trail

Golden Ears Pkwy

Day Use Area

Alouette Dam

SEE INSET

Mike Lake Rd

To western fire roads

Fern Cres

Alouette River

Blue Mtn

MIKE LAKE AREA

To Alouette Mtn

Lake Trail

Incline Trail

Mike Lake

Mike Lake Trail

Dock

Mike Lake Rd

Fire road

To 240 St

Mike Lake Trail

0    250    500 m

0    1    2    3 km

The park has an extensive system of riding, mountain biking and hiking trails, but four of the easier ones are recommended for birders:

- **Mike Lake Trail**. The walking distance is 4.2 km from the park entrance to Mike Lake. The trail around the lake is about 3 km. This walk takes 2 to 3 hours and has an elevation gain of 100 m. You can also drive right to the lake.
- **Alouette Mountain Hiking Trail**. The walking distance from the top of Incline Trail via Lake Beautiful to Alouette Mountain is 10 km, which takes about 5 hours. This is the best access to the mountain hemlock forest and subalpine habitats.
- **Gold Creek Corridor**. The walking distance from the West Canyon parking lot to the Lake Viewpoint is 3 km and takes about 2 hours, with an elevation gain of 150 m.
- **West Canyon to Alder Flats**. The walking distance is 5 km and the hike takes about 3 hours, with minimal elevation change. **Note:** *Please remember that the backcountry in this park is extremely rugged. Only experienced and properly equipped mountaineers should attempt hiking in this area.*

## BIRD SPECIES

Some 141 species have been recorded in Golden Ears Provincial Park. Bird study began here in 1962, at which time an annotated checklist of the southern portion of Garibaldi Provincial Park (now Golden Ears) was prepared. A more extensive report by Al Grass was published in 1989. The Mike Lake area of the park is the richest bird habitat, supporting 91 out of the 141 species, followed by the Gold Creek Corridor. May and June are the most productive birding months in the park. A good day's birding at this time of year can produce 55 to 65 species.

*Sooty Grouse* is seen at all elevations, but the best area is along the Alouette Mountain or West Canyon trails. The grouse is often heard hooting in spring but can be extremely difficult to locate.

*Barred Owls* are residents and are best seen at Mike Lake or Alouette Campground on the Tiarella Nature Trail (venturevancouver.com/image/tiarella-nature-trail-golden-ears-provincial-park). Both the *Black* and *Vaux's Swift* are summer residents often seen on cool, cloudy days, especially along Gold Creek Corridor (Lower Falls Trail). Six species of woodpeckers have been seen here, including the *Red-breasted Sapsucker*. Look for sapsucker wells on western hemlock bark near Mike Lake, Spirea Nature Trail and Alouette Campground.

The *Warbling Vireo* is quite abundant, especially around Mike Lake. Warbler migration in spring includes the *Wilson's*, *MacGillivray's* and *Yellow-rumped* (both *Audubon* and *Myrtle* races). The *Black-throated Gray* and *Townsend's Warbler* are summer residents.

The conifer–loving Golden–crowned Kinglet is often found with Ruby–crowned Kinglets.
Jim Martin

Both *Red* and *White-winged Crossbills* are found here (highly cyclic in abundance, but often in good numbers), especially at Alouette Campground, Alouette Mountain and Gold Creek Corridor. Other finches include the *Black-headed Grosbeak*, *Pine Siskin* and *Purple Finch*.

*Written by Al Grass, 2001. Revised by Al and Jude Grass, 2015.*

# 33. BIRDING FROM BC FERRIES

## MAIN FERRY ROUTES — INTRODUCTION

THE BRITISH COLUMBIA FERRY SYSTEM PROVIDES A NUMBER OF "MOBILE platforms" that will take birdwatchers into semi-pelagic waters, as well as habitats not easily viewed from shore. The ferry routes to Vancouver Island from Horseshoe Bay and Tsawwassen, and the Gulf Island route that makes stops at

Galiano, Mayne, North Pender and Salt Spring islands (also departing from Tsawwassen), can offer good bird and marine mammal viewing opportunities in addition to superb coastal scenery. On a year-round basis, the ferry routes that traverse Active Pass are the best. Active Pass is a noted seabird and **Bald Eagle** "hot spot" between Galiano and Mayne islands and has been given the international designation as an

View from Galiano Island of one of the BC Ferries going through Active Pass. Mark Habdas

**Important Bird Area**. For details, see the Active Pass Important Bird Area website (activepassiba.ca). The best birdwatching periods are during the spring and fall migrations and during winter, roughly between late September until about mid-May.

At the time of writing, BC Ferries operates four routes across the Strait of Georgia. This strait is part of the Salish Sea, the name officially adopted in 2009 by the Province of British Columbia and the State of Washington. The Salish Sea includes Puget Sound and the Strait of Juan de Fuca at the south end, the Strait of Georgia in the middle and Johnstone Strait at the north end. This designation commemorates the Salish First Nations' long attachment to this body of water.

The long jetty built to access the Tsawwassen Ferry Terminal also provides excellent birdwatching opportunities on the extensive mud flats (see Section 13 of this guide).

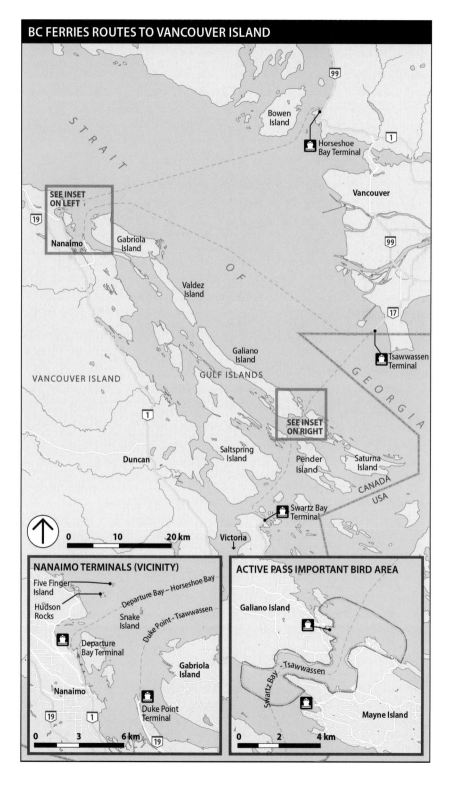

## BC FERRIES ROUTES TO VANCOUVER ISLAND

99

Bowen
Island

Horseshoe
Bay Terminal

1

Vancouver

S T R A I T

19

SEE INSET
ON LEFT

Nanaimo

Gabriola
Island

99

Valdez
Island

17

Tsawwassen
Terminal

Galiano
Island

O F

VANCOUVER ISLAND

GULF ISLANDS

G E O R G I A

SEE INSET
ON RIGHT

1

Duncan

Saltspring
Island

Pender
Island

Saturna
Island

CANADA
USA

Swartz Bay
Terminal

0    10    20 km

Victoria

### NANAIMO TERMINALS (VICINITY)

Five Finger
Island

Hudson
Rocks

Departure Bay – Horseshoe Bay

Snake
Island

Duke Point - Tsawwassen

Departure
Bay Terminal

Gabriola
Island

Nanaimo

19   1

Duke Point
Terminal

0    3    6 km

19

### ACTIVE PASS IMPORTANT BIRD AREA

Galiano Island

Swartz Bay - Tsawwassen

Mayne Island

0    2    4 km

# DIRECTIONS

*Note: Ferry routes stay fairly constant. However, since schedules and fares occasionally change, it's important to plan your travel by carefully checking the BC Ferries website (bcferries.com) or contacting them by phone prior to your departure. This is particularly important for the Gulf Islands ferries, as service is limited and they will fill up quickly on holiday and summer weekends.*

*Similarly, if you are taking a bus to the ferry terminal, be sure to check the most up-to-date schedules by accessing the TransLink website (translink.ca) or phoning them.*

*For contact information for BC Ferries and buses, please see the* **Public Transit and Weather Information** *section of this guide.*

## Ferry Routes Available

The three major routes connecting Vancouver and Vancouver Island are Horseshoe Bay–Departure Bay (Nanaimo), Tsawwassen–Duke Point (also Nanaimo) and Tsawwassen–Swartz Bay (Victoria).

The ferries serving the Gulf Islands of Galiano, Mayne, North Pender and Salt Spring depart from Tsawwassen on the mainland and from Swartz Bay (Victoria) on Vancouver Island.

*Notes: Concession fares for BC seniors are currently available Monday through Thursday. For those wanting to make a return trip without getting off the ferry at Swartz Bay or Departure Bay, passengers can remain on board and purchase a return ticket at the Purser's Office. Take a lunch, or take advantage of the food, beverage and other services on board.*

## To Reach Horseshoe Bay from Downtown Vancouver

Drive west on Georgia Street through Stanley Park and cross the Lions Gate Bridge to West Vancouver. Follow Marine Drive West to Horseshoe Bay (the longer, scenic, semi-waterfront route) or follow the signs up Taylor Way to Highway 1 (the faster route, known locally as the Upper Levels Highway) and proceed west to Horseshoe Bay. The route to Horseshoe Bay and the ferry terminal is well marked. Ferries to Nanaimo leave about every 2 hours. Crossing time is about 1 hour 40 minutes.

There is regular bus service from downtown Vancouver to the Horseshoe Bay Ferry Terminal. To access the most up-to-date information on bus schedules and routes, please see the TransLink website (translink.ca) or check the **Public Transit and Weather Information** section of this guide.

## To Reach Tsawwassen from Downtown Vancouver

Drive south on Highway 99 (Oak Street) and follow the signs for BC Ferries/Victoria. Exit onto Highway 17A, about 1 km south of the George Massey Tunnel under the Fraser River. After several kilometres, Highway 17A merges onto Highway 17 and takes you directly to the Tsawwassen Ferry Terminal.

There is regular bus service from downtown Vancouver, via Richmond, to the Tsawwassen Ferry Terminal. To access the most up-to-date information on bus schedules and routes, please see the TransLink website (translink.ca) or check the *Public Transit and Weather Information* section of this guide.

# BIRD SPECIES

## Horseshoe Bay to Departure Bay (Nanaimo)

Sailing time: 1 hour 40 minutes. This northern open-water crossing is somewhat dull for birders in comparison to the southern routes. This said, as the ferry approaches Nanaimo, the rocky islets of the Five Finger Island, Snake Island and Hudson Rocks are the nesting areas for small numbers of *Canada Geese*, *Glaucous-winged Gulls*, *Black Oystercatchers* and *Pigeon Guillemots* and, from time to time, *Pelagic* and *Double-crested Cormorants*. From October through to April, when Pacific herring gather in preparation to spawn, large numbers of gulls, loons, cormorants and *Bald Eagles* congregate in this area and follow the fish shoals. *Brandt's* (winter), *Double-crested* and *Pelagic Cormorants* (year-round and more inshore) are frequent. Favourite cormorant resting areas are easily spotted by the

Bonaparte's Gulls sometimes come very close to shore. Colin Clasen

white guano deposits they leave behind. The *Surfbird*, *Black Turnstone* and *Marbled Murrelet* (often in pairs) are present during the winter, but they are difficult to see due to their small size and cryptic colouration.

At the Horseshoe Bay terminal, but less so at Departure Bay, *Glaucous-winged Gulls* and a small flock of *Barrow's Goldeneyes* (in winter) often feed on the infestations of "blue" mussels attached to the floating wharves and pilings.

## Tsawwassen to Swartz Bay (Victoria)

Sailing time: 1 hour 40 minutes. Once you board this ferry, walk around the outer decks, which provide excellent vantage points for checking out the bird species resting on the breakwater and pilings near the ship. During the winter months, *Brandt's Cormorant* often "hauls out" here, as do a variety of gulls.

About 35 minutes out from Tsawwassen, the ferry approaches the entrance to Active Pass, a designated Important Bird Area. During the winter months, depending on the movements of the shoals of Pacific herring and leading up to their spawning in March/April, huge numbers of fish-eating birds are attracted to these food concentrations. Within Active Pass, there is often a nice variety of seabirds, especially between September and May. During this period, six species dominate: *Bonaparte's Gull* (early to mid-April), *Brandt's Cormorant*, *Pacific Loon*, *Common Murre*, *Glaucous-winged* and *Mew Gull*. The *Common Loon*, *Double-crested Cormorant*, *Surf* and *White-winged Scoters*, *California Gull* and *Western Grebe* are frequent winter residents. Look for *Harlequin Ducks* close to or perched on rocks near the shore. A number of pairs of *Bald Eagles* nest in the vicinity of Active Pass. During stormy periods, the mix of species can change considerably, as many additional species may seek shelter in the pass.

## Tsawwassen to Duke Point (Nanaimo)

Sailing time: 2 hours. Once the ferry has departed the terminal, this route traverses the Strait of Georgia (mid-Salish Sea) until it rounds Entrance Island Lighthouse and the approach to Duke Point. Few birds frequent these waters but in stormy weather the *Sooty Shearwater*, *Jaeger* and *Fork-tailed Storm-Petrel* occasionally transit this area. During migration, small flocks of *Northern Phalaropes* often follow floating debris (flotsam) along tide lines.

The mid-strait is where the birdwatcher needs to become a cetacean and pinniped watcher, as Dall's porpoise, white-sided dolphin, killer whale (orca) and the occasional minke whale are seen quite regularly. Harbour seal (quite common near shore and around ferry terminals), California and Steller (northern) sea lion, and increasingly northern elephant seal, can also be spotted along this route during the fall to spring period.

During the ferry's approach to Duke Point, the high cliffs of Gabriola Island

Caspian Tern with an eel photographed at the Tsawwassen ferry jetty. Colin Clasen

(on the port side) are regularly frequented by a pair of *Peregrine Falcons*. *Double-crested* and *Pelagic Cormorants*, *Glaucous-winged Gulls* and *Pigeon Guillemots* nest here. If the herring are in residence (February–March), the bird dynamics can be spectacular, with as many as 500 *Bald Eagles* and thousands of seabirds bingeing on this feast.

## SOUTHERN GULF ISLANDS ROUTES

This island-hopping route offers the birdwatcher or naturalist a splendid opportunity for a one-day round trip to Galiano, Mayne, North Pender or Salt Spring Island. The outward voyage from Tsawwassen departs mid-morning, and then stops at each of these islands in succession (ending at Salt Spring), then reverses its route arriving back at Tsawwassen at about dinnertime. You have to choose one of these islands and remain there until the ferry returns. On each island, there are great opportunities to see the sights, birdwatch, flower watch or whatever else your heart may desire, all within easy walking distance of each ferry terminal.

Remember that **BC seniors travel for half fare Monday through Thursday**, so this is a very "thrifty" opportunity. Take a lunch, or take advantage of the food, beverage and other services on board.

The best season for seabird watching is from September to May (see Active Pass comments above). The songbird migration roughly coincides with the spring flowers blooming, being best during April to mid-May. After this, the soils begin to dry out, with the flower show quickly fading.

BC Ferries staff (Purser's Office) are quite knowledgeable about these islands and the facilities available.

**Note**: *For the most up-to-date information, please refer to the BC Ferries website (bcferries.com), click "Schedules," then "Southern Gulf Islands Schedules." For the trip over, read the subsection entitled "Vancouver Departures (Tsawwassen to Galiano, Mayne, Pender, Salt Spring and Saturna Islands)." (However, for the purposes of our suggested day trip, disregard the Saturna Island part, as that requires a separate ferry departing from Swartz Bay.) For the return trip, read the subsection "Salt Spring Island Departures (Long Harbour)."*

Based on the 2015 schedule, you can choose one of the following stopovers:

## Galiano Island: Sturdies Bay (shore time about 6 hours)

The information kiosk at Sturdies Bay has copies of the trail map produced by the Galiano Parks and Recreation Commission. With 6 hours at your disposal, Bluffs Park is easily walkable. Walking time is about 1 hour. This park offers a spectacular vantage point to view the western entrance to Active Pass. The distance is about 3 km (6 km round trip) and can be reached by a number of routes. The nicest is via a forest trail from the Whaler Bay Trailhead. Walking along Burrill and Bluff roads will also get you to Bluffs Park.

Bellhouse Provincial Park is about a 1 km walk from Sturdies Bay via Burrill and Jack roads. This point of land provides a good vantage spot to view seabirds, marine mammals and an early spring Garry oak flower meadow. If you backtrack and follow Burrill Road west, there are a number of other water access and vantage points of the western entrance to Active Pass, including one at Mary Anne Road. This is another good place to view marine birds and mammals.

## Mayne Island: Village Bay (shore time about 4.5 hours)

Visitors to Mayne Island can take advantage of a community bus service (fare is by donation) that will take you to most places on the island. There is a brochure available on the island, and it indicates the many walking trails and other features of interest. Access to the south shore of Active Pass is restricted for some locations; enquire locally.

Common Murres can be found within Active Pass during the winter months. Joan Lopez

### North Pender Island: Otter Bay (shore time about 3 hours)

Roesland Park and Roe Islet beyond are part of the Gulf Islands National Park Reserve. Both can be reached on foot from the Otter Bay Ferry Terminal via the South Otter Bay Road. Walking time is about 45 minutes, and the distance is about 3 km. Enquire locally, or utilize Pender Island's unique car-stop program, with designated locations where locals will give "hitchhikers" a lift to places of interest.

### Salt Spring Island: Long Harbour (shore time about 1.5 hours)

Shore time here is brief. From the picnic area just outside the ferry terminal, there is a short, paved trail to a nice lookout. This trail offers a good leg stretch and a scenic walk through an arbutus and Douglas-fir forest. There are also picnic tables adjacent to the beach across from the ferry terminal.

*Written and updated by Bill Merilees, 2015.*

# SEASONAL STATUS OF VANCOUVER BIRDS

**Area covered:** Metro Vancouver from the International Boundary (including Point Roberts, WA) North to 49° 35' N. West to the eastern shoreline of Howe Sound (including Bowen Island) and to the middle of the Strait of Georgia. East to 122° 33' W (260th Street in Langley and Maple Ridge), including all of Golden Ears Provincial Park.

**The Checklist:** This checklist is divided into two parts—a list of 268 regularly occurring species (reported annually) and a list of 152 casual and accidental species (not reported every year).

For the regular species, we present bar graphs indicating the seasonal occurrence and relative abundance of each. For the casual and accidental species, because not all sightings have been critically reviewed, we cannot say exactly how many sightings there are for each. Therefore, we have indicated for each season whether the species is accidental (1 record) or casual (2 or more records), without indicating dates for individual sightings.

*Original computer design by Tom Brown, Kyle Elliott and Rick Toochin.*
*Modified by Larry Cowan, 2015.*

## Key: Seasonal "Regularly Occurring" chart

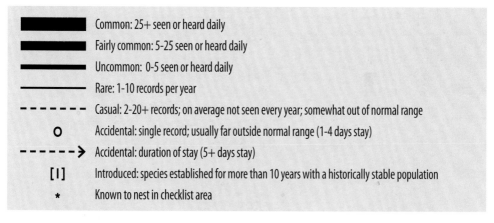

| | |
|---|---|
| ▬▬▬ | Common: 25+ seen or heard daily |
| ▬▬▬ | Fairly common: 5-25 seen or heard daily |
| ▬▬▬ | Uncommon: 0-5 seen or heard daily |
| —— | Rare: 1-10 records per year |
| - - - - - - | Casual: 2-20+ records; on average not seen every year; somewhat out of normal range |
| O | Accidental: single record; usually far outside normal range (1-4 days stay) |
| - - - - -> | Accidental: duration of stay (5+ days stay) |
| [I] | Introduced: species established for more than 10 years with a historically stable population |
| * | Known to nest in checklist area |

## Key: Seasonal "Casual and Accidental" chart

| | |
|---|---|
| **ca** | Casual: 2-20+ records; on average not seen every year; somewhat out of normal range |
| **acc** | Accidental: single record; usually far outside normal range (1-4 days stay) |

Opposite: The Audubon variety of the Yellow–rumped Warbler has a yellow throat.
Jim Martin

## SEASONAL "REGULARLY OCCURRING"

| Regularly Occurring | J | F | M | A | M | J | J | A | S | O | N | D |
|---|---|---|---|---|---|---|---|---|---|---|---|---|
| Grtr White-fronted Goose | | | | | | | | | | | | |
| Snow Goose | | | | | | | | | | | | |
| Brant | | | | | | | | | | | | |
| Cackling Goose | | | | | | | | | | | | |
| Canada Goose* | | | | | | | | | | | | |
| Mute Swan* [I] | | | | | | | | | | | | |
| Trumpeter Swan | | | | | | | | | | | | |
| Tundra Swan | | | | | | | | | | | | |
| Wood Duck* | | | | | | | | | | | | |
| Gadwall* | | | | | | | | | | | | |
| Eurasian Wigeon | | | | | | | | | | | | |
| American Wigeon* | | | | | | | | | | | | |
| Mallard* | | | | | | | | | | | | |
| Blue-winged Teal* | | | | | | | | | | | | |
| Cinnamon Teal* | | | | | | | | | | | | |
| Northern Shoveler* | | | | | | | | | | | | |
| Northern Pintail* | | | | | | | | | | | | |
| Green-winged Teal* | | | | | | | | | | | | |
| Canvasback | | | | | | | | | | | | |

| | J | F | M | A | M | J | J | A | S | O | N | D |
|---|---|---|---|---|---|---|---|---|---|---|---|---|
| Redhead | | | | | | | | | | | | |
| Ring-necked Duck* | | | | | | | | | | | | |
| Greater Scaup | | | | | | | | | | | | |
| Lesser Scaup | | | | | | | | | | | | |
| Harlequin Duck* | | | | | | | | | | | | |
| Surf Scoter | | | | | | | | | | | | |
| White-winged Scoter | | | | | | | | | | | | |
| Black Scoter | | | | | | | | | | | | |
| Long-tailed Duck | | | | | | | | | | | | |
| Bufflehead | | | | | | | | | | | | |
| Common Goldeneye | | | | | | | | | | | | |
| Barrow's Goldeneye | | | | | | | | | | | | |
| Hooded Merganser* | | | | | | | | | | | | |
| Common Merganser* | | | | | | | | | | | | |
| Red-breasted Merganser | | | | | | | | | | | | |
| Ruddy Duck* | | | | | | | | | | | | |
| Ring-necked Pheasant* [I] | | | | | | | | | | | | |
| Ruffed Grouse* | | | | | | | | | | | | |
| Sooty Grouse* | | | | | | | | | | | | |
| | J | F | M | A | M | J | J | A | S | O | N | D |

| | J | F | M | A | M | J | J | A | S | O | N | D |
|---|---|---|---|---|---|---|---|---|---|---|---|---|
| Red-throated Loon | | | | | | | | | | | | |
| Pacific Loon | | | | | | | | | | | | |
| Common Loon | | | | | | | | | | | | |
| Yellow-billed Loon | | | | | | | | | | | | |
| Pied-billed Grebe* | | | | | | | | | | | | |
| Horned Grebe | | | | | | | | | | | | |
| Red-necked Grebe | | | | | | | | | | | | |
| Eared Grebe | | | | | | | | | | | | |
| Western Grebe | | | | | | | | | | | | |
| Clark's Grebe | | | | | | | | | | | | |
| Brandt's Cormorant | | | | | | | | | | | | |
| Double-crested Cormorant* | | | | | | | | | | | | |
| Pelagic Cormorant* | | | | | | | | | | | | |
| American White Pelican | | –➤o | | | | | | | | | | |
| Brown Pelican | | o | | | | | | | | | | |
| American Bittern* | | | | | | | | | | | | |
| Great Blue Heron* | | | | | | | | | | | | |
| Great Egret | | | | | | | | | | | | |
| Cattle Egret | | | | | | | o | | | | | |
| Green Heron* | | | | | | | | | | | | |

| | J | F | M | A | M | J | J | A | S | O | N | D |
|---|---|---|---|---|---|---|---|---|---|---|---|---|
| Blk-crowned Night-Heron* | | | | | | | | | | | | |
| Turkey Vulture | | | | | | | | | | | | |
| Osprey* | | | | | | | | | | | | |
| Golden Eagle* | | | | | | | | | | | | |
| Northern Harrier* | | | | | | | | | | | | |
| Sharp-shinned Hawk* | | | | | | | | | | | | |
| Cooper's Hawk* | | | | | | | | | | | | |
| Northern Goshawk* | | | | | | | | | | | | |
| Bald Eagle* | | | | | | | | | | | | |
| Red-tailed Hawk* | | | | | | | | | | | | |
| Rough-legged Hawk | | | | | | o | | | | | | |
| Virginia Rail* | | | | | | | | | | | | |
| Sora* | | | | | | | | | | | | |
| American Coot* | | | | | | | | | | | | |
| Sandhill Crane* | | | | | | | | | | | | |
| Black-bellied Plover | | | | | | | | | | | | |
| American Golden-Plover | | | | | | | | | | | | |
| Pacific Golden-Plover | | | | | | | | | | | | |
| Semipalmated Plover* | | | | | | | | | | | | |
| Killdeer* | | | | | | | | | | | | |
| Black Oystercatcher* | | | | | | | | | | | | |
| American Avocet* | | | | | | | | | | | | |

| | J | F | M | A | M | J | J | A | S | O | N | D |
|---|---|---|---|---|---|---|---|---|---|---|---|---|

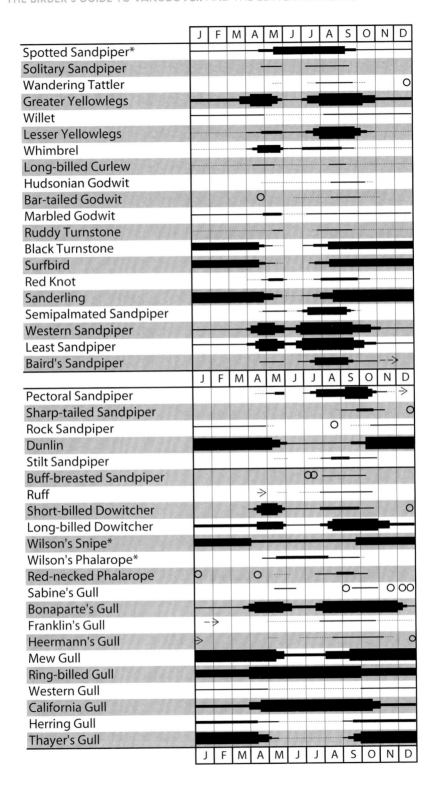

| | J | F | M | A | M | J | J | A | S | O | N | D |
|---|---|---|---|---|---|---|---|---|---|---|---|---|
| Spotted Sandpiper* | | | | | | | | | | | | |
| Solitary Sandpiper | | | | | | | | | | | | |
| Wandering Tattler | | | | | | | | | | | | |
| Greater Yellowlegs | | | | | | | | | | | | |
| Willet | | | | | | | | | | | | |
| Lesser Yellowlegs | | | | | | | | | | | | |
| Whimbrel | | | | | | | | | | | | |
| Long-billed Curlew | | | | | | | | | | | | |
| Hudsonian Godwit | | | | | | | | | | | | |
| Bar-tailed Godwit | | | | | | | | | | | | |
| Marbled Godwit | | | | | | | | | | | | |
| Ruddy Turnstone | | | | | | | | | | | | |
| Black Turnstone | | | | | | | | | | | | |
| Surfbird | | | | | | | | | | | | |
| Red Knot | | | | | | | | | | | | |
| Sanderling | | | | | | | | | | | | |
| Semipalmated Sandpiper | | | | | | | | | | | | |
| Western Sandpiper | | | | | | | | | | | | |
| Least Sandpiper | | | | | | | | | | | | |
| Baird's Sandpiper | | | | | | | | | | | | |
| Pectoral Sandpiper | | | | | | | | | | | | |
| Sharp-tailed Sandpiper | | | | | | | | | | | | |
| Rock Sandpiper | | | | | | | | | | | | |
| Dunlin | | | | | | | | | | | | |
| Stilt Sandpiper | | | | | | | | | | | | |
| Buff-breasted Sandpiper | | | | | | | | | | | | |
| Ruff | | | | | | | | | | | | |
| Short-billed Dowitcher | | | | | | | | | | | | |
| Long-billed Dowitcher | | | | | | | | | | | | |
| Wilson's Snipe* | | | | | | | | | | | | |
| Wilson's Phalarope* | | | | | | | | | | | | |
| Red-necked Phalarope | | | | | | | | | | | | |
| Sabine's Gull | | | | | | | | | | | | |
| Bonaparte's Gull | | | | | | | | | | | | |
| Franklin's Gull | | | | | | | | | | | | |
| Heermann's Gull | | | | | | | | | | | | |
| Mew Gull | | | | | | | | | | | | |
| Ring-billed Gull | | | | | | | | | | | | |
| Western Gull | | | | | | | | | | | | |
| California Gull | | | | | | | | | | | | |
| Herring Gull | | | | | | | | | | | | |
| Thayer's Gull | | | | | | | | | | | | |

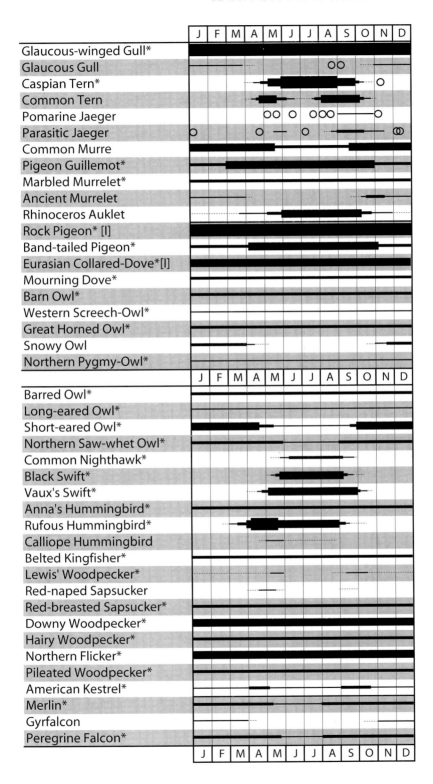

| | J | F | M | A | M | J | J | A | S | O | N | D |
|---|---|---|---|---|---|---|---|---|---|---|---|---|
| Glaucous-winged Gull* | | | | | | | | | | | | |
| Glaucous Gull | | | | | | | | | | | | |
| Caspian Tern* | | | | | | | | | | | | |
| Common Tern | | | | | | | | | | | | |
| Pomarine Jaeger | | | | | | | | | | | | |
| Parasitic Jaeger | | | | | | | | | | | | |
| Common Murre | | | | | | | | | | | | |
| Pigeon Guillemot* | | | | | | | | | | | | |
| Marbled Murrelet* | | | | | | | | | | | | |
| Ancient Murrelet | | | | | | | | | | | | |
| Rhinoceros Auklet | | | | | | | | | | | | |
| Rock Pigeon* [I] | | | | | | | | | | | | |
| Band-tailed Pigeon* | | | | | | | | | | | | |
| Eurasian Collared-Dove*[I] | | | | | | | | | | | | |
| Mourning Dove* | | | | | | | | | | | | |
| Barn Owl* | | | | | | | | | | | | |
| Western Screech-Owl* | | | | | | | | | | | | |
| Great Horned Owl* | | | | | | | | | | | | |
| Snowy Owl | | | | | | | | | | | | |
| Northern Pygmy-Owl* | | | | | | | | | | | | |

| | J | F | M | A | M | J | J | A | S | O | N | D |
|---|---|---|---|---|---|---|---|---|---|---|---|---|
| Barred Owl* | | | | | | | | | | | | |
| Long-eared Owl* | | | | | | | | | | | | |
| Short-eared Owl* | | | | | | | | | | | | |
| Northern Saw-whet Owl* | | | | | | | | | | | | |
| Common Nighthawk* | | | | | | | | | | | | |
| Black Swift* | | | | | | | | | | | | |
| Vaux's Swift* | | | | | | | | | | | | |
| Anna's Hummingbird* | | | | | | | | | | | | |
| Rufous Hummingbird* | | | | | | | | | | | | |
| Calliope Hummingbird | | | | | | | | | | | | |
| Belted Kingfisher* | | | | | | | | | | | | |
| Lewis' Woodpecker* | | | | | | | | | | | | |
| Red-naped Sapsucker | | | | | | | | | | | | |
| Red-breasted Sapsucker* | | | | | | | | | | | | |
| Downy Woodpecker* | | | | | | | | | | | | |
| Hairy Woodpecker* | | | | | | | | | | | | |
| Northern Flicker* | | | | | | | | | | | | |
| Pileated Woodpecker* | | | | | | | | | | | | |
| American Kestrel* | | | | | | | | | | | | |
| Merlin* | | | | | | | | | | | | |
| Gyrfalcon | | | | | | | | | | | | |
| Peregrine Falcon* | | | | | | | | | | | | |

| | J | F | M | A | M | J | J | A | S | O | N | D |
|---|---|---|---|---|---|---|---|---|---|---|---|---|

221

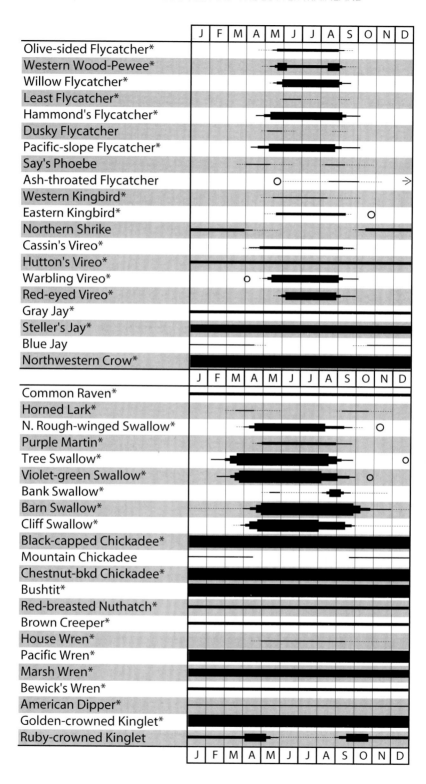

|  | J | F | M | A | M | J | J | A | S | O | N | D |
|---|---|---|---|---|---|---|---|---|---|---|---|---|
| Olive-sided Flycatcher* | | | | | | | | | | | | |
| Western Wood-Pewee* | | | | | | | | | | | | |
| Willow Flycatcher* | | | | | | | | | | | | |
| Least Flycatcher* | | | | | | | | | | | | |
| Hammond's Flycatcher* | | | | | | | | | | | | |
| Dusky Flycatcher | | | | | | | | | | | | |
| Pacific-slope Flycatcher* | | | | | | | | | | | | |
| Say's Phoebe | | | | | | | | | | | | |
| Ash-throated Flycatcher | | | | | | | | | | | | |
| Western Kingbird* | | | | | | | | | | | | |
| Eastern Kingbird* | | | | | | | | | | | | |
| Northern Shrike | | | | | | | | | | | | |
| Cassin's Vireo* | | | | | | | | | | | | |
| Hutton's Vireo* | | | | | | | | | | | | |
| Warbling Vireo* | | | | | | | | | | | | |
| Red-eyed Vireo* | | | | | | | | | | | | |
| Gray Jay* | | | | | | | | | | | | |
| Steller's Jay* | | | | | | | | | | | | |
| Blue Jay | | | | | | | | | | | | |
| Northwestern Crow* | | | | | | | | | | | | |
| Common Raven* | | | | | | | | | | | | |
| Horned Lark* | | | | | | | | | | | | |
| N. Rough-winged Swallow* | | | | | | | | | | | | |
| Purple Martin* | | | | | | | | | | | | |
| Tree Swallow* | | | | | | | | | | | | |
| Violet-green Swallow* | | | | | | | | | | | | |
| Bank Swallow* | | | | | | | | | | | | |
| Barn Swallow* | | | | | | | | | | | | |
| Cliff Swallow* | | | | | | | | | | | | |
| Black-capped Chickadee* | | | | | | | | | | | | |
| Mountain Chickadee | | | | | | | | | | | | |
| Chestnut-bkd Chickadee* | | | | | | | | | | | | |
| Bushtit* | | | | | | | | | | | | |
| Red-breasted Nuthatch* | | | | | | | | | | | | |
| Brown Creeper* | | | | | | | | | | | | |
| House Wren* | | | | | | | | | | | | |
| Pacific Wren* | | | | | | | | | | | | |
| Marsh Wren* | | | | | | | | | | | | |
| Bewick's Wren* | | | | | | | | | | | | |
| American Dipper* | | | | | | | | | | | | |
| Golden-crowned Kinglet* | | | | | | | | | | | | |
| Ruby-crowned Kinglet | | | | | | | | | | | | |

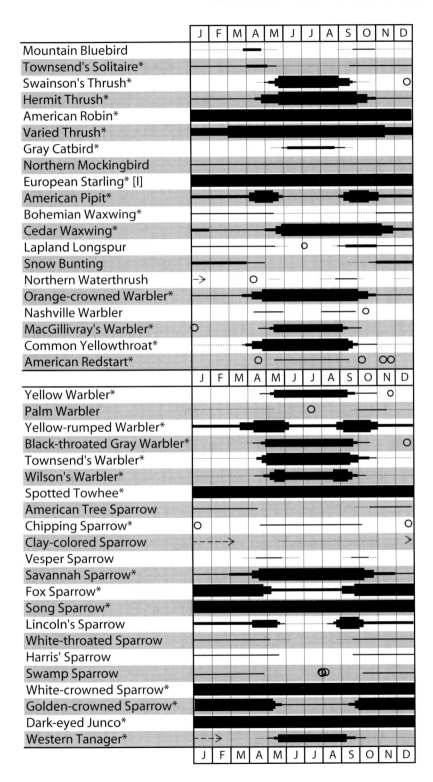

|  | J | F | M | A | M | J | J | A | S | O | N | D |
|---|---|---|---|---|---|---|---|---|---|---|---|---|
| Black-headed Grosbeak* | | | | | | | | | | | | |
| Lazuli Bunting* | | | | | | | | | | | | |
| Red-winged Blackbird* | | | | | | | | | | | | |
| Western Meadowlark* | | | | | | | | | | | | |
| Yellow-headed Blackbird* | | | | | | | | | | | | |
| Rusty Blackbird | | | | | | | | | | | | |
| Brewer's Blackbird* | | | | | | | | | | | | |
| Brown-headed Cowbird* | | | | | | | | | | | | |
| Bullock's Oriole* | | | | | | | | | | | | |
| Gray-crowned Rosy Finch | | | | | | | | | | | | |
| Pine Grosbeak | | | | | | | | | | | | |
| Purple Finch* | | | | | | | | | | | | |
| House Finch* | | | | | | | | | | | | |
| Red Crossbill* | | | | | | | | | | | | |
| White-winged Crossbill | | | | | | | | | | | | |
| Common Redpoll | | | | | | | | | | | | |
| Pine Siskin* | | | | | | | | | | | | |
| American Goldfinch* | | | | | | | | | | | | |
| Evening Grosbeak* | | | | | | | | | | | | |
| House Sparrow* [I] | | | | | | | | | | | | |
|  | J | F | M | A | M | J | J | A | S | O | N | D |

Ruddy Turnstone in typical breeding plumage. Tak Shibata

# SEASONAL "CASUALS & ACCIDENTALS"

| Casuals & Accidentals | Winter | Spring | Summer | Autumn |
|---|---|---|---|---|
| Emperor Goose | ca | ca | acc | ca |
| Ross' Goose | ca | ca | - | ca |
| Garganey | - | acc | acc | acc |
| Baikal Teal | acc | - | - | acc |
| Tufted Duck | ca | ca | ca | ca |
| King Eider | ca | ca | ca | ca |
| Common Eider | acc | acc | acc | acc |
| Smew | acc | acc | - | - |
| Rock Ptarmigan | ca | - | acc | ca |
| White-tailed Ptarmigan | - | - | acc | ca |
| Laysan Albatross | acc | acc | acc | - |
| Northern Fulmar | - | - | acc | acc |
| Sooty Shearwater | - | - | - | ca |
| Short-tailed Shearwater | - | - | - | ca |
| Black-vented Shearwater | - | acc | - | - |
| Fork-tailed Storm-Petrel | acc | - | acc | ca |
| Leach's Storm-Petrel | - | - | - | acc |
| Magnificent Frigatebird | - | - | acc | - |
| Least Bittern | - | - | acc | - |
| Snowy Egret | - | ca | - | - |
| White-tailed Kite | - | ca | acc | - |
| Broad-winged Hawk | - | acc | - | ca |
| Swainson's Hawk | - | ca | ca | acc |
| Yellow Rail | - | - | acc | - |
| Common Gallinule | - | acc | acc | - |
| Lesser Sand-Plover | - | - | acc | - |
| Snowy Plover | - | acc | ca | - |
| Black-necked Stilt | - | ca | - | - |
| Mountain Plover | - | - | - | ca |
| Spotted Redshank | - | acc | - | acc |
| Wood Sandpiper | - | - | - | acc |
| Upland Sandpiper | - | acc | ca | ca |
| Little Curlew | - | - | acc | - |
| Bristle-thighed Curlew | - | acc | - | - |
| Far Eastern Curlew | - | - | - | acc |
| Great Knot | acc | - | - | - |
| Red-necked Stint | - | acc | ca | ca |
| Little Stint | - | - | ca | ca |
| Temminck's Stint | - | - | - | acc |
| | Winter | Spring | Summer | Autumn |

| | Winter | Spring | Summer | Autumn |
|---|---|---|---|---|
| White-rumped Sandpiper | - | - | ca | ca |
| Curlew Sandpiper | - | - | acc | ca |
| Spoonbill Sandpiper | - | - | acc | - |
| Red Phalarope | acc | - | acc | ca |
| Black-legged Kittiwake | ca | ca | ca | ca |
| Tufted Puffin | - | - | ca | ca |
| Ivory Gull | acc | - | - | - |
| Black-headed Gull | ca | ca | ca | ca |
| Little Gull | acc | ca | ca | ca |
| Laughing Gull | - | - | acc | - |
| Iceland Gull | ca | ca | - | ca |
| Slaty-backed Gull | ca | ca | - | ca |
| Black Tern* | - | ca | ca | ca |
| Arctic Tern | - | ca | ca | ca |
| Forster's Tern | - | - | ca | ca |
| Elegant Tern | - | - | ca | acc |
| South Polar Skua | - | - | - | ca |
| Long-tailed Jaeger | - | acc | acc | ca |
| Cassin's Auklet | acc | acc | ca | ca |
| Oriental Turtle-Dove | acc | - | - | - |
| Flammulated Owl | - | acc | - | - |
| Northern Hawk-Owl | ca | ca | - | ca |
| Burrowing Owl* | ca | ca | acc | ca |
| Spotted Owl* | - | - | - | acc |
| Great Gray Owl | ca | ca | - | ca |
| Boreal Owl | acc | acc | - | acc |
| Lesser Nighthawk | - | - | acc | - |
| Common Poorwill | - | - | - | acc |
| White-throated Swift | - | - | - | acc |
| Ruby-throated Hummingbird | - | acc | acc | - |
| Black-chinned Hummingbird | - | - | - | - |
| Costa's Hummingbird | acc | acc | acc | acc |
| Acorn Woodpecker | - | - | acc | - |
| Williamson's Sapsucker | - | - | acc | - |
| Yellow-bellied Sapsucker | ca | ca | - | ca |
| Am. 3-toed Woodpecker* | ca | ca | ca | ca |
| Blk-backed Woodpecker | - | - | - | acc |
| Prairie Falcon | ca | ca | - | ca |
| Alder Flycatcher | - | - | ca | - |
| Black Phoebe | - | acc | acc | acc |
| Eastern Phoebe | - | acc | acc | - |
| Tropical Kingbird | - | - | - | ca |
| Scissor-tailed Flycatcher | - | - | acc | - |
| | Winter | Spring | Summer | Autumn |

| | Winter | Spring | Summer | Autumn |
|---|---|---|---|---|
| Loggerhead Shrike | ca | ca | - | ca |
| Philadelphia Vireo | - | - | - | acc |
| Yellow-green Vireo | - | - | - | acc |
| Western Scrub-Jay* | ca | ca | ca | ca |
| Black-billed Magpie* | ca | ca | ca | ca |
| Clark's Nutcracker | acc | acc | acc | ca |
| Cave Swallow | - | - | - | acc |
| Sky Lark | acc | - | - | - |
| Boreal Chickadee | acc | - | - | acc |
| White-breasted Nuthatch | ca | ca | acc | ca |
| Pygmy Nuthatch | - | - | - | ca |
| Rock Wren | ca | ca | acc | ca |
| Sedge Wren | - | - | - | acc |
| Blue-gray Gnatcatcher | acc | - | acc | acc |
| Red-flanked Bluetail | acc | - | - | - |
| Northern Wheatear | - | - | acc | - |
| Western Bluebird* | acc | acc | acc | acc |
| Veery | - | ca | ca | - |
| Dusky Thrush | acc | acc | - | - |
| Fieldfare | acc | - | - | - |
| Sage Thrasher | acc | ca | - | acc |
| Brown Thrasher | acc | acc | acc | acc |
| Siberian Accentor | acc | - | - | - |
| Eastern Yellow Wagtail | - | - | - | acc |
| White Wagtail | - | ca | - | acc |
| Red-throated Pipit | acc | - | acc | acc |
| Chestnut-collrd Longspur | - | - | acc | - |
| Smith's Longspur | - | - | - | acc |
| McCown's Longspur | acc | - | - | - |
| McKay's Bunting | acc | - | - | - |
| Ovenbird | - | ca | ca | - |
| Golden-winged Warbler | - | - | - | acc |
| Black-and-white Warbler | ca | ca | ca | ca |
| Prothonotary Warbler | - | - | - | acc |
| Tennessee Warbler | ca | ca | ca | - |
| Virginia's Warbler | - | acc | - | - |
| Hooded Warbler | - | - | acc | - |
| Northern Parula | - | acc | acc | - |
| Magnolia Warbler | - | acc | ca | ca |
| Blackburnian Warbler | - | acc | acc | - |
| Chestnut-sided Warbler | - | acc | ca | acc |
| Blackpoll Warbler | - | acc | acc | ca |
| | Winter | Spring | Summer | Autumn |

227

| | Winter | Spring | Summer | Autumn |
|---|---|---|---|---|
| Black-throated Blue Warbler | - | acc | - | - |
| Black-throatd Green Warbler | - | - | acc | - |
| Hermit Warbler | - | ca | - | - |
| Canada Warbler | - | acc | - | - |
| Painted Redstart | acc | - | - | acc |
| Yellow-breasted Chat | acc | ca | ca | acc |
| Green-tailed Towhee | - | acc | acc | - |
| Brewer's Sparrow | - | ca | ca | acc |
| Lark Sparrow | - | ca | ca | acc |
| Black-throated Sparrow | - | ca | ca | - |
| Sagebrush Sparrow | - | ca | - | acc |
| Lark Bunting | - | - | acc | ca |
| Grasshopper Sparrow | - | acc | acc | acc |
| Baird's Sparrow | - | - | acc | - |
| Le Conte's Sparrow | - | - | - | ca |
| Nelson's Sparrow | - | - | - | acc |
| Rose-breasted Grosbeak | acc | acc | ca | ca |
| Indigo Bunting | - | - | ca | acc |
| Painted Bunting | - | - | - | acc |
| Bobolink | - | ca | ca | ca |
| Common Grackle | acc | acc | acc | acc |
| Hooded Oriole | acc | acc | - | acc |
| Dickcissel | | acc | | |
| Baltimore Oriole | - | - | acc | - |
| Brambling | ca | acc | - | ca |
| Cassin's Finch | ca | ca | - | ca |
| Hoary Redpoll | acc | acc | - | - |
| Lesser Goldfinch | acc | - | - | acc |
| | Winter | Spring | Summer | Autumn |

| Extirpated [ I - introduced ] |
|---|
| American Black Duck* [I]    California Quail* [I] |
| Gray Partridge*[I]   Yellow-billed Cuckoo   Crested Myna* [I] |

American Wigeon pair courting. Virginia Hayes

SELECTED LIST OF
VANCOUVER BIRD SPECIES

There are two main approaches that can be followed in a birdwatching guide. The first approach emphasizes a locality: "Which species of birds can I expect to find in a particular area?" This approach has been followed in the main chapters of this guide. The second approach emphasizes a specific bird species: "Where can I find a particular species?" This approach, which is especially useful to visitors from other areas, is the subject of this section.

Many of the bird species found in the Vancouver area are common not only in this area, but over a large part of North America. No special directions are needed to find these birds, because the observer is likely to find them in a short time anyway. However, there is a long list of species that are either uncommon or rare locally (and thus sought after by local birdwatchers), or that may be common locally, but are rare or absent in much of the rest of Canada and the US (and hence sought after by visiting birders). This list combines the two categories. The choice of species included is subjective, but the list includes all those that local bird experts are asked about most frequently.

Casual and accidental species (those occurring, on average, less than once a year in the Vancouver area) are not included here, because they are too unpredictable.

**1. Pacific Loon** Uncommon from October to late May, but a common transient; it prefers deep water and strong tidal currents and is rarely seen in shallow water. Lighthouse Marine Park in Point Roberts is the best place to view this bird. Large flocks also occur offshore from Reifel Migratory Bird Sanctuary in late April, but are usually too far offshore for good viewing. This species can also be seen in large flocks from fall through late spring in Active Pass, on the Tsawwassen to Swartz Bay ferry route. *Photo: Juvenile Pacific Loon. Ilya Povalyaev*

**2. Yellow-billed Loon** Very rare from October to May, but recorded almost annually, scarce in recent years. Shallow marine waters are its preferred habitat. Identification can be tricky; be aware of immature Common Loons with pale bills. *Photo: Yellow-billed Loon. Ilya Povalyaev*

Opposite: Bonaparte's Gull hitching a ride on a log boom. Joan Lopez

**3. Red-necked Grebe**  Common from mid-August to mid-May. Widely distributed, with the best locations including Point Roberts, the Tsawwassen and Roberts Bank jetties and Stanley Park. In September, several thousand moult in Boundary Bay (far offshore); a good place to view them is from Blackie Spit, south Surrey and Lily Point in Point Roberts. *Photo: Breeding pair of Red-necked Grebes. John Lowman*

**4. Western Grebe**  Uncommon far offshore from mid-August to May. Widely distributed in marine and estuarine waters, but considerably less common and seen in much smaller numbers than they were 25 years ago. Large flocks used to occur at English Bay. Areas that are still good to view this species are sometimes Canoe Pass (Westham Island), the waters between the Tsawwassen ferry jetty and Roberts Bank coal terminal, and off of Blackie Spit and the White Rock Pier. Check flocks carefully for Clark's Grebe, which is very rare in this area. *Photo: Western Grebe with a fresh catch. Virginia Hayes*

**5. Eared Grebe**  Rare from September to May, casual the rest of the year. The vast majority of sightings in the Vancouver area are from the White Rock Pier, where a few birds winter annually. Other locations to check include Iona Beach Regional Park and the Tsawwassen ferry jetty. *Photo: Eared Grebe in breeding plumage. Colin Clasen*

**6. Brandt's Cormorant**  Fairly common from September to June, casual the rest of the year. This species prefers deep salt water. The best sites to see it are the Grebe Islets off Lighthouse Park, the Burnaby Shoal channel marker off Brockton Point in Stanley Park, and the Tsawwassen ferry jetty breakwater and pilings. Large flocks can also often be seen flying by Lighthouse Marine Park at Point Roberts, or in Active Pass on the Tsawwassen to Swartz Bay ferry route. *Photo: Brandt's Cormorant. Tak Shibata*

**7. American Bittern**  An uncommon resident of extensive marsh areas. During the summer, this species can be heard "pumping," especially at sunrise and sunset, in the Pitt-Addington Marsh Wildlife Management Area, the marshes of Sturgeon Banks off the Richmond west dyke, or Reifel Migratory Bird Sanctuary. The best sites in the winter are along the dykes at Brunswick Point or Reifel, especially on high tides, when the birds are forced closer to shore. *Photo: American Bittern at Reifel. Jim Martin*

**8. Green Heron** Rare breeder, uncommon post-breeding migrant in August and September, when northward dispersing juveniles augment the small local population. This species is possible at almost any slough, pond or slow-moving lowland stream. DeBoville slough might be the most reliable location. Other places to search are the Southlands area in south Vancouver, Reifel Migratory Bird Sanctuary, the Pitt-Addington Marsh Wildlife Management Area, Minnekhada Regional Park, Colony Farm Regional Park and Ambleside Park. *Photo: Green Heron. Jim Martin*

**9. Black-crowned Night-Heron** Up to six birds winter regularly from mid-August to May in the trees bordering Fuller's Slough at the Reifel Migratory Bird Sanctuary. This is the only reliable location in BC to see this species. *Photo: Black-crowned Night-Heron at Reifel. Jim Martin*

**10. Trumpeter Swan** Common from mid-November to late March, when large flocks frequent farm fields and tidal marshes. The best places to check are Westham Island, the fields east of Roberts Bank and fields along Burns Drive, Delta (see the Burns Bog section). Use of fields by swans is dependent on crop rotation, with the swans preferring potato fields. Tundra Swan is rare and should be looked for in these flocks. Be cautious with identification of the two species (voice is the best distinction). During the past few summers, a few Trumpeter Swans have resided in the Katzie Marsh at Grant Narrows Regional Park (see the section on the Pitt-Addington Marsh Wildlife Management Area). *Photo: Pair of Trumpeter Swans. Mike Tabak*

**11. Cackling Goose** A fairly recent split from Canada Goose. Small numbers winter, and during spring (April) and fall (September and October), migration flocks are occasionally seen overhead; they are detected by their high-pitched calls, short necks and stubby bills. More common in the eastern Fraser Valley, Langley to Chilliwack. *Photo: Cackling Goose. Ilya Povalyaev*

**12. Brant** Fairly common from November to mid-March, common in April, rare the rest of the year. The best site to see this species is Boundary Bay Regional Park, where flocks of up to 100 or more feed on the eelgrass beds. Other good sites to check include the waters between the Tsawwassen ferry jetty and the Roberts Bank coal terminal, the White Rock waterfront and Point Roberts. Look for a genetically distinct subspecies, the Gray-bellied Brant, which is distinguished by its pale breast (it resembles eastern birds); it has recently been identified with more frequency in Boundary Bay. *Photo: Brant eating seaweed at the Tsawwassen ferry jetty. Colin Clasen*

**13. Eurasian Wigeon** Uncommon from mid-October to April. This species can be anywhere there are large numbers of American Wigeon. The best location is Roberts Bank coal terminal, where a thorough search through the thousands of American Wigeon could turn up greater than 100 Eurasians. Other good sites include Reifel Migratory Bird Sanctuary, Boundary Bay Regional Park, Ambleside Park and Blackie Spit. *Photo: Eurasian Wigeon. Virginia Hayes*

**14. Tufted Duck** First recorded in 1961, then seen annually for many years, but decidedly scarcer in the last decade. The large wintering scaup flock no longer uses Lost Lagoon, which used to frequently host Tufted Duck. The best site to see this species is Iona Beach Regional Park; however, any wintering scaup flock should be thoroughly searched. *Photo: Tufted Duck. Jim Martin*

**15. Harlequin Duck** Fairly common from October to May, uncommon the rest of the year, when non-breeders frequent rocky shorelines. The best spots to check are Stanley Park (between Ferguson Point and Prospect Point), Ambleside Park, the west end of the White Rock Promenade, Tsawwassen ferry jetty and Point Roberts. During winter it is regular in small numbers along the rocky shorelines of North and West Vancouver. *Photo: Male Harlequin Duck. Jim Martin*

**16. Long-tailed Duck** Common from late October to mid-April, rare the rest of the year. This species is usually found in salt water, well offshore. Good places to search are Point Roberts, Stanley Park, the Iona South Jetty, the Tsawwassen ferry jetty and the White Rock waterfront. *Photo: Female Long-tailed Duck. Jim Martin*

**17. Barrow's Goldeneye** Abundant from mid-October to May, rare the rest of the year. They usually feed in large flocks off rocky shorelines. The best sites are Stanley Park and Ambleside Park, but they can be found almost anywhere along the shores of Burrard Inlet or English Bay This species is scarce in the Fraser delta but could be seen at Point Roberts or the Tsawwassen ferry jetty. The West Vancouver shoreline occasionally has summering individuals. *Photo: Barrow's Goldeneye pair flying. Liron Gertsman*

**18. Bald Eagle** Once rare, eagles have increased tenfold in number in the last 30 years. They are now common throughout the region from November to May, uncommon the rest of the year. Breeding sites, some with obvious nests, include Reifel Migratory Bird Sanctuary, Stanley Park, Lighthouse Park and Pitt-Addington Marsh Wildlife Management Area. During the winter, this bird is difficult to miss if you bird anywhere in the Fraser delta. Hundreds can be seen along the Squamish River (about 1 hour north of Vancouver) in December and January and the Harrison River (about 1.5 hours east of Vancouver) in November and December. Hundreds roost in the Burns Bog area from December to March. Most birds depart from July to October for salmon-spawning streams in the north. *Photo: Bald Eagle. Mike Tabak*

**19. Rough-legged Hawk** Uncommon from October to April in open country, especially in the farmlands of the Fraser delta. The best sites to check are the fields north of Boundary Bay (especially along 64th and 72nd streets), Westham Island, the fields east of Roberts Bank, Sea Island and the Pitt-Addington Marsh Wildlife Management Area. *Photo: Rough-legged Hawk. Jim Martin*

**20. Peregrine Falcon** Uncommon resident, more difficult to find from June to July. This species is often seen hunting shorebirds and small ducks in the Fraser delta. The best sites to check are Iona Island, Reifel Migratory Bird Sanctuary, Roberts Bank and the entire shoreline of Boundary Bay. They are often seen near the Ironworkers Memorial (Second Narrows) Bridge, which links Vancouver and North Vancouver. *Photo: Peregrine Falcon. Michelle Lamberson*

**21. Gyrfalcon** Very rare from late November to March, when one or two will usually show up in the Fraser delta. This species is most often seen in the fields north of Boundary Bay, the fields east of Roberts Bank (carefully scan the first few power pylons near the causeway), fields east of Mud Bay (40th Avenue), on Westham Island and rarely on Sea and Iona islands. In recent years, one has frequented the Viterra Grain Terminal at the south end of the Iron Workers (Second Narrows) Bridge. Gyrfalcons often have very large winter territories and can be difficult to locate. *Photo: Gyrfalcon. Mike Tabak*

**22. Sooty Grouse** A fairly common resident of the North Shore Mountains. This species is easily heard when the males are booming in the spring, but they are high in the trees and can be very difficult to see. Later in the summer, females with chicks can often be found on the sides of the access roads of Cypress and Mount Seymour provincial parks (early morning is best). During the winter, when they live high up the mountains in coniferous forests, they are next to impossible to find. Other places to check are the UBC Research Forest, Burnaby Mountain Conservation Area and Minnekhada Regional Park. *Photo: Sooty Grouse. John Lowman*

**23. Sandhill Crane** Rare resident. Two or three pairs breed in the Pitt-Addington Marsh Wildlife Management Area and Burns Bog, a pair at Reifel Migratory Bird Sanctuary and a pair in recent years at the Richmond Golf Course. They can be observed (and heard) most easily from Rannie Road in Pitt Meadows, or the fields just to the south between April and August. Flock(s) of up to 30 birds used to occur in the fields around Burns Bog and can often be seen in fields along 68th Street south of River Road. Small numbers of wild migrants, attracted by the resident birds, drop in to the Reifel Sanctuary in April and May and mid-August to September, and a small flock has wintered at Reifel in recent years. *Photo: Sandhill Crane landing. John Lowman*

**24. American Golden-Plover** Rare from August to October. This species can be found by scanning the Black-bellied Plover flocks that frequent the Boundary Bay area during fall. Search freshly plowed fields lacking deep furrows on Westham Island and the fields around Boundary Bay, especially during high tide. Pacific Golden-Plover is also a rare migrant in the area, and identification should be made with caution; juvenile Americans vary in colour and many approach Pacific Golden—primary extension, jizz (hard to determine without lots of experience!) and call are other clues. This species is not present in the winter but could possibly be seen in mid-summer. *Photo: American Golden-Plover juvenile. Jim Martin*

**25. Black Oystercatcher** Uncommon resident of rocky shorelines and jetties. The best locations to view this species are the Grebe Islets and the Tsawwassen ferry jetty, where they breed. Other locations to check, especially during the winter, are the mouth of Cypress Creek in West Vancouver and the Ferguson Point area in Stanley Park. *Photo: Black Oystercatcher. Ilya Povalyaev*

**26. Wandering Tattler** Rare from late July to late September, when it frequents rocky shorelines and jetties. The best location to search for this species is the Iona South Jetty. Other sites that infrequently have tattlers include the Tsawwassen ferry jetty, the Grebe Islets, Lighthouse Park and the Point Roberts Marina jetty. *Photo: Wandering Tattler. Liron Gertsman*

**27. Whimbrel** Regular in May, scarce from April to September, casual the rest of the year. On a high tide, they tend to roost in grassy fields near the intersection of 176th Street and 8th Avenue in South Surrey. Flocks of over 100 birds have been seen at each of these locations in early spring. Other places to check include Blackie Spit and Iona Beach Regional Park. *Photo: Whimbrel. Ilya Povalyaev*

**28. Long-billed Curlew** Rare from mid-April to mid-May and mid-August to mid-September, casual the rest of the year. Reported regularly in April, usually calling in over flight at Sea or Iona islands, also occasionally at Boundary Bay. Best locations to check are Blackie Spit, Roberts Bank and the Pitt Wildlife Management Area. An individual bird has wintered at Blackie Spit for many years, often in the company of Marbled Godwit. *Photo: Long-billed Curlew. Liron Gertsman*

**29. Hudsonian Godwit** Very rare from late August to early October, casual from May to mid-August. The best locations to check are the Boundary Bay foreshore, Reifel Migratory Bird Sanctuary and Roberts Bank. *Photo: Hudsonian Godwit. Mike Tabak*

**30. Marbled Godwit** Rare during May through September, casual the rest of the year. The best locations to check are Blackie Spit, the Boundary Bay foreshore and Roberts Bank. In recent years, small numbers have wintered at Blackie Spit. Godwits should be checked carefully, since Bar-tailed Godwits have been observed on numerous occasions from August to October, especially along the Boundary Bay Foreshore (probably the best site in Canada to search for this species). *Photo: Marbled Godwit. Mike Tabak*

**31. Surfbird** Uncommon from late August to May, when it frequents rocky shorelines, often in the company of Black Turnstone. Surfbirds are most often seen on the Grebe Islets near Lighthouse Park (occasionally on the rocks of the park itself and the mouth of Cypress Creek, West Vancouver). Low tide is essential to find this species, since high tide covers their feeding sites. Other locations that infrequently have Surfbird include the Tsawwassen ferry jetty, the Iona South Jetty and Point Roberts. *Photo: Surfbird. David Schutz*

**32. Red Knot** Uncommon. Small numbers during September and October with maximum daily counts <5, rare spring migrant in May, casual the rest of the year. The best way to find this species is to scan through the Black-bellied Plover flocks that frequent the Boundary Bay area and the Roberts Bank coal terminal. *Photo: Red Knot. Tak Shibata*

**33. Sharp-tailed Sandpiper** Rare fall migrant, with most of the sightings occurring from mid-September to late October. The Vancouver area is probably the best area in North America (except for Alaska) to observe this species. Almost every bird that passes through is in juvenile plumage and often found in the company of Pectoral Sandpiper. The two best sites to check are the west field at Reifel Migratory Bird Sanctuary and the foreshore of Boundary Bay between 96th and 104th streets. Observed less frequently at Iona Island sewage ponds. Nearly all sightings are from these locations. *Photo: Sharp-tailed Sandpiper. Liron Gertsman*

**34. Rock Sandpiper** Very rarely reported from November to May, when it frequents rocky shorelines with the Black Turnstone and Surfbird, but in much smaller numbers, making it difficult to pick out. This species is most often seen at the Grebe Islets near Lighthouse Park and the mouth of Cypress Creek in West Vancouver. Low tide is essential to find this species, since high tide covers their feeding sites. Other sites to check include the Ferguson Point area in Stanley Park, the Tsawwassen ferry jetty and Point Roberts. *Photo: Rock Sandpiper. Ilya Povalyaev*

**35. Stilt Sandpiper** Rare in August and September, fluctuating from a few individuals to dozens between seasons. Casual during late spring. The best sites to search for this bird are the Iona Island sewage ponds, Reifel Migratory Bird Sanctuary and 12th Avenue Lagoon at Boundary Bay Regional Park. *Photo: Stilt Sandpiper. Jim Martin*

**36. Buff-breasted Sandpiper** Rare in late August and September, when it often frequents turf farms, other short-grass habitats and freshly plowed fields. It occurs in very small numbers and is not seen every year. The best sites to search are the turf farm on the west side of 72nd Street in Delta (especially during high tide) and the Boundary Bay foreshore between 104th and 96th streets. There are also a few records from the Iona Island sewage ponds. *Photo: Buff-breasted Sandpiper. Jim Martin*

**37. Ruff** First recorded in 1971, seen most years, with one to four records each year. Most records occur from August through October, but there are a few spring records as well. The majority of sightings are from the Iona Island sewage ponds, the Reifel Migratory Bird Sanctuary and Boundary Bay, especially near the "Mansion" west of 96th Street. *Photo: Ruff. Mike Tabak*

**38. Parasitic Jaeger**  Rare spring migrant from mid-May to early June and an uncommon fall migrant in September and October. A good location to see this species is off Lighthouse Marine Park in Point Roberts. Other good sites include the end of the Iona South Jetty, the Tsawwassen ferry jetty and Spanish Banks. Pomarine and Long-tailed Jaeger have also been reported in Vancouver but are very rare and identification should be made with caution. *Photo: Parasitic Jaeger. Glenn Bartley*

**39. Franklin's Gull**  Rare from August to November, casual during the rest of the year. The best location to look for this species is Iona Island Regional Park. Other locations with repeated sightings are Blackie Spit, Point Roberts and the crab pier at Jericho Beach Park (Spanish Banks). *Photo: Franklin's Gull. Mike Tabak*

**40. Heermann's Gull**  Regular (fairly common) from mid-August to early November, with most sightings during September and early October at Light-house Marine Park in Point Roberts. Numbers fluctuate from year to year, as this is the northern limit of this species' fall dispersal. Rare elsewhere but occasionally seen from the Iona South Jetty, the Tsawwassen ferry jetty and Spanish Banks. *Photo: Heermann's Gull. Tak Shibata*

**41. Thayer's Gull**  Common from October to March. This species can easily be found in gull flocks around the Vancouver Landfill. They are fairly easy to see foraging around the Iona sewage ponds from November to February, and in flooded agricultural and school/playing fields throughout Richmond, especially during rains. They often roost in fields along Burns Drive and between Highway 99 and River Road along 64th and 68th streets in Delta. Small numbers are also found at the lower Capilano River beside Ambleside Park and even foraging in parks with grass playing fields. Distinguish with care from Herring Gull, which is outnumbered at least 20 to 1 by Thayer's. *Photo: Thayer's Gull. Mike Tabak*

**42. Western Gull**  Rare from October to May, casual during the rest of the year. Likely quite rare in our area. This species is often found in large flocks of Glaucous-winged Gull. Search anywhere large numbers of gulls are roosting, often in fields around the dump in Delta. Identification should be made with caution, since Glaucous-winged x Western hybrids outnumber pure Western Gull. Clean head, big bill, dark mantle, black undersurface of primaries are good starting points in identifying this species. *Photo: Western Gull. Mike Tabak*

**43. Glaucous Gull**  Rare from November to March, when mainly first- or second-year plumaged birds are found in large gull flocks. The best site for this species is near the Vancouver Landfill. The landfill is closed to the public, but searching the flocks of roosting gulls nearby may reveal this bird. Gulls often roost in fields along Burns Drive, north of the interchange of Highway 99 and Highway 10, and between Highway 99 and River Road along 64th and 68th streets. Glaucous Gull might also be found at Iona Beach Regional Park. *Photo: Glaucous Gull. Ilya Povalyaev*

**44. Pigeon Guillemot**  Fairly common from March to November, uncommon the rest of the year. A few birds breed at the base of the cliffs at Prospect Point in Stanley Park, in the pilings around the Tsawwassen ferry jetty and under the Burrard Dry Dock Pier/Lonsdale Quay in North Vancouver. Lighthouse Park is also a good year-round location. During the winter, they can be found at Point Roberts, off of the Maplewood Conservation Area, off Brockton Point in Stanley Park and around the Grebe Islets and Lighthouse Park in West Vancouver. *Photo: Pigeon Guillemot. John Lowman*

**45. Marbled Murrelet**  Uncommon resident. This species appears to be declining rapidly in the Vancouver area. Small numbers occur during the summer and probably breed (observed flying out of old-growth forest) in the Capilano, Seymour and Coquitlam river watersheds, which are closed to public access. The best places to search during the summer are the West Vancouver shoreline and Indian Arm. During the winter, they might be seen from Point Roberts, Stanley Park, Ambleside Park, Iona Island South Jetty or Lighthouse Park. Sightings are also possible on the Tsawwassen to Swartz Bay ferry route. These are small birds—bring a scope! *Photo: Marbled Murrelet. Ilya Povalyaev*

**46. Ancient Murrelet**  Rare from mid-October to April. Most reliably seen from late November to early January on the Tsawwassen to Schwarz Bay ferry route (outside the checklist area). Most sightings of this species are from Lighthouse Marine Park in Point Roberts during October and November. They have also been seen from the Iona Island South Jetty and Stanley Park. *Photo: Ancient Murrelet. Tak Shibata*

**47. Rhinoceros Auklet**  Fairly common from mid-June to early October, off Lighthouse Marine Park in Point Roberts. Uncommon to rare at other sites, such as off the end of the Iona Island South Jetty, Tsawwassen ferry jetty, Stanley Park and Lighthouse Park, the Grebe Islets and English Bay (off Cecil Green, UBC). *Photo: Rhinoceros Auklet. John Lowman*

**48. Eurasian Collared-Dove** Common resident. It is unbelievable how fast this species has spread in the last decade. Now seen throughout the Fraser delta, especially in open agricultural areas. *Photo: Eurasian Collared-Dove. Colin Clasen*

**49. Barn Owl** Uncommon resident of agricultural lands and open country. Can be fairly easily seen by driving roads slowly on a nice night. The area south of Steveston Highway between Gilbert Road and No. 5 Road in Richmond, the roads on Westham Island, Sea Island and around Boundary Bay are also good. Stopping and squeaking improves success. Can be found during the day by entering occupied barns (with owners' permission!). *Photo: Barn Owl perched at Maplewood. John Lowman*

**50. Western Screech-Owl** A now very rare resident of forested areas. This species has declined dramatically, likely due to a combination of habitat loss and, especially, predation from Barred Owls and possibly eastern gray squirrels (egg predation). They seem to prefer areas of mixed forest, preferably near streams. Most recent sightings are from wooded ravines in Langley. *Photo: Western Screech-Owl in Langley. Colin Clasen*

**51. Snowy Owl** Uncommon in winter from mid-November to April, when it frequents shorelines and fields. One or two appear most winters, but larger numbers (10 to 30) occur during irruption years, which happen about every fourth year. The best location to see this species is the Boundary Bay foreshore between 72nd and 64th streets, where they tend to sit on the logs on the foreshore. Other areas include Roberts Bank, Brunswick Point, Westham Island and Iona Island. *Photo: Snowy Owl. Mike Tabak*

**52. Northern Pygmy-Owl** Rare resident of the North Shore Mountains. Cypress and Mount Seymour provincial parks, where they often perch on treetops, are the best places to search. They are most often seen in winter (October to April), but can be found in summer too. They have also been reported from Lighthouse Park, the Maplewood Conservation Area and the Pitt-Addington Marsh Wildlife Management Area. This small owl will often respond to imitations of its call during daylight hours. Some individuals will hunt at bird feeders during the winter. *Photo: Northern Pygmy-Owl with vole at Maplewood. John Lowman*

241

**53. Spotted Owl** Extirpated from the Vancouver Checklist Area, and fewer than 10 pairs remain in the province. *Photo: Spotted Owl. Glenn Bartley*

**54. Long-eared Owl** Rare, non-breeding visitor and winter resident. Occurs in thick mature hedgerows adjacent to old field habitat in the Fraser delta. During the winter, with careful searching of hedgerows and thickets, look for signs such as accumulated whitewash, and you may be lucky to find them at Sea Island, Serpentine Fen, Brunswick Point, Richmond West and Boundary Bay Dykes. Formerly a very rare breeder but no recent records. *Photo: Long-eared Owl. Virginia Hayes*

**55. Northern Saw-whet Owl** Uncommon resident that, like the Long-eared Owl, is more easily found during the winter at roost sites. It breeds in coniferous forest in areas such as Stanley Park, Lighthouse Park, Pacific Spirit Regional Park and Campbell Valley Regional Park. During the winter, it is most easily seen at Reifel Migratory Bird Sanctuary, where between one and six may reside. Consult staff as to the most likely locations. Searching conifers and hedgerows (especially overhanging conifer branches) on Sea Island may be productive. *Photo: Northern Saw-whet Owl. Jim Martin*

**56. Black Swift** Fairly common but erratic from mid-May to mid-September. The best places to search are Cypress and Mount Seymour provincial parks and the Pitt-Addington Marsh Wildlife Management Area. Black Swifts often show up in the lowlands during periods of inclement weather with low clouds. Possible anywhere during migration. *Photo: Black Swift. Jim Martin*

**57. Vaux's Swift** Fairly common from late April to mid-September. Most frequently seen at Cypress and Mount Seymour provincial parks, Lighthouse Park and the Pitt-Addington Marsh Wildlife Management Area. A visit in late April to Iona Island during a low-pressure system often yields a few. Possible anywhere during migration. *Photo: Vaux's Swift. Greg Gillson*

**58. Anna's Hummingbird** Common resident. This species has undergone a dramatic increase in numbers and range and now occurs all year, anywhere in the checklist area with feeders. Any hummer seen from October to February is invariably this species. *Photo: Anna's Hummingbird. John Lowman*

**59. Red-breasted Sapsucker** Uncommon resident usually found in dense coniferous forest. Most common at altitudes above 800 m. The best locations are Mount Seymour and Cypress provincial parks, Lighthouse Park, Burnaby Mountain Conservation Area, Minnekhada Regional Park and the Pitt-Addington Marsh Wildlife Management Area. Possible anywhere in winter, especially after heavy snows or a cold spell. A partial altitudinal migrant, but seen most often in the mountains, even in winter. *Photo: Red-breasted Sapsucker. Peter Candido*

**60. Three-toed Woodpecker** Rare resident in subalpine forest. The only consistent locality is Cypress Provincial Park, occasionally along the Yew Lake Trail, but more often along the Howe Sound Crest Trail, which involves fairly strenuous hiking (and has yielded very few recent reports). These trails are off-limits during the winter while the ski hill is in operation, as they are located outside the ski area boundary. *Photo: Three-toed Woodpecker. Mike Tabak*

**61. Hammond's Flycatcher** Fairly common from late April to September, when it breeds in high-elevation coniferous forest or low-elevation mixed forest. Cypress and Mount Seymour provincial parks, Stanley Park, Lighthouse Park, Campbell Valley Regional Park and Minnekhada Regional Park are good places to search. *Photo: Hammond's Flycatcher. Jim Martin*

**62. Pacific-slope Flycatcher** Fairly common in summer from late April to mid-August, when it breeds in coniferous forest. Much more numerous than Hammond's, especially at lower elevations. It prefers coniferous forests with a deciduous understorey, but breeds in most forested areas around Vancouver. Stanley Park, Lighthouse Park, Campbell Valley Regional Park, Point Roberts and Minnekhada Regional Park are good places to search. *Photo: Pacific-slope Flycatcher. Jim Martin*

**63. Eastern Kingbird** Uncommon from June to late August. Found regularly only in the Pitt-Addington Marsh Wildlife Management Area (specifically Grant Narrows Regional Park and along Rannie Road), where several pairs nest every year. Rare summer visitor to other riparian areas in the checklist area (Colony Farm Regional Park). *Photo: Eastern Kingbird. John Gordon*

**64. Northern Shrike** Uncommon from mid-October to April. Found in open country, usually on telephone wires or the tops of shrubs. The most likely spots include Sea and Iona islands, the Pitt-Addington Marsh Wildlife Management Area, Colony Farm Regional Park, Westham Island, Reifel Migratory Bird Sanctuary and the fields and dykes around Brunswick Point and Boundary Bay. *Photo: Northern Shrike. Jim Martin*

**65. Western Scrub-Jay** Casual. In the last decade, this bird has been reported almost annually, usually in treed residential areas with feeders. Has bred in Maple Ridge. In fall, it seeks acorns. *Photo: Western Scrub-Jay adult feeding young in Maple Ridge in June 2014—the first photographic proof of this species successfully breeding in southwestern BC. John Gordon*

**66. Hutton's Vireo** Fairly common resident of low-elevation mixed forest. Found in most of our larger urban parks. Often heard singing its persistent song from March to May, during the winter it is usually silent, except for scolding calls. This species often accompanies flocks of chickadees and kinglets. Be cautious with identification, since a briefly observed vireo can easily resemble a Ruby-crowned Kinglet. Stanley Park, Richmond Nature Park, Pacific Spirit Park, Lighthouse Park, Point Roberts, Burnaby Lake Regional Park, Burnaby Mountain Conservation Area, Queen Elizabeth Park, Mundy Park and Campbell Valley Regional Park are good places to look. *Photo: Hutton's Vireo. Liron Gertsman*

**67. Cassin's Vireo** Uncommon migrant from mid-April to mid-May and mid-August to early September in low-elevation mixed forest. Rare breeder in our area as it prefers dry forest. This species can arrive in early April, but caution should be used to identify a singing bird, since local Purple Finch early in the year sing slow notes like the song of the vireo. Minnekhada Regional Park, Deer Lake Regional Park, Stanley Park, Pacific Spirit Regional Park and Lighthouse Park are good places to search. *Photo: Cassin's Vireo. Tak Shibata*

**68. Purple Martin** Uncommon from May to September. This species had not been recorded in Vancouver for 22 years prior to 1994. Thanks to hundreds of volunteers maintaining nest box programs at several sites, this bird made a good comeback to the checklist area, with hundreds of pairs breeding. They return late April and depart early September, but may abandon sites for a few days at a time in inclement weather. The largest colony is at the Maplewood Conservation Area, with other sites established at Iona Island, Reifel Sanctuary, Blackie Spit and Rocky Point Park in Port Moody. *Photo: Purple Martin male. John Lowman*

**69. Chestnut-backed Chickadee** One of the most common species in coniferous forest. In winter it may occur in adjacent deciduous forest when feeding with flocks of Golden-crowned Kinglet and Black-capped Chickadee. Good locations include Stanley Park, Campbell Valley Regional Park, Lighthouse Park, Pacific Spirit and Minnekhada Regional Parks, and Cypress and Mount Seymour provincial parks. Largely absent (casual) from Lulu and Sea islands and western Delta. *Photo: Chestnut-backed Chickadee. John Gordon*

**70. Bushtit** Common resident of residential areas, hedgerows and woodlots and forest edges, but not in extensive forest areas. Often seen in flocks of 35 to 40 in winter. Jericho Beach Park, Stanley Park, Queen Elizabeth Park, Ladner Harbour Park, Colony Farm Regional Park, Burnaby Lake Regional Park, Campbell Valley Regional Park and Reifel Migratory Bird Sanctuary are good places to look. *Photo: Female Bushtit. Colin Clasen*

**71. Bewick's Wren** Common resident, found in hedgerows, brush, woodlots and forest edges and openings. Conspicuous when singing in late February to May; in other months, this bird sticks to cover. Good locations include Stanley Park, Pacific Spirit Regional Park, Jericho Beach Park, Ladner Harbour Park, Colony Farm Regional Park, Burnaby Lake Regional Park and Reifel Migratory Bird Sanctuary. *Photo: Bewick's Wren. Michelle Lamberson*

**72. American Dipper** Uncommon resident of fast-flowing creeks and rivers on the North Shore, where it breeds. The most reliable site is at the Capilano Fish Hatchery in North Vancouver. Also found along the Seymour River and Lynn Creek (both on the North Shore). In some years, one will spend the winter at Beaver Creek in Stanley Park. *Photo: American Dipper with a bug. Michelle Lamberson*

**73. Townsend's Solitaire** Rare in winter, casual in summer. This species is most reliable in late April and early May, when small numbers migrate through the Vancouver area. Recently, the most reliable area is Queen Elizabeth Park, but one could show up anywhere. Other likely locations include Minnekhada Regional Park/Addington Marsh and the Pitt-Addington Marsh Wildlife Management Area. During the winter, this species is sometimes seen in residential areas on the North Shore. *Photo: Townsend's Solitaire at Grant Narrows. Colin Clasen*

**74. Varied Thrush** Common resident. Breeds in locations with higher-elevation coniferous forest, such as Cypress and Mount Seymour provincial parks. These birds then move to lower elevations in the winter and can be found in almost any wooded area, park or residential neighbourhood, especially on the North Shore. *Photo: Varied Thrush. Peter Candido*

**75. Gray Catbird** Regular from late May to August at the Pitt-Addington Marsh Wildlife Management Area at Grant Narrows Regional Park, where several pairs breed in the riparian thickets bordering the marsh. They can be found along the wooded dyke at Grant Narrows and in the large stand of black cottonwood along Rannie Road, about 2 km south of the park. Very rarely reported from elsewhere in the checklist area. *Photo: Gray Catbird on Nature Dyke Trail at Grant Narrows. Colin Clasen*

**76. Black-throated Gray Warbler** Fairly common from May to mid-September in lower-elevation broadleaf or mixed forest. Best areas include Campbell Valley Regional Park, Minnekhada Regional Park, Deer Lake Park, Stanley Park, Pacific Spirit Regional Park and the Maplewood Conservation Area. *Photo: Black-throated Gray Warbler. Tak Shibata*

**77. Townsend's Warbler** Common from May to mid-September in higher-elevation coniferous forest, where it is easily heard but hard to spot high in the treetops; it is casual in winter in lowland forest. Cypress and Mount Seymour provincial parks, Stanley Park and Lighthouse Park are some of the best spots to search. *Photo: Townsend's Warbler. Jim Martin*

**78. MacGillivray's Warbler** Common from mid-May to early September in suitable habitat, when it nests in dense shrubbery and tangles along streams, power line rights-of-way or in young regenerating forest. Spots to check include Minnekhada Regional Park, the Pitt-Addington Marsh Wildlife Management Area and Cypress and Mount Seymour provincial parks. When not singing, it is easily overlooked, as it tends to stay deep in shrubby cover. *Photo: MacGillivray's Warbler. Tak Shibata*

**79. Western Tanager** Fairly common from mid-May to mid-September in low-elevation coniferous forest. Like the Black-headed Grosbeak, it can be overlooked due to its robin-like song and habit of staying within the tree canopy. Good places to search include Queen Elizabeth Park (in spring migration), Campbell Valley Regional Park, Minnekhada Regional Park, the Pitt-Addington Marsh Wildlife Management Area, Stanley Park and any large forested area on the North Shore. *Photo: Western Tanager. Liron Gertsman*

**80. Black-headed Grosbeak** Common from early May to September in low-elevation deciduous forest, forest edge and woodlots (<800 m). Often overlooked due to its robin-like song and habit of staying within the tree canopy. Good places to search include Colony Farm Regional Park, Campbell Valley Regional Park, Minnekhada Regional Park, Ladner Harbour Park, Burnaby Lake Regional Park and Pacific Spirit Regional Park. *Photo: Black-headed Grosbeak. Virginia Hayes*

**81. Lazuli Bunting** Rare from June to mid-August, when it breeds in open shrubby country. The most reliable area is Colony Farm Regional Park, where it nests each year. Can occur in suitable habitat in other areas, especially in Delta (North 40 Park Reserve), Surrey (Serpentine Floodplain) and Langley (Glen Valley). *Photo: Lazuli Bunting. Liron Gerstman*

**82. American Tree Sparrow** Rare from October to mid-March, when it is seen in hedgerows or weedy fields in open country. Reifel Migratory Bird Sanctuary, Serpentine Fen, Brunswick Point, Iona Island and the areas surrounding Boundary Bay are good places to search for this species. *Photo: American Tree Sparrow. John Gordon*

**83. Lapland Longspur** Rare from September to April, uncommon fall migrant in late September and early October. Frequents open fields and shorelines. The best places to search include Jericho Beach Park, Iona Island South Jetty, Roberts Bank jetty and fields nearby, fields and dykes on Westham Island, Brunswick Point and around Boundary Bay. *Photo: Lapland Longspur at Colony Farm. Colin Clasen*

**84. Snow Bunting** Uncommon from November to April, when it frequents sparsely vegetated shorelines. The two best locations to search are the Iona Island South Jetty and the Tsawwassen ferry jetty. It has also been reported from Jericho Beach Park, Ambleside Park and Blackie Spit. *Photo: Snow Buntings bathing. Mike Tabak*

**85. Yellow-headed Blackbird** Uncommon from May to late August. This species is only reliable at the very small breeding colony at the outer ponds of Iona Island Regional Park. Rare during the winter, when it might be found in large mixed blackbird flocks in the Fraser delta. *Photo: Yellow-headed Blackbird at Iona. Colin Clasen*

**86. Bullock's Oriole** Uncommon from mid-May to mid-August. This species nests in stands of black cottonwood or Lombardy poplar. Good places to search include Grant Narrows Regional Park, Colony Farm Regional Park, Ladner Harbour Park and east of Farm Slough at Blackie Spit. *Photo: Bullock's Oriole. Liron Gertsman*

**87. Gray-crowned Rosy-Finch** Rare in winter (mainly October to April). Your best bet is to search the higher elevations of Cypress or Mount Seymour provincial parks in late October or early November, before the snow becomes too deep for hiking. These locations should also be checked in late April during spring thaw, when this bird will feed at the edges of the melting snow. Can be found away from the North Shore Mountains in open country, usually within a day or two after heavy snowfalls in the mountains, but they are extremely scarce. They have been seen at Jericho Beach Park, Iona Island South Jetty and the Tsawwassen ferry jetty. *Photos taken on Mount Seymour. Top to bottom: Gray-crowned Rosy-Finch (interior variety). Gray-crowned Rosy-Finch (coastal variety). Liron Gertsman*

**88. Pine Grosbeak** Rare in winter, casual in summer. Like the Gray-crowned Rosy Finch, your best bet to find this species is to search the subalpine forest of Cypress or Mount Seymour provincial parks in late October or early November. Could occur at any location during irruption years. Queen Elizabeth Park has some recent winter reports. *Photos, top to bottom: Pine Grosbeak, red variant. Pine Grosbeak, russet variant. David Schutz*

*Written by Wayne Weber. Revised by Dan Tyson and Kyle Elliott, 2001. Revised by Tom Plath, Mike Tabak, Mike Toochin, Dan Tyson and Mark Wynja, 2015.*

# ONLINE RESOURCES TO INCREASE YOUR BIRDING SUCCESS

**VANBCBIRDS** (YAHOO GROUP) IS A FREE ONLINE BIRDING GROUP WITH over 600 members in the Metro Vancouver area. Birders of all experience levels can read about the sightings of other birders, post their own sightings and feel comfortable asking any type of question about birds and birding-related subjects. The link for signing up is: groups.yahoo.com/neo/groups/vanbcbirds/info.

**eBird** is a free international online database service operated by the Cornell Lab of Ornithology and National Audubon Society. It's a convenient way to keep a permanent record of your bird sightings and help monitor the abundance and distribution of bird populations. Log on to the website (ebird.org/content/Canada), then click on the "Explore Data" tab at the top, then click on "Sign in or Register" above the "View and Explore Data" title.

This service includes the very valuable "eBird Rare Bird Alert" option, which automatically sends email alerts to you about new sightings reported on eBird in your region. To activate this option in your eBird account, click on "Manage My Alerts" at the bottom right, type in "Metro Vancouver" in the "Rare Bird Alerts" box and click "Subscribe."

**BC Rare Bird Alert** is a free blog with regional reports to click on, including one for "Vancouver and Fraser Valley" (bcbirdalert.blogspot.ca).

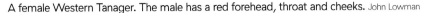

A female Western Tanager. The male has a red forehead, throat and cheeks. John Lowman

# REPORTING WING-TAGGED AND LEG-BANDED BIRDS OF PREY

## WING TAGS

Wing tags have been placed on a variety of birds of prey caught at and around airports in Vancouver, Seattle and Portland, with a different colour being used at each airport. The wing-tagged species are mostly the **Red-tailed Hawk, Rough-legged Hawk** and **Barn Owl**, along with small numbers of the *Snowy Owl, Short-eared Owl, Great Horned Owl, American Kestrel, Peregrine Falcon, Cooper's Hawk, Sharp-shinned Hawk* and *Merlin*.

If you spot a wing-tagged bird, please report it to the appropriate contact person (see below). When you report your sighting(s), please state the tag colour, the letter/number on it and which wing the tag was on. Also state the location where the bird was seen, as precisely as possible. Please include a photo if available.

> **White wing tags** (caught at Vancouver airport)
> Contact Gary Searing: 250-656-1889, gfs@airportwildlife.ca
>
> **Blue and Yellow wings tags** (caught at SeaTac airport)
> Contact Bud Anderson: 360-757-1911, falconresearch@gmail.com
>
> **Orange wing tags** (caught at Portland airport)
> Contact Carole Hallett: carole.hallett@gmail.com

## COLOURED PLASTIC LEG BANDS

If you sight a *Cooper's Hawk* with a plastic leg band, please note the colour of the band(s) and which leg it is on (left, right or both). If there are multiple bands, note which colours are on top and bottom, and make a note of the geographic location of the sighting.

> **Vancouver area contact**: Jason Brogan: jason.m.brogan@gmail.com
> **Victoria area contact**: Andy Stewart: 250-743-1328, andy.stewart@shaw.ca

# BIRDING AND BIRD PHOTOGRAPHY ETIQUETTE

NATURE VANCOUVER RECOGNIZES THE DESIRE OF BOTH BIRDERS AND bird photographers to get as good a look as possible at our fine feathered friends—it is only natural. We also feel it is only natural for the birds to want to be admired from a respectful distance, so they can go about their normal activities with minimal disturbance by people.

## CODE OF BIRDING ETHICS

Therefore, with the best interests of the birds in mind, we recommend following the "Code of Birding Ethics" of the American Birding Association. The full version of their code can be found on their website (aba.org/about/ethics.html).

However, here are some of their key recommendations:

- "Everyone who enjoys birds and birding must always respect wildlife, its environment, and the rights of others. In any conflict of interest between birds and birders, the welfare of the birds and their environment comes first."
- "To avoid stressing birds or exposing them to danger, exercise restraint and caution during observation, photography, sound recording, or filming."
- "Limit the use of recordings and other methods of attracting birds, and never use such methods in heavily birded areas or for attracting any species that is Threatened, Endangered, or of Special Concern, or is rare in your local area."
- "Keep well back from nests and nesting colonies, roosts, display areas, and important feeding sites."
- "Before advertising the presence of a rare bird, evaluate the potential for disturbance to the bird, its surroundings, and other people in the area, and proceed only if access can be controlled, disturbance can be minimized, and permission has been obtained from private land-owners. The sites of rare nesting birds should be divulged only to the proper conservation authorities."
- "Do not enter private property without the owner's explicit permission."
- "Practice common courtesy in contacts with other people. Your exemplary behavior will generate goodwill with birders and non-birders alike."
- "If you witness unethical birding behavior, assess the situation, and intervene if you think it prudent. When interceding, inform the person(s) of the inappropriate action and attempt, within reason, to have it stopped. If the behavior continues, document it, and notify appropriate individuals or organizations."

## AREA OF SPECIAL CONCERN: BOUNDARY BAY FROM 64TH STREET TO 112TH STREET

Some very undesirable consequences have arisen when people try to get too close to the birds, to get better looks and photographs. Nowhere is this more evident than at Boundary Bay. Things came to a head in the winters of 2012–13 and 2013–14, when large numbers of *Snowy Owls* appeared along the foreshore and throngs of viewers came to observe the spectacle. Most people stayed on the dyke, where they could get excellent looks and/or photos of the owls roosting on driftwood logs close by.

Unfortunately, the marsh was also patrolled by individuals who felt the need to get even closer. There were many incidences of the birds being harassed. There were reports of people repeatedly flushing them; using loud, continuous recording playbacks; clapping, whistling or hooting to get them to wake up; and using baits as attractants. (Other species that are often targeted in a similar way are the *Short-eared Owl*, *Long-eared Owl*, *Northern Harrier* and *Bald Eagle*.)

The vast majority of experienced birders and photographers consider such behaviour unethical. Not only is it unethical, but it is also against the law to harass the birds. Eventually, conservation officers were called to the scene. Signage was installed, asking viewers to respect the wildlife and remain on the dyke. Many offenders are relative newbies who are innocently unaware of what comprises acceptable behaviour, but unfortunately, there are a few who deliberately choose to ignore ethics, guidelines and laws.

To report violations, please see the next section, *Reporting Obvious Harassment of Wildlife*.

Everyone is welcome to view the wonderful sights at Boundary Bay, but **please respect the birds**! They have very little space left in which to feed and rest.

*Main text written by Colin Clasen, 2015.*
*"Area of Special Concern" text written by Carlo Giovanella and Ilya Povalyaev, 2015.*

# REPORTING OBVIOUS HARASSMENT OF WILDLIFE

IF YOU FEEL YOU ARE WITNESSING *OBVIOUS* WILDLIFE HARASSMENT IN THE Metro Vancouver area, the proper authority to contact (at the time of writing) is:

**Conservation Officer Service Reporting Line**: 1-877-952-7277

You will be asked to provide key details about the violator, including date, time, location and vehicle licence plate. Photos and videos of violators and their vehicles can also be very helpful.

While the well-being of the birds is obviously important, so is your own. Therefore, do not put your own safety at risk in a situation like this by confronting the violator. Instead, contact the Conservation Officer.

# NATURE-RELATED ORGANIZATIONS

## GENERAL NATURE GROUPS

### Nature Vancouver

naturevancouver.ca

PO Box 3021, Vancouver, BC  V6B 3X5

Nature Vancouver offers regular birding field trips, as well as monthly Birders' Nights with guest speakers, held the first Thursday of every month (except June, July and August). Visitors are welcome. The website also describes their Botany, Geology and Marine Biology programs and other activities offered by Nature Vancouver.

### NatureKids BC
### (formerly Young Naturalists' Club of British Columbia)

naturekidsbc.ca / info@naturekidsbc.ca / 604-985-3059

1620 Mt. Seymour Road, North Vancouver, BC  V7G 2R9

This exciting nature discovery and environmental action program invites young people (ages 5–12) to discover nearby nature, through natural history programs, field trips and *NatureWILD Magazine*.

## BC Nature (Federation of British Columbia Naturalists)

bcnature.ca / manager@bcnature.ca / 604-985-3057

1620 Mount Seymour Road, North Vancouver, BC V7G 2R9

BC Nature is a federation of 53 natural history clubs around the province, including Nature Vancouver, WildResearch, Burke Mountain Naturalists, Delta Naturalists, White Rock and Surrey Naturalists, Alouette Field Naturalists and Friends of Semiahmoo Bay. Many clubs have weekly birding field trips and bird lists for their local areas.

## HOSTED BIRDING LOCATIONS

### British Columbia Waterfowl Society

(Managers of the George C. Reifel Migratory Bird Sanctuary since 1963)

reifelbirdsanctuary.com / 604-946-6980

5191 Robertson Road, Delta, BC V4K 3N2

The Reifel Sanctuary, in the heart of the Fraser River estuary, has nearly 300 ha of managed wetlands, natural marshes and low dykes, with several kilometres of flat, wheelchair-accessible trails. Along the trails, there are several small "bird blinds" or "hides," which are designed with small, slat-like windows, so visitors can view the birds outside without disturbing them. This is the winter home of *Lesser Snow Geese* and is one of Canada's top bird-watching sites. It's also the easiest place in southwestern BC to see several species, including the *Sandhill Crane*, *Black-crowned Night-Heron* and *Northern Saw-whet Owl*. Membership in the society provides free year-round admission to the sanctuary, a 10 percent discount on gift shop purchases, and quarterly issues of the society's newsletter, "Marshnotes," which features sanctuary highlights and conservation issues of local interest. Open daily from 9 a.m. to 4 p.m.

### WBT Wild Bird Trust of BC

(Operators of the Conservation Area at Maplewood Flats)

wildbirdtrust.org / Site office 604-903-4471

2645 Dollarton Highway, North Vancouver (2 km east of the Ironworkers Memorial Bridge)

Executive office 604-922-1550 / Mailing address #124, 1489 Marine Drive, West Vancouver, BC V7W 1B9

This conservation area is comprised of 30 ha, including a 2 ha freshwater marsh and over 3 km of wheelchair-accessible trails, with occasional resting benches and a viewing platform. Free bird survey at 8 a.m. the first Saturday of each month. Home to the largest *Purple Martin* colony on the mainland, with over 90 nest boxes. Phone for information about membership, guided walks, bird surveys, school programs, special events and volunteering. Membership includes their bi-annual publication *Wingspan*, with feature articles on various nature-related topics.

## Stanley Park Ecology Society (SPES)

stanleyparkecology.ca / 604-257-6908

Stanley Park Dining Pavilion, 2nd Floor, 610 Pipeline Road, Vancouver, BC V6G 1Z4 (Mailing address: PO Box 5167, Vancouver, BC V6B 4B2)

SPES has been a registered charity since 1988. In June 1997, SPES and the Vancouver Park Board entered into a Joint Operating Agreement. As the primary provider of land-based education interpretive services in Stanley Park, SPES's role includes education, research and conservation action. This includes monthly bird walks on the last Sunday of every month (except December).

SPES also advises the Vancouver Park Board on conservation issues within Stanley Park, with an emphasis on wildlife, habitat and species at risk. The Park Board provides several facilities, including the Stanley Park Nature House on Lost Lagoon (see website for details) and the Dining Pavilion offices. SPES is funded by grants, private donations and memberships, program revenues and service fees. In addition, they rely on their dedicated volunteers, committed staff and board members and the generous support of local businesses and foundations.

## BIRDING—ONLY GROUPS

## British Columbia Field Ornithologists

bcfo.ca / PO Box 45111 Dunbar, Vancouver, BC V6S 2M8

BCFO is a not-for-profit, charitable organization that is committed to the study, preservation and enjoyment of British Columbia's wild birds. Its members are birders and ornithologists, from novice to expert. BCFO administers the Provincial Bird Records Committee, supports a Young Birders program, offers research grants and regularly features members' photography on its website. It also provides expert commentary on birds when asked by the media.

BCFO members are provided with subscriptions to the quarterly newsmagazine *BC Birding* and the annual journal *British Columbia Birds*, participation in annual conferences and expert-led field trips to bird-rich locations around the province and participation in various bird surveys, as well as conservation and research projects involving amateur and professional ornithologists.

# VALUABLE ONLINE BIRD RESEARCH INFORMATION

## British Columbia Breeding Bird Atlas
birdatlas.bc.ca

BC's first Breeding Bird Atlas provides accounts of the 320 species breeding in BC, including distribution maps and photos. Based on field data collected from 2008 to 2012 by over 1,300 volunteer birdwatchers, this atlas is the single most comprehensive, current information source on the status of BC's breeding birds. The entire contents—maps, species accounts, graphs, tables, raw data and more—are available free of charge. This is one of the largest volunteer-based initiatives in British Columbia's history and a major new resource for conservation.

## Biodiversity Centre for Wildlife Studies
wildlifebc.org / bcfws@shaw.ca / 250-477-0465
3825 Cadboro Bay Road, PO Box 55053, Victoria, BC V8N 6L8

This centre has the largest wildlife library in the province, including the largest and most active nest record scheme in Canada, with free online access to valuable birding data. Bird records are a major part of the wildlife collection, and the annual Breeding Bird Reports are an important part of the ongoing study of birds in BC. This data helps to make informed decisions about wildlife conservation and management in the province.

# HANDS-ON RESEARCH-BASED GROUPS

## WildResearch
wildresearch.ca / info@wildresearch.ca
2258 Oxford Street, Vancouver, BC V5L 1G1

WildResearch operates the Iona Island Bird Observatory, using bird banding to monitor how birds use Iona Beach Regional Park, to provide estimates of survival and population trends and to create training, educational and volunteer opportunities for members of the community. They conduct spring, fall and winter bird monitoring programs and offer annual pelagic trips out of Ucluelet on Vancouver Island.

## Vancouver Avian Research Centre (VARC)
birdvancouver.com / info@birdvancouver.com / 604-218-1191
4115 East Braemar Road, North Vancouver, BC V7K 3C9

VARC operates the Colony Farm bird banding station in Port Coquitlam.

Dedicated to wild bird research, conservation and education, they conduct bird monitoring and banding and provide research, demonstration, education, volunteer opportunities and visitor programs.

## REHABILITATION AND RESCUE GROUPS

### The Orphaned Wild Life (O.W.L.) Rehabilitation Society
owlcanada.org / owlrehab@dccnet.com / 604-946-3171
3800 72nd Street, Delta, BC  V4K 3N2
   O.W.L.'s primary goal is to rehabilitate and release sick, injured and orphaned birds of prey. Open 7 days a week, 10 a.m. to 3 p.m.

### Wildlife Rescue Association of British Columbia
wildliferescue.ca / info@wildliferescue.ca / office: 604-526-2747
**Emergency phone: 604-526-7275**
5216 Glencairn Drive, Burnaby, BC  V5B 3Cl
   WRA cares for and rehabilitates orphaned, injured or pollution-damaged wildlife. Care Centre open 7 days a week (including holidays), 8 a.m to 5:30 p.m.
   Office open Monday to Friday, 9 a.m. to 5:30 p.m.

## GROUPS OFFERING CASUAL OUTINGS AND/ OR NATURE INFORMATION

### Alouette Field Naturalists
Pitt Meadows and Maple Ridge area
604-463-8743

### Burke Mountain Naturalists
bmn.bc.ca
554 Yale Road, Port Moody  V3H 3K3

### Burns Bog Conservation Society
burnsbog.org / info@burnsbog.org /  604-572-0373 or 1-888-850-6264
#4, 7953 120th Street, Delta, BC  V4C 6P6

## Delta Naturalists' Society

dncb.wordpress.com

Box 18136, 1215C - 56th Street, Delta, BC  V4L 2M4

Casual birders visit different locations each week, usually within the Lower Mainland or nearby Washington State.

## Friends of Semiahmoo Bay Society

birdsonthebay.ca / information@birdsonthebay.ca / 604-536-3552

## Friends of Cypress Provincial Park

cypresspark.ca / info@cypresspark.ca

PO Box 91053, West Vancouver, BC  V7V 3N3

## Langley Field Naturalists

langleyfieldnaturalists.org / langleyfieldnaturalists@shaw.ca

## Lighthouse Park Preservation Society

lpps.ca / lighthouseparkps@gmail.com

## Stanley Park Ecology Society

stanleyparkecology.ca / 604-257-6908

PO Box 5167, Vancouver, BC  V6B 4B2

## White Rock and Surrey Naturalists Society

www.facebook.com / WRSnaturalists / wrsn@shaw.ca

Box 75044 RPO, White Rock, Surrey, BC  V4A 0B1

Good comparison of Pelagic Cormorant (left) and Double–crested Cormorant (right).
Joan Lopez

# PUBLIC TRANSIT AND WEATHER INFORMATION

## PUBLIC TRANSIT INFORMATION

The schedules, routes or fares for public transportation and ferries can change at any time. Therefore, for the most reliable and up-to-date information possible, we recommend contacting the following sources.

### TransLink
translink.ca / 604-953-3333
 Up-to-date and reliable bus, SkyTrain and SeaBus information and schedules for Vancouver and vicinity.

### West Vancouver Transit
westvancouver.ca/transportation-roads/blue-bus / 604-985-7777

### Pacific Coach Lines
pacificcoach.com / 604-662-7575 or 1-800-661-1725
 Regular buses from Vancouver to Victoria, via Tsawwassen/Swartz Bay ferry.

### BC Ferries
bcferries.com / 1-888-223-3779
 Ferry schedules change seasonally and on holidays; therefore please check schedules carefully.

## WEATHER INFORMATION

### Online and Newspaper Weather Information
Federal government: weather.gc.ca
The Weather Network: theweathernetwork.com
*Vancouver Sun*: vancouversun.com/weather
*The Province* (Vancouver): theprovince.com/weather

For tide information, please see the separate *Tides* section in this guide.

# TIDES

TIDE LEVELS ARE VERY IMPORTANT WHEN LOOKING FOR WATER BIRDS and shorebirds. Probably the easiest way to check the seven-day tide levels and times is to go to the Fisheries and Oceans Canada website (waterlevels.gc.ca) and choose one of the six measuring sites in the Metro Vancouver area: Vancouver, Point Atkinson, Port Moody, New Westminster, Tsawwassen or White Rock. If you want a full year of tide predictions, you can either purchase the "Canadian Tide and Current Tables," available at most marinas, or go online and enter "Fisheries and Oceans Canada, Tide Tables" and get them for free. Select Volume 5, which covers the Strait of Georgia. By calling 1-877-775-0790, you can listen to recorded tidal predictions, but there is only one local choice, "Point Atkinson."

You can also check the weather section of the *Vancouver Sun* and the *Province*, which are the two largest daily newspapers.

The largest average tidal exchanges occur during the June and December solstices. The smallest average tidal exchanges occur during the March and September equinoxes. In summer, the lowest tides occur midday and the highest tides occur in the evening. In winter, the lowest tides occur through the night and the highest tides occur midday.

Abbreviations used for tides: m=metre and ft=foot.

Tidal fluctuations in waters around Vancouver are large, from as little as minus 0.3 m (minus 1 ft) to as much as 4.9 m (16.1 ft) within a 24-hour period. Daily high tides vary from about 3.6 m (11.8 ft) to 4.9 m (16.1 ft).

On a sandy or muddy shoreline, most waterfowl are best seen during moderately high tides of 3.7 m (12 ft) and higher, although the **Green-winged Teal** and sometimes other dabbling ducks often congregate to feed on tidal flats.

Shorebirds are generally best seen during tides of about 3 m (10 ft) to 3.8 m (12.5 ft). During lower tides, there is so much exposed mud and sand that shorebirds get spread out over an enormous area and are not as easy to see. High tides push them nearer to shore, where they can often be seen more easily. On the other hand, maximum tides of 4.6 m (15 ft) or more minimize the exposed mud and sand, forcing shorebirds to other areas that may be inaccessible to birders. However, high tides push some shorebirds into inland ponds near the ocean, at easily accessible locations like the George C. Reifel Migratory Bird Sanctuary and Iona Regional Park.

Plan to arrive *at least* 1 hour (2 hours may be better) before the expected high tide. The water can move in surprisingly fast. Just as there is an optimum viewing period during a rising tide (1 to 2 hours *before* a high tide), it can also be good during a falling tide (1 to 2 hours *after* a high tide), when shorebirds start returning to the increasingly exposed mud and sand. Furthermore, when there is only a small difference in height between high tide and low tide, the birds will be kept closer to the shoreline longer, allowing for a longer period of good viewing.

**Note:** *If there are rocks or high points a short distance from shore that are easily accessible during a low tide,* **pay attention to the incoming tide** *(especially if it is rising fast) to avoid being cut off from shore.*

Tides are also important when viewing shorebirds and waterfowl along a rocky coastline. At low tide, exposed or shallow beds of mussels and barnacles may attract sea ducks, turnstones, oystercatchers, gulls and other birds. Birding locations in this book that are particularly tide sensitive include Boundary Bay, Blackie Spit, Iona Beach Regional Park and Iona South Jetty, Boundary Bay Regional Park and the Compensation Lagoon at the Tsawwassen Ferry Terminal.

Optimum tides for viewing shorebirds are: base of Iona jetty, 3.5 m to 3.7 m (11.5 ft to 12 ft); 12th Avenue Lagoon at Boundary Bay Regional Park, 3.8 m and flooding to 4 m (12.5 ft to 13 ft); northern Boundary Bay between 88th and 96th streets, 4 m (13 ft). In front of "the Mansion" (a very large brown house) where there is a deep channel, birding is good even on a low tide.

*Written by Catherine J. Aitchison from information provided by Hue MacKenzie, Richard Swanston and Brian Self, 2001. Updated by Colin Clasen and reviewed by Joan Lopez, Rob Lyske, Ilya Povalyaev, Bev Ramey and Richard Swanston, 2015.*

Long–tailed Ducks are usually easiest to find at the White Rock Pier. Joan Lopez

# BLACK BEARS, COUGARS AND OTHER WILD ANIMALS

BLACK BEARS, COUGARS AND OTHER WILD ANIMALS SHARE OUR PARKS and wilderness areas with us and should be treated with the utmost respect and consideration. Always stay at a safe distance and never feed any wild animal. From time to time, depending on seasonal conditions, you may encounter black bears or cougars anywhere in the region covered by this guide. The most likely general areas for either species are Cypress and Mount Seymour provincial parks on the North Shore Mountains, Golden Ears Provincial Park, Minnekhada Regional Park and (for black bears) Burns Bog in Delta.

You are far more likely to encounter a black bear than a cougar, because cougars tend to blend in with their environment and stay well hidden, but it is wise to be alert for both. Fortunately, attacks by black bears or cougars are very rare.

## BLACK BEAR AND COUGAR AVOIDANCE AND DETERRENCE

- To help prevent black bear or cougar encounters, **make whatever type of noise you can**, to alert the animals that you are in the area. That includes talking, singing, clapping, or breaking sticks, especially where a bear or cougar might not otherwise smell, hear or see you coming.
- Look around for animals in the distance. Be alert for fresh tracks, scat, diggings, overturned rocks, claw marks on trees, rotten trees torn apart or other signs of recent black bear or cougar presence. Also be cautious if you see a large dead animal, because a black bear or cougar may be nearby.
- If you are in a group, keep all group members in sight of each other, remain on established trails and only venture out during daylight hours. Stay in the open whenever possible.

## BASIC ADVICE FOR ENCOUNTERING A BLACK BEAR OR COUGAR

- If a black bear or cougar is spotted, all group members and other people in the area should be alerted immediately, and the group should stay close together.
- Never approach an animal or its young.
- Retreat to a safe location, take an alternative route to avoid the animal, or wait until it has moved well away from the area.

- Stay calm.
- Do not run, because that could trigger an attack.
- Back away slowly.
- Make yourself appear as large as possible by staying upright, waving your hat, coat or other objects above your head and, if you are with a group, gathering all group members close together. You are trying to convince the animal you are a threat, not prey.
- Do not turn your back on the animal.
- Always give the animal an avenue of escape.
- If it is a black bear, *do not* make eye contact.
- If it is a cougar, *do* make and maintain eye contact.
- If you have bear spray, be sure you know how to use it and ensure that it has not expired.

## IF A BLACK BEAR OR COUGAR CHARGES OR ATTACKS

The *specific* advice offered by the sources we consulted depends on many variables, including the following:

1. How close the animal is (perceptions differ on what "close" means).
2. Whether it is a bluff charge or a real charge.
3. Whether it is exhibiting defensive behaviour or predatory behaviour (the experts say telling the difference takes "skill" and "experience").
4. Whether it is a black bear or a cougar.
5. Whether there are cubs present.

> **Important:** Giving proper advice for all combinations of these variables is beyond the scope of this guide. Therefore, **for much more detailed advice for specific situations, we *strongly* recommend that you review the latest information from the experts, including the sources listed below.**

There is one piece of *general* advice offered by all of the sources we consulted, regarding an actual physical attack by either a black bear or cougar. That advice is to FIGHT BACK as hard as you can. Use whatever is available as a weapon, including rocks, sharp sticks, tree branches, hiking poles, binoculars, cameras, tripods, knives and bear spray. Aim for the animal's eyes/nose/mouth/face/ears.

*Note: The above list contains items of advice that were common to most of the references we consulted. To avoid repeating those common items, in the references below, we only added comments that were unique or were phrased differently, especially regarding what type of voice to use.*

## REFERENCES FOR BLACK BEAR ENCOUNTERS

- **BC Ministry of Environment**, Conservation Officer Service, Bear Aware (www. env.gov.bc.ca/cos/info/bearaware/bear_encounters.html): *"Talk in a gruff voice."*
- **BC Parks** (www.env.gov.ba.ca/bcparks): *"Talk softly so it knows what you are."*
- **Parks Canada** (www.pc.gc.ca/eng/docs/v-g/oursnoir-blackbear/page3.aspx): *"Talk in a soft voice."*
- **WildSafeBC** (wildsafebc.com): *"Speak to the bear in a loud, low voice, saying things like 'whoa bear—you'd better back off.'"*
- **Get Bear Smart Society** (bearsmart.com/play/bear encounters): *"Identify yourself by speaking in a calm, appeasing tone."*
- **Center for Wildlife Information** (centerforwildlifeinformation.org/BeBear-Aware/BearEncounters/bearencounters.html): *"Talk firmly in a low-pitched voice."*
- **North Shore Black Bear Society** (northshorebears.com/encounters): *"Speak calmly."*
- **Mountain Nature** (www.mountainnature.com/wildlife/bears): *"Speak calmly so that it knows you are a human . . . Back away slowly . . . Keep talking calmly."*
- **City of Maple Ridge, Bear Aware** (mapleridge.ca/322/Bear-Aware): *"Speak to the bear in a calm, firm voice."*

## REFERENCES FOR COUGAR ENCOUNTERS

Cougars generally stalk and attack from behind and may target a person who gets separated from the group. Therefore, if a cougar is spotted, all group members should stay close together. Unfortunately, little is known about what triggers a cougar attack.

- **The Cougar**, by Paula Wild (Douglas & McIntyre, 2013). The following are quotes from Chapter 9, "Keeping Safe in Cougar Country," and the Appendix, "Cougar Safety Checklist."

*"It's important to remember that eye contact between people and bears is totally different than eye contact between people and cougars. Most bear attacks are defensive (accidental) and eye contact should be avoided. The majority of cougar attacks are predatory and eye contact is vital."*

*"If a cougar exhibits defensive behaviour . . . raise your arms in the air, speak calmly but firmly and slowly back away."*

*"If a cougar is watching, following or approaching, immediately act aggressively by throwing sticks, yelling, baring your teeth and growling."*

*"Make loud continuous noise by yelling or using a whistle or air horn."*

- **WildSafeBC** (wildsafebc.com) *"Maintain eye contact and speak to it in a loud firm voice. If a cougar shows aggression, or begins following you, respond aggressively in all cases as cougars see you as a meal: keep eye contact, yell and make loud noises, and show your teeth."*

- **BC Ministry of Environment** (www.env.gov.bc.ca/wld/documents/cougsf. htm) *"Talk to the cougar in a confident voice. Pick all children up off the ground immediately as they frighten easily and their rapid movements may provoke an attack. Speak loudly and firmly."*

- **International Society for Endangered Cats in Canada** (www.wildcatconservation.org) *"If you meet a cougar, do not run. Yell, throw rocks and speak loudly and firmly."*

- **Wild Aware Utah** (wildawareutah.org) *"Talk firmly in a loud voice. Fight back if you are attacked! If you are aggressive enough, the cougar will probably flee."*

BC Parks also has an informative four-page brochure that you can obtain for free from their website by entering "BC Parks Bears and Cougars" into your search engine.

*Written by Catherine J. Aitchison, 2001. Updated by Colin Clasen, 2015.*

Opposite: The distinctive underwing pattern of this Willet was captured perfectly. Jim Martin

Top: Whimbrel occur annually in small numbers. John Gordon
Bottom: Pacific Golden-Plover in breeding plumage. Liron Gertsman

# INDEX